Migrant Returns »

Migrant Returns » Manila, Development, and Transnational Connectivity

ERIC J. PIDO

Duke University Press   Durham and London   2017

© 2017 Duke University Press
All rights reserved
Printed in the United States of America on acid-free paper ∞
Interior designed by Courtney Leigh Baker
Typeset in Minion Pro and Myriad Pro by Graphic Composition, Inc.,
Bogart, Georgia

Library of Congress Cataloging-in-Publication Data
Names: Pido, Eric J., author.
Title: Migrant returns : Manila, development, and transnational connectivity /
Eric J. Pido.
Description: Durham : Duke University Press, 2017. | Includes bibliographical
references and index.
Identifiers: LCCN 2016050802 (print)
LCCN 2016056122 (ebook)
ISBN 9780822363538 (hardcover : alk. paper)
ISBN 9780822363699 (pbk. : alk. paper)
ISBN 9780822373124 (ebook)
Subjects: LCSH: Return migration—Philippines. | Filipino Americans—Migrations.
| Philippines—Emigration and immigration. | United States—Emigration and
immigration.
Classification: LCC JV8685 .P536 2017 (print) | LCC JV8685 (ebook) | DDC
305.9/069109599—dc23
LC record available at https://lccn.loc.gov/2016050802

Cover art: A real estate agent presents a sample two-bedroom condominium at the
Avida sales pavilion in Mandaluyong City, Manila, 2013. (REUTERS/Cheryl Ravelo)

Contents

Abbreviations vii   Preface ix

Introduction An Ethnography of Return 1

PART I: DEPARTURES

1. The Balikbayan Economy Filipino Americans and
the Contemporary Transformation of Manila 29

2. The Foreign Local Balikbayans, Overseas Filipino
Workers, and the Return Economy 49

3. Transnational Real Estate Selling the
American Dream in the Philippines 72

PART II: RETURNS

4. The Balikbayan Hotel Touristic Performance
in Manila and the Anxiety of Return 115

5. The Balikbayan House The Precarity
of Return Migrant Homes 131

6. Domestic Affects The Philippine Retirement Authority,
Retiree Visas, and the National Discourse of Homecoming 148

Conclusion Retirement Landscapes
and the Geography of Exception 163

Epilogue 179   Notes 187   References 197   Index 209

Abbreviations

BPO
Business process outsourcing

BSP
Bangko Sentral ng Pilipinas

CALABARZON
Cavite, Laguna, Batangas, Rizal, and Quezon region

CBD
Central business district

CREBA
Chamber of Real Estate and Builders' Associations Inc.

DOT
Department of Tourism

IMF
International Monetary Fund

MRT
Manila Rapid Transit

NCR
National Capital Region

OFW
Overseas Filipino Worker

PEZA
Philippine Economic Zone Authority

PLDT
Philippine Long Distance Telephone Company

PRA
Philippine Retirement Authority

PRAMA
Philippine Retirement Authority Members Association Inc.

PRI
Philippine Retirement Incorporated

SEZ
Special Economic Zone

SRRV
Special Resident Retiree's Visa

TEZ
Tourism Economic Zones

TFC
The Filipino Channel

Preface

I can vividly remember my mother and father arguing after a phone call from the Philippines when I was an adolescent. They each took shifts pacing back and forth between the kitchen and dining room, while the other huddled over the tile countertop. My parents were anxiously trying to come to a decision about the family estate that my paternal grandfather left my father after he passed away just weeks before. *Estate* is too generous a term. Rather, the property constituted a meager lot of land that directly faced the Panay Gulf in Hinigaran, a small municipality almost precisely at the center of the province of Negros Occidental. Even today, dozens of fishermen arrive on the beaches each morning, dragging their battered *bangkas* through the sand, to sell their daily catch. The same boats that inspired my father to dream about worlds across the ocean, over half a century ago, remain. Although small, my father's land was precious.

This book brings shape to the meaning of property and the lived materiality suturing migration together with home. That brief, yet anxiety-filled conversation would linger on in my mind for over a decade, and the questions it produced would result in the pages of this book. What if my parents kept the land? Who would tend to it while we were away? Would they live in the Philippines for part of the year, far away from their children here in the United States? And what of those families who had taken up living on my father's land? After decades of living there, raising their children, and sharing a life, what would become of them?

Little did I know at the time that many of these questions were set in motion by the Immigration Act of 1965. This legislation, which enabled tens of thousands of Filipinos, including my parents, to emigrate to the United States, produced a pivotal moment in U.S. immigration history. Along with transforming the demographics of American society, it reinvigorated the colonial relationship between the United States and the Philippines by re-institutionalizing a gateway through which a network of Filipino migrants could make their way into the United States and settle in the postcolonial metropole. This gateway was the mechanism that would later produce the *balikbayan* subject. These subsequent economies of travel and remittances were possible only because the balikbayans who migrated to the United States after 1965 were largely composed of two distinct groups: one group that was uniquely skilled and educated, so that they were viewed as a desirable pool of migrants who could fill various labor gaps throughout the U.S. economy, and another group able to immigrate to the United States regardless of their lack of skills and education owing to stipulations within the act that allowed family members to be reunited with family who had already settled in various parts of the United States (Hing 1993; Choy 2003). In fact, the majority of the migrants who entered the United States through the Immigration Act of 1965 were permitted to immigrate through the family reunification provision. Subsequently, the wave of Filipino immigration after 1965 produced a dual chain of migration to the United States (Liu, Ong, and Rosenstein 1991). Yet while Filipinos were one of the largest immigrant groups to migrate to the United States as a result of this particular legislation, only a small handful of literature discusses the specific impact of this key legislation on the Filipino Americans who continue to create a number of vibrant ethnic spaces throughout the larger U.S. landscape.

These daily negotiations and the impossibility of finding a balance are reminiscent of perhaps the most influential scholar in the overlapping fields of ethnic and racial studies. At the turn of the twentieth century, W. E. B. Du Bois (2008) put words to the veil that masked the lives and culture of black folk. Du Bois argued that the experiences of African Americans in the United States were made entirely invisible to the eyes of the dominant culture surrounding them. Simultaneously, and in an intensely ambivalent fashion, this veil also provided African Americans with some ability to conceal themselves, in a sense, from the larger white society. Paul Gilroy would later describe Du Bois's analogy as the distinct sociality "swathed within the folds of the veil of colour" (1993, 123). Invisibility, which has often been understood in Filipino American literature as a negative consequence of imperialist amnesia and cultural aphasia, might also be understood as a generative force. It also enables and facilitates the transnational routes of Filipino migration between the Philippines and the United States, continually linking Filipinos in the United States with their immediate and extended families in the Philippines. This project stands on the shoulders of early works by Benito M. Vergara (2009), Rick Bonus (2000), and Martin Manalansan (2003) as an attempt to make sense of the invisibility both imposed on and employed by Filipinos in the United States and how this invisibility manifests itself into the spaces that Filipinos throughout the diaspora inhabit. It seeks to articulate an analytic of the veil as a tool to understand and convey the ambivalent experiences of Filipino transnationalism.

I rely on the work of Inderpal Grewal (2005) in seeking to move beyond what she regards as a prevailing discourse within cultural and ethnic studies that views migration and immigration solely through the frame of the United States as an imperialist nation-state. Rather, like Grewal, I too am exploring how the idea of America has "produced many kinds of agency and diverse subjects" for Filipinos and trying to make sense of how this idea functions "as a discourse of neoliberalism making possible struggles for rights through consumerists' practices and imaginaries that came to be used both inside and outside the territorial boundaries of the United States" (2). The metaphor of the veil forces readers of different backgrounds to suspend a U.S.-centric framework when viewing Filipinos in the United States and, instead, complicates traditional and fictitious binaries such as those imposed between American and immigrant, colonizer and colonized, and oppressed and oppressor.

What tends to be overlooked in the literature on race and diaspora are those immigrant communities, like balikbayans, who are able to imagine, in a very real sense, a return to their homeland. Yet while this return is possible and continuously present, by the very act of settling abroad in the United States, balikbayans are transformed and are at once local and foreign to the Philippines. Their status as U.S. citizens provides them with an ambivalent recognition among Filipinos in the Philippines. Balikbayans no longer simply return to the Philippines, a sentiment made apparent by one of the many balikbayans I interviewed for this book: "Coming back here is not like coming home. Things are very different." The uniqueness of balikbayans is in the manner in which they carry the weight of the obligations and indebtedness of the balikbayan economy on their shoulders when they return. In this way, balikbayans are exiled through the transformation of not only themselves but the very idea of home and homeland as well.

Much like the subject and approach of this text, my gratitude stretches both near and far, and across many geographic and temporal lines. As for many children of immigrants, the practice and language of academia did not come naturally for me. Moments of intellectual clarity or writing acumen were not always apparent, and if it were not for the immense thoughtfulness of mentors who intervened throughout my life, in both fleeting and sustained ways, I would not always have known that I could one day write a book. And so I cannot be more sincere when I say thank you to Julie Silianoff for calling me a writer in the eighth grade.

At the University of California at Berkeley, first and foremost, I am grateful to Catherine Ceniza Choy for her gentle and steadfast guidance. While it is never easy to give an equal measure of encouragement and criticism, her thoughtful feedback and brilliance throughout the years continue to provide me with direction and assurance. I am also indebted to a number of faculty and graduate students in the Department of Regional and City Planning for providing an intellectual home away from ethnic studies and nurturing my curiosity around space and place. I especially want to thank Teresa Caldeira for her book *City of Walls*, which inspired an entire chapter in this book, and for her guidance throughout the early formulation of this work. And I am also grateful to Ananya Roy for creating an intellectual community of graduate students around her course The City, making herself available for hours after class each week to facilitate a discussion with us, and, of course, for the immense inspiration she provided after reading each draft of my work. Last, I will always be thankful to that community of graduate students, who are now colleagues, for the immensely generative conversations and collegiality that was so pivotal for me during that particular moment: Reem Alissa, Yael Allweil, Guatam Bhan, Jia-Ching Chen, Mona Damluji, Alexander Schafran Fukuma, Joseph Godlewski, Mike Gonzales, Sylvia Nam, and Carmen Rojas.

Just as every sentence begins with a single letter, this book began with a single page that I wrote as a fellow at what is now called the Institute for the Study of Societal Issues. I have no idea who or where I would be without the financial and emotional support provided by the institute and the intellectual giants who created that tiny, yet powerful, space. Each week, I relied on the commitment of my colleagues to diligently read my work, provide me with clarity, and share with me a remarkable enthusiasm that enabled me to completely and wholeheartedly pursue my ideas and work. To my colleagues, Becky Alexander, Emily Gleason, Juan Herrera, Sarah Lopez, Carmen Martinez-Calderon, Nathan McClintock, Tamera Lee Stover, and Nicol U: your courage and brilliance continue to awe me as much today as all those years ago. None of this would have been possible without David Minkus and Deborah Lustig, who vetted countless pages of our work, provided the tangible feedback so rare at Berkeley, and sustained us with food and laughter each week for two entire years. And last, but most significantly, I am completely indebted to Christine Trost for providing me with the opportunity to be a research fellow at the institute and continuing to offer me her guidance and compassion as a fellow. I am only sorry that she will never completely know just how much her mentorship taught me.

In addition to graduate school, where the majority of this work solidified, a host of generous souls have helped to move this project forward in various ways by reading drafts, giving professional advice, or transforming my perspective. At the University of Washington, I am indebted to two of my Filipino colleagues and mentors. Much of this book was written as an imaginary conversation with Vicente Rafael and Rick Bonus. Their pioneering work provided me with a language that allowed me to connect both sides of the Pacific. I am especially grateful to Vince for continuing to champion my work and intellectual curiosity. I am also immensely thankful to Susan Kemp for her constant encouragement, incomparable kindness, and keen insightfulness in introducing me to both Doreen Massey and Rick. And I will be forever grateful to Tony Ishisaka for making a home for me in his office and providing a foundation for me as both a scholar and a person.

In Ithaca, I will always be thankful to the Sociology Department at Ithaca College for the space and resources provided to me, but especially to Sue-Jae Gage for the warmth she provided not only to me but also to my colleagues Hollie Kulago and Jeffreen Hayes. I continue to be inspired by the indomitable presence of all three of you. Thank you, Alicia Swords, for your friendship, and Rebecca Plante, for your tireless mentorship and generosity of spirit. And I will always be filled with utmost gratitude to Razack Karriem, Clement Lai, and Kelly Fong (and Mochi) for your genius and camaraderie but, most of all, for providing me with constant sustenance and a warm home away from Aura.

In reference to the vibrant collegiality among Filipino American scholars, I once overheard a colleague in Asian American studies joke that "the Filipino tide lifts all boats." Indeed. Throughout the years I have been indebted to the (now) generations of very visible Filipino and Filipino American studies scholars. Along with those I have already mentioned: thanks to Theo Gonzalves and Rick Baldoz for their generosity in giving

advice and laughter. To Jody Blanco, Lieba Faier, Vernadette Vicuna Gonzalez, Roderick Labrador, Dawn Bohulano Mabalon, Victor Mendoza, Anthony Ocampo, and Robyn Rodriguez, I am so grateful for your constant
willingness to share wisdom, read and comment on drafts, and offer pa-
tient responses during panels. Oliver Wang's work on mobile DJs in Daly
City provided the scholarly foundation for moving beyond the geographic
boundaries of the Bay Area. In my department at San Francisco State, it
has been an incredible honor to work alongside and be a witness to the
incomparable influence of my colleagues Daniel Phil Gonzales and Allyson
Tintiangco-Cubales. And finally, I owe a great deal to Martin Manalansan.
When I began reading about Filipinos in the United States in college, the
number of books I could collect barely filled half of a single bookshelf.
Now the products of this work could fill an entire bookcase, and its influence stretches across disciplines and epistemologies. Traces of Martin's
influence, his inexhaustible generosity and immeasurable guidance, can be
found in almost all of the work that has come out of the field in the last two
decades. For this especially, I am truly grateful.

At San Francisco State University, I cannot thank my colleagues enough
for welcoming both me and my work to the department. I am so grateful to
Grace J. Yoo, Laureen Chew, Lorraine Dong, and Amy Sueyoshi for helping me navigate through the early stage of my academic career. Ben Ko-
bashigawa, Isabelle Thuy Pelaud, Christen Sasaki, Valerie Soe, and Wesley
Ueunten, your kindness toward me and ceaseless commitment to challenge
every shape and form of authority and power will always figure as my intellectual and ethical compass. I am especially thankful to Jonathan H. X. Lee
for his giving spirit and his constant willingness to share so much of what
he knows and has with me. And, finally, to my brilliant friend Anantha
Sudhakar: thanks for the hours of writing together, the perfectly worded
insights, laughter, and lovely meals.

A special thank you to my editor, Courtney Berger, for seeing the promise of this work even though I had yet to even complete my dissertation,
for her diligent responses, and for her impeccable professionalism. I am
also grateful to her for selecting excellent readers; their comments provided wonderful clarity and helped to make significant improvements to
the book. And to the rest of the staff at Duke University Press, thank you to
Erin Hanas, early on, and to Sandra Korn for their facilitation of the pub-
lishing process and for their equally impressive professionalism.

In closing, I want to thank my numerous family members in both the

United States and the Philippines, most recently for offering up rooms to rest, chauffeuring me to interviews, helping me to navigate through Manila, and providing Aura and me with food again and again during months of fieldwork in the Philippines; for this I will always be thankful. And to my immediate family: my sister, Lynn; my brothers, Eviner and Erwin; and, most of all, my parents, Elmer and Juliet. Literally thousands of their insights and exchanges throughout my life have shaped how I see the world, my community, and myself; so much of this can be found strewn as fragments throughout this book. Finally, I will never be grateful enough to Aura Abing, for every moment and every thing. This book is for you.

Introduction » An Ethnography of Return

The PRA [Philippine Retirement Authority] should find ways to boost the growth of the booming retirement industry in the Philippines. [The world's] graying population is rapidly increasing. . . . The Philippines is in a very good position to take advantage of this potential. . . . As one of the flagship projects of the Philippine government, I want [the] PRA to boost its efforts to develop and promote the Philippines as a retirement haven and contribute to the increase of foreign investments. —Former Philippine president Gloria Macapagal-Arroyo

In 2007 the former president of the Philippines, Gloria Macapagal-Arroyo, made an appearance at the unveiling of three colossal retirement villages in the Batangas region, a large province just eighty kilometers south of the country's capital region, Metro Manila (see figure I.1). The mere mention of these multimillion-dollar property ventures, christened with names like the Imperial Silvertown, Chateau Evercrest Retirement Project, and Batulao Monte Grande, evokes a particular retirement fantasy. The manner in which the word *retirement* proliferates in the vast inventory of brochures and websites produced by the Philippine Retirement Authority (PRA), and the global campaigns initiated to sell such developments, tends to evoke a particular meaning of return for its consumers: one that is simultaneously foreign and local. They can certainly expect to experience a wide range of amenities, all of which are now commonplace to tourism throughout the globe. Yet while retirement in the Philippines has often been associated with non-Filipinos, the way these villages cater to localized aspirations at-

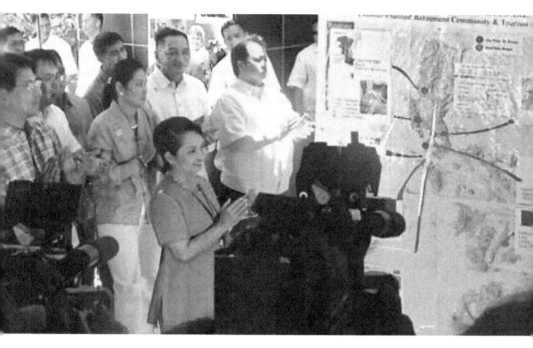

FIGURE I.1 Former Philippine president Gloria Macapagal-Arroyo with Philippine Retirement Authority chair Edgar Aglipay and guests in Batangas in 2007. Courtesy of the Philippine Retirement Authority.

tached to the ideals of retirement makes these developments unique. Each of the retirement hubs also includes churches, schools, clinics, and even entire hospitals. These resources collectively enable consumers not only to retire in the traditional sense but also to reside with the possibility of starting a business, having more children, and raising them in the Philippines. "Retiring in the Philippines," suggests Jerry, a former police officer in San Francisco who has already contributed a significant portion of his 401(k) to a property in one of the retirement villages, "is like having a second chance at living life."

Maligned both by ongoing accusations of corruption and by a national economy mired in debt, the former president touted the importance of capitalizing on aspirations to retire in the Philippines. Macapagal-Arroyo is certain that the materialization of these aspirations will pave the way for the future development of the country. Raising her voice in exuberant conviction, she extolled this opportunity to the handful of press and dignitaries present: "I want [the] PRA to boost its efforts to develop and promote the Philippines as a retirement haven and contribute to the increase of foreign investments" (quoted in Pelovello 2008).

The country's reputation for violence and corruption, however, continues to hinder the Philippine tourism industry's attempts to lure travelers to visit, let alone retire in, the Philippines. Unsettling tales of crime, malfeasance, disorder, and inaccessibility—the same tropes that generally shape the discourse of travel throughout cities in the Global South—have had a particularly detrimental effect on tourism in the Philippines. They have also dogged the national economy for decades. However, newer patterns of migration and economic alignment are enabling tourism and, by extension, retirement in the Philippines to be reimagined.

The reintroduction of capital throughout the Global South, precipitated by new modes of global mobility, has produced a vast rearrangement of economic ties among countries: the renewing of competition for resources among former Old World adversaries, the rise of newer ones, and the refashioning of global connectivity via a set of increasingly complex and unpredictable channels. As a result, the traditional logics around the primacy of the United States and western Europe as the universal end point for settlement and professional ambition have come into serious question. Likewise, the accumulation of finance capital created by these trends has expanded the consumer classes throughout Asia, including those living in countries traditionally seen as marginal to consumptive behavior (see Hoang 2015). The purchase of luxuries, however, necessitates the desire to protect and maintain what one has acquired. As such, the global increase in consumption has brought with it new forms of social exclusion and the need to reinforce older systems of social segregation (see Caldeira 2000). Contemporary urban development throughout the Global South over the last three decades has been increasingly shaped by the logic of this dialectic.

The convergence of these concurrent social and economic processes has reinvigorated specific sectors within larger economies, namely, the production of amenities for leisure and entertainment aimed at local populations. This brings us back to the former Philippine president's attendance at the unveiling in Batangas. The PRA projects that the country's flagship retirement villages alone, like those in Batangas, will contribute up to $44 billion to the country's economy in the coming years (Mollman 2007).[1] The PRA is the latest in a line of governmental entities throughout the region looking to exploit the potential for capital that is increasingly being produced by shifting trends in local consumerism. To keep pace with other retirement hubs throughout Southeast Asia, PRA executives have been exploring alternatives to advertising to prospective clients in Japan, Korea, and Europe, instead relying on an older strategy to confront the most pressing obstacles to economic development in the Philippines; they continue to depend on the country's most important and unique resource: Filipinos living abroad.

For the Philippines, what constitutes the local immediately comes into question in relation to Filipinos living abroad who are not returning to the Philippines. These *balikbayans* constitute one of the largest tourist populations visiting the Philippines. The Department of Tourism in the Philippines officially defines the term *balikbayan* in two distinct ways. First, there are "Philippine nationals who are temporarily residing abroad," a group primarily composed of laboring bodies exported by the Philippine government as Overseas Filipino Workers. Then there is the more privileged cohort of Filipinos "who acquired foreign citizenship and permanent status abroad" and who are generally referred to as *balikbayans* within the local vernacular. This latter group of former Philippine citizens functions as the focal point of this project.

For the former president, the retirement industry occupies a critical place in her plan for developing the country's economy; balikbayans have become an integral component within this larger plan. As Arroyo's speech poignantly intimates, an increasing number of balikbayans are purchasing property in their homeland as a second home or in hopes of future repatriation. This figure is so vast that a number of PRA executives optimistically project that the Philippines will become home to almost one million retirees by 2015 (Mollman 2007). As the cover of the *Balikbayan* travel magazine conveys, once executives and developers began to grasp the immense economic potential posed by linking balikbayans to the retirement industry, a dynamic shift took place in the Philippine economy. Multinational property developers operating in the Philippines no longer catered exclusively to foreign nationals. New government agencies were constructed. As previously mentioned, the maintenance of an elite consumer class usually depends on the construction of amenities and services focused around and enabled by the security system and the further segregation of wealth from poverty. Together with private developers, immense resources of the state are being deployed to build networks that will support a vast infrastructure of elite residential complexes and retirement villages throughout the country specifically catering to Filipinos living abroad. Spurred on by

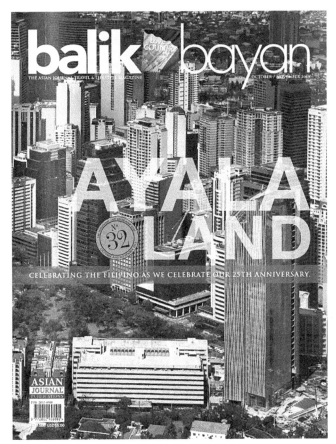

FIGURE I.2
Balikbayan is a "bi-monthly travel and lifestyle journal for balikbayans and Filipino expats from the USA and other parts of the world" published by *Asian Journal*.

government incentives, real estate corporations are continuing to design elaborate and innovative strategies to generate capital from balikbayans and their investments. The immense effort directed toward this redirection of economic policy and development has finally made the dream of an elite lifestyle a distinct possibility for returning Filipino migrants.

Migrant Returns examines how balikbayans have come to play a central role in the development of the Philippine economy, their negotiation of this new role, and the ambivalence produced by it. This book addresses two interrelated questions, which delve into larger concerns regarding the political, economic, and affective tracings of global migration. The first illuminates conceptualizations around contemporary globalization by examining the manner in which the Philippine government utilizes balikbayans to sustain the country's foothold within the global economy. Second, this work engages debates around the processes through which globalization occurs. I argue that a depiction of the colossal urban transformation accompanying the return of balikbayans conveys the very materiality of transnational connectivity between Filipino Americans in the United States and the Philippines.

The multiscaled nature of this dynamic is explored through an examination of the actions and discourses of three interrelated groups of social actors: the Philippine state, the various real estate corporations and realtors composing the transnational real estate industry between the Philippines and the United States, and Filipino returnees themselves. At times, the actions and discourses presented by these three social actors are initiated by distinct and even conflicting motivations and goals. In other instances, however, they complement one another or overlap. The impact of this interaction on the urban landscape of the Philippines illuminates new ways of conceptualizing global migration.

Migration, the movement of human beings from one geographically delimited space to another, is propelled in part by the imperatives of capitalism. Karl Marx famously described the workings of capitalism as that intractable process in which "all that is solid melts into air, all that is holy is profaned, and men at last are forced to face with sober sense the real conditions of their lives and their relations with their fellow men" (Marx 1978, 25). Because our contemporary social reality is constituted by the exchange of money and the logic of finance, everything is transformed into values, and, as Marx suggests, human relationships have been replaced with "object relationships." There is nothing that articulates this image more vividly than migration. Movement—departure, diaspora, exile, settlement, and return, all in search of capital—comes to define the very identities of those who migrate, and "as individuals express their life, so they are" (Schmitt 1987, 8).

At the same time, migration is equally driven by the force of migrant desire, or what Arjun Appadurai (1996) calls the "work of the imagination." This work, an imaginative laboring, drives innovation: designs, formulas, knowledge systems, images, and patterns. The outcome, the labor of the imagination, draws together these intensities into entire systems of culture and meaning: art and literature, architecture and environmental design, forms of urbanism, technologies, and media communications. It also forms the trajectory of migration's many circuits and networks. All of those singularities, multiplicities, objects, and experiences—which are provisional, fluid, and stable—merge together into an infrastructure of a functional tandem that configures our social reality. The conjunction of these systems is sometimes complicit with the logic of capitalism. But, in other moments, these systems, including those constituting migrations, may also operate alongside and outside the circuits of the global economy. It is critical to this analysis that both individuals and communities continue to be placed at the center of this imaginative laboring.

This book is a multisite ethnography of the transformations produced by a system of imaginative laboring that has taken place for decades. The culmination of this labor is deriving a distinct form of return migration. This migration is changing the economic region of Metro Manila in ways both material and affective. While conservative estimates suggest that 2.5 million Filipino migrants have permanently returned to the Philippines over the past fifteen years, this number fails to capture the exact size of this "graying population" who continually make their way back to the Philippines each year outside of formal, governmentally regulated channels or without the explicit intent of staying for good.[2] Having settled somewhere abroad for several decades, these Filipinos find their way back to their homeland in various configurations. Until the mid-2000s, Filipino emigrants looking to retire in the Philippines constituted less than 10 percent of visitors to the country. Since then, however, boosted by incentives to invest in residential property coupled with the country's ever-redeveloping urban landscape, that number has been steadily rising.

Repeated Turning

This book seeks to disentangle what Anna Tsing (2005) calls the "sticky materiality" produced by globalized capital from the imaginative laboring that animates it. It attempts to embody that which has become objectified through capitalism by articulating the subjectivity constituted by return, returning, and returns. Because of the general emphasis on the capitalist imperative within scholarship and popular discourse, so clearly depicted by the images invoked above, our understanding of migration tends to frame movement around binaries: core and periphery, receiver and sender, capitalist enterprise and exploited labor. Subsequently, a critique of migration is often attentive only to locating and singling out those scripts, both conspicuous and hidden, that are in direct opposition to the capitalist and universalizing entrapments of modernity. Thus, there remains only one version shaping the narrative of migration, capital, and resistance to it.

Yet, as we already know, there are many narratives to history. This book explicitly addresses this multiplicity; it is an ethnography of multiple modernities. Migration, often the paintbrush of a particular modernity, is constituted by bodies, objects, practices, and ideas *in motion*. And through this very movement, each of these entities continues to change. In this way, migration is also a metric, one that measures both space and time. It charts the "staging of modernity" both in terms of location and also as a demarcation separating what is ahead from that which was left behind (see Mitchell 2000). Yet, because of the simplistic binary that continues to enclose our conception and critique of globalization, *home* is situated, epistemically, as the counterpoint of modernity. It remains stationary. Home is a point of origin, fixed and unmediated by time or space. It remains that which is left behind.

The *return to home*, then, is usually understood, at best, as a mere fantasy or as practices of nostalgia. In this way, it is usually formed by the narrative of longing but never fully realized in practice. At worst, return is characteristically considered to be evidence of the very failure to become modern. Those who do in fact return might as well have never left. Yet, if globalization continually seeks to unify time, space, and everything in between within a trajectory of persistent modernity, how can it then be the case that home remains still?

Inderpal Grewal (2005) employs the phrase "transnational connectivities" to emphasize the manner in which governmentality, which she describes as the culmination of "subjects, technologies, and ethnical practices," permeates and becomes fused within transnational networks and connections.[3] From this vantage point, home is a constantly shifting archive, attempting to grapple onto and capture multiple imaginaries, aspirations, and social formations (Schein 1999). In this way, home is less a geographically delimited and physical space. Rather, more accurately, it is a *process* containing a set of connectivities, which continue to traverse the globe and vacillate between places.

Benito M. Vergara's (2009) work on Filipinos who have settled in Daly City, California, describes the daily connections maintained by Filipinos with their homeland. To make sense of the imaginative laboring produced by these connectivities, Vergara employs the term "repeated turning."

Borrowing from the sense of obligation evoked within Khachig Tölölyan's (1996) conception of diaspora, Vergara (2009, 4) argues that "whether manifested as political activism, assertions of ethnic pride, nostalgia, consumerism, or just vague remembering, the repeated turning is obliquely opposed to the narrative of assimilation. The tension between this remembrance and the demands of citizenship in the new homeland, the obligations in different directions, constitute a predicament for the Filipino immigrant."[4] Return, here, is crucially envisaged as moments of perpetual occurrence. The case of Filipinos physically returning to their homeland, understood through a process of repeated turning, poignantly demonstrates how often the act of returning performed by migrants is simply a manifestation of much longer and more extensive processes as opposed to a single event or stage.

Migrant Returns can be interpreted as the continuation of Vergara's seminal examination of the transnational subjectivity constructed by particular flows of migrations to the United States after 1965. Because of this structural moment in the economic and political history of the United States, a fundamentally different kind of skilled and educated labor was selectively integrated into the country's labor market. Stephen Graham and Simon Marvin (2001) explain how contemporary forms of "splintering urbanism" are built on the foundation laid by previous technologies, urban policies, and settlement, which produced "pathways" under which newer capacities formed. Moments of intensive immigration, especially those occurring immediately after 1965, are paramount to conceiving the ways in which migration, and return in particular, constructed contemporary pathways for material and affective investments in the Philippine economy.[5]

By situating the concept of return through a theoretical framing of repeated turning, I am imploring my audience to continuously interrogate the idea of migration, semantically, conceptually, and in terms of scale. From 2006 to 2010, I followed a particular cohort of Filipino women and men who, for various reasons, were returning to their homeland to purchase property, secure their physical possessions and investments in the Philippines, or oversee the building of their homes on property they had already bought. A significant portion of this work is concerned with the way in which these women and men articulate their experiences of return, their narratives of interacting with Filipinos who were once seen as compatriots but who have become "different." These stories—conveyed in numerous ways: ubiquitous jokes, exasperated tirades, shameful confessions, and idle gossip—construct a vital archive for challenging fundamental assumptions around migration, globalization, and modalities of power.

Apart from a handful of scholars, including Vergara, the steadily growing literature on Filipinos has devoted less attention to this generation of Filipinos who migrated and settled in the United States after 1965. This is partially due to the institutionalized effects of racializing Asian Americans as model minorities during this period. The homogenization of this particular cohort of Filipinos, some of whom were highly educated and skilled and just as many of whom were not, has been internalized by much of the critical scholarly research on people of color in the United States.[6] As a result, the Filipino immigrants who eventually found their way into one of the many suburban neighborhoods in various parts of the United States have become emulsified into a singular, middle-class population that does not readily fit into the counterhegemonic and postcolonial discourse emerging alongside the literatures related to ethnic and Asian American studies. Rather than engaging alternatives to this racializing discourse, the recent scholarship on contemporary flows of Filipino migration between the Philippines and the United States after 1965 has been primarily concerned with a critical examination of the gendered division of labor among the working class from the Philippines.[7]

Yet a critical examination of the American middle class often embodied by immigrants who arrived after 1965 presents multiple points to intervene within discourses on globalization and the prevailing shadow of American imperialism. It reveals the manner in which fundamental notions of neoliberalism were imposed on migrating bodies of Asian immigrants as they settled in the United States as a direct result of economic imperatives to fill labor shortages in the U.S. labor market. Just as importantly, it disrupts the spatial-temporal notion that modernity began beyond the boundaries of the Philippines. On the contrary, several Philippine scholars have carefully described how colonial education and the inculcation of the English language had, after only a generation, successfully produced copies of Americans who were sometimes "more American than Americans" (San Juan 1998). One of the fundamental "structures of feeling" produced in the United States and relayed throughout its various colonial metropoles, especially in the Philippines, was the ideal of being middle class and, in particular, the ideology of "classlessness" it evoked and enabled.[8] Before stepping foot in the United States, through the manner in which these ideologies were forcibly incorporated within Philippine society, Filipinos had already acquired the tools to navigate American society. The confluence of culture, colonial education, the English language, Hollywood films, and American commodities had constructed a map to aid this navigation, and the pursuit of the middle class became the compass (see, for example, Capino 2010).

The refusal, then, to view nostalgia as simply an enactment of longing for an imagined past disrupts lingering notions that conceive of migrant identities being dependent on place. My use of *homeland* is not confined to the geographic limitations of the Philippine nation-state but more specifically refers to a spatial-temporal *process*. When im/migrants imagine their homelands, as Appadurai's (1996) conceptions of scapes shows, these images and visions are constantly mediated and distilled not only through memories, which are also contingent and changing, but through a vast array of communicative technologies and global media relayed from place to place. Here I am expanding on Ien Ang's (1994) interpretation of Paul Gilroy's (1993) *Black Atlantic*. Ang argues that "the experience of migration brings with it a shift in perspective. . . . [F]or the migrant it is no longer 'where you're from,' but 'where you're at' which forms the point of anchorage" (1994, 10). Nostalgia, in this way, performed through a litany of religious practices, parties and festivals, phone calls and e-mails, and foodways, is not in reference to an exact moment or place. Nostalgia is an anchor providing moments of assurance as immigrants navigate between places.

Finally, this framework contrasts with much of the scholarship on return migration, which often relies on traditional conceptions of migration as being produced through particular "cycles" or resulting from a set of "stages."[9] Because of the dominant economic reasoning used to explain the processes of globalization and migration discussed previously, return migration is just another iteration of global market forces producing supply and demand, and push and pull. Rather, I argue that return, whether voluntary, forced, or generational, is also governed by the thrust of imaginative laboring. The flow of migration, its destinations and pit stops, may follow the larger circuits of economic imperatives, but the materialization through which this motion takes shape is the result of migrants' drives: their desires, aspirations, and dreams for themselves and their families, and the possibility of other futures. In the chapters that follow, I chart the traces of these transnational connectivities as they materialize throughout the landscape and built environment of Manila.

Imagining the Global-Modern

The idea of a global economy elicits another kind of paradoxical imaginary: one that is all encompassing and yet ever expanding. Often, even those who write about the global economy have a difficult time articulating its boundaries and the very processes enabling its colossal machinery. One dominant logic informing the language of globalization suggests that mandates necessitated by irrepressible market forces compel those at the helm of multinational corporations and developed nation-states to yield to and unify under its demands lest they fall to the wayside or be trampled beneath its weight. This rhetoric, and the kind of scholarship it elicits, is continually challenged by the task of giving equal attention to the ways in which globalization affects the everyday lives of individuals. Yet, through this very formula, this faceless multitude has become irrelevant. They are understood to be powerless in determining how the global economy evolves, and their choices, actions, and resistance are inevitably reappropriated and reintegrated into the global market.

We, however, are constantly reminded that communities, as marginalized as they may be, continue to shape and even determine, at times, the direction in which the larger global economy moves. These communities and the transnational convergence of their specific practices—socioeconomic, political, and cultural—produce the very interventions that confront, reshape, enable, or become consumed by the global economy and the processes of globalization. Decades of migrating and returning Filipinos and the cumulative capital that they bring and reinvest provide one example. I am focusing on how the return of Filipino immigrants to the Philippines after 1965 and the decades of remittances, both financial and social, have enabled the production of what I call the *balikbayan economy*, the transnational circulation of diasporic labor and capital between the United States and the Philippines. While the vast majority of the literature on international migration examines labor flows and settlement into various receiving countries, I employ the idiom of *migrant return* to convey the complex process through which many immigrants maintain ties with their homelands and eventually travel back either to visit or to resettle.

These *returns* have not only reconfigured the physical and economic landscape of the migrants' homeland but also impacted larger processes of globalization. In the example above, Arroyo's presence at the unveiling of the retirement villages conveys the often-indistinguishable relationship between the public and the private spheres in the Philippines, what executives in the PRA calls the "twin strategy" or "triangular relations" (Toyota and Xiang 2012). It illustrates a moment in which governmental leaders, corporate executives, and business owners (triangular relations) unite in an attempt to exploit the capital returns of balikbayans. Meanwhile, what becomes apparent is that balikbayans, in many ways, continue to complicate and even resist assumed market-oriented logics. Such contradictions are endemic in "actually existing neoliberalism"; when applied to specific places, like the Philippines, these practices are often "contested, negotiated, and adapted . . . with oftentimes uncanny collusions with political, economic, and social formations" (Ortega 2012).[10]

The intersection between property development and structural adjustment programs features prominently throughout the development of Southeast Asian economies. Metro Manila has become a paramount example of debt financing in the Global South. As the Philippines and a host of other developing economies ceaselessly borrow from global lending institutions as a means of improving their credit portfolios and enhancing their relationships with trading partners in the rest of the world, property development figures as an integral mechanism through which governments can stabilize their local economies. Through a vast network of building projects, such as dams, roads and highways, and commercial districts, all of which are financed through debt, foreign investments continue to increase, and local governments "partner" with private entities as a means of exploiting these fleeting moments of financial boom.[11]

The hundreds of corporate investors, transnational real estate brokers, and government officials present during Arroyo's speech in Batangas attest to the significant role that property development performs in developing national and global economies. The input of foreign investments, critically fueled by decades of remittances sent by Filipinos working abroad, enabled the Philippine economy to offset losses created by an equal number of years of borrowing. Over a period of time, this relative stability sustained a foundation to grow property markets around the country's most vibrant urban centers (see Rimmer and Dick 2009). When the Asian region suffered a severe economic crisis in 1997, this embedded pattern of debt financing, coupled with flows of remittances, sheltered the Philippines from collapse (see de Dios and Hutchcroft 2003).

The concept of the *balikbayan economy* introduces a rubric for analyzing the spatial-temporal patterns of migration and investment that have characterized the rapidly transforming National Capital Region of the Philippines. I use the term *spatial-temporal* as a way of connecting these patterns to historical moments of colonialism and neocolonialism, specifically the period when the United States formally colonized the Philippines, that explain why and how balikbayans are emerging as a key component in developing the Philippine economy. The pervasive manner in which the Philippines was reconstructed as a colonized subject of U.S. imperialism produced not only persistent configurations of economic and military dependence but also, perhaps more significantly, fantasies of achieving a particular kind of American modernity (see Tadiar 2004).

These fantasies, and the imaginative labor they performed, generated waves of emigration from the Philippines. From a total population of approximately 100 million people, 2013 government statistics indicate more than 10 million Filipinos were working overseas. Of these, more than 1.2 million were classified as "irregular," either working on tourist visas or laboring as undocumented residents overseas, while more than 4.2 million were "temporary," commonly referred to as OFWs. At the other end of the spectrum, 4.9 million permanent emigrants were settled in different parts of the world (Commission on Filipinos Overseas 2013). This latter figure includes balikbayans living permanently in places like the United States but not the generations of Filipino Americans who have been residing in the United States since the early part of the twentieth century. The number of Filipinos emigrating to the United States surged after the passage of the Immigration and Nationality Act of 1965 (also known as the Hart–Celler Act). Since then, the number of Filipinos residing in the United States has officially risen to more than 3.4 million, the largest group of permanent Filipino emigrants residing outside of the Philippines.[12]

After decades of living in the United States and accumulating a limited amount of wealth there, many of these Filipinos are visiting and returning to their homeland. The tourism and retirement industries are devoting more and more resources to ensure that a significant portion of these balikbayans will invest in the country's property market. Yet tales of crime and corruption, along with larger aspirations to achieve modernity, are standing in the way of these returns. For instance, Edgar Aglipay, the previous chairman of the PRA, discussed the hindrances constraining the growth of both tourism and retirement in the Philippines. He stated that media reports continually portrayed the Philippines as a crime-laden, chaotic, and dirty country teeming with kidnappers. "'We have a bit of a problem here, because of perception,' he explained to members of the Philippine media. 'It's the negative impression. That's our biggest concern in trade missions abroad, the common question is how safe is the Philippines. More often than not the doubters have never been to the country.' These 'negative impressions,' the Philippine Retirement Agency (PRA) general manager Fernando Z. Francisco agreed, 'have hampered efforts to get investors and retirees to visit'" (Alave 2007). These problems, which encouraged the initial generations of Filipinos to leave the Philippines and settle abroad, especially after 1965, have now become the obstacles inhibiting Filipinos from actively investing in a return to their homeland. Now that this "graying" generation is facing retirement and, contrary to images of model minority successes, continuing to struggle economically in the United States, a triad of government agents, multinational corporations, and financial institutions is attempting to capitalize on a particular moment of crisis. These entities have coalesced and are investing significant resources to convince balikbayans to overcome their long-held reservations around permanently returning to their homeland and to decide to purchase property in order to retire in the Philippines.

Building toward a Modern Economy

In attempting to define and articulate what exactly constitutes *the modern*, whether it is the modern world, modernity, or even the postmodern, we would only force ourselves to trudge through an endless and arguably pointless debate (see Mitchell 2000). And yet we instinctively return to this question because the term has become ubiquitous. We find it conditioning every facet of our social world. It becomes either a standard to which we aspire or a distinction separating us from what we hope to have left behind. The irony of the modern is that in the moment when we feel that we have broached the threshold into modernity, we find ourselves desiring through constant technological innovation and the pervasive anxiety induced by thoughts of insecurity to become modern once again.[13] The modern may be many things, perhaps endlessly, but it is certainly elusive. The following chapters in this book provide a cartography mapping the eventual intersections of two simultaneously operating modernities. Balikbayans, launched toward the United States by aspirations originally precipitated through decades of American coloniality and education, left a homeland that was also enacting its own fantasies of modernity.

Not unlike Casablanca beginning in the 1940s (see Rabinow 1989) or Brasília during the late 1950s (see Holston 1989), Metro Manila began its march toward modernity in the 1960s when Ferdinand Marcos instituted a series of public projects throughout the city in hopes of aligning the Philippines with other developing nation-states that were outwardly aspiring to Western democratic rule. From the late 1960s to his removal in 1986, the Marcos administration oversaw the construction of a number of landmarks in the capital city. These urban designs played a crucial role in attracting foreign investment and, more importantly, providing evidence that the country merited economic restructuring by the World Bank and the International Monetary Fund. For example, this period saw the creation of Epifanio de los Santos Avenue, the main artery of transit cutting across almost the entire region.

Marcos's wife, Imelda, was arguably equally influential. Her aspirations to a certain modernity were also made visible through her numerous contributions to the architectural landscape, including the multimillion-dollar Cultural Center Complex, the Philippine National Convention Center, and the National Film Center, all built on reclaimed land on the edge of Manila Bay. The construction of the Cultural Center alone spanned almost two decades (1966–1982). Replicating the same modernist framework of urban renewal occurring throughout the rest of developing world, Marcos's mandate for a "New Society" resulted in the state-administrated removal of thousands of "squatters" from informal settlements (Shatkin 2004).

These imperatives led to the creation of the Metropolitan Manila Commission in 1975, which would oversee the first coherent master plan for Metro Manila. For the first time since American colonial rule, Metro Manila provided a master city plan entitled *Metropolitan Manila: Towards a City of Man* (Marcos 1985). Not only did this plan oversee the construction of Epifanio de los Santos Avenue but also the Manila South and North Expressways and the light rail transit system, which would produce the "vector of speed" that would lend itself to further separating the privileged and mobile elite by elevating them above the widespread poverty below.[14] And, similar to what would become characteristic of neoliberal urban governance, the city's renewal was made possible only through a complexly interweaving system of payoffs that ultimately contributed to bankrupting the country (Hackworth 2006). The misuse of public funds to commence building these grandiose plans caused a number of projects to stall or fail permanently owing to financial mismanagement or outright fraud (Manapat 1991).

Another implementation that set Marcos apart from his predecessors was the creation of the Housing Settlement and Regulatory Commission, the precursor to the Housing and Land Use Regulatory Board. While previous leaders imposed their rule through proxies at the local level who would give preferential treatment to specific contracts in which these leaders had a vested interest, Marcos implemented one central governmental authority for land use management, zoning decisions, and the approval of building permits. The commission was the first centralized governmental institution to possess exclusive jurisdiction over local decisions concerning land use in Metro Manila.

The commission's early failures represent many of the hurdles created by the entrenched culture of land ownership in the Philippines. The commission had agreed that there was a need for land reform and enacted the Urban Land Reform Programme of 1979, which clearly stipulated that property development in Metro Manila needed to fall in line with government plans and, as such, real estate purchases needed to be registered with and approved by the government. A tide of opposition rose among the landholding elite, and a number of real estate contractors and owners, as well as business owners, protested that the government regulation mandated by the commission would lead the Philippine economy into collapse (Connell 1999, 420). In response, Marcos intervened and decided to redirect and focus land reform on "depressed areas," namely, those affected by "squatters," which amounted to only 1.1 percent of Metro Manila's total land area (Van Naerssen, Ligthart, and Zapanta 1996).

This political response was intended less to remove impoverished populations from "borrowed land" than to divert internal migration away from Metro Manila toward the peripheries and decrease urban cramming. In time, because of the spatial constraints created by overuse and crowding, government incentives to develop the semiperiphery of Metro Manila during the 1970s and 1980s led to the influx of manufacturing and middle- and lower-class settlements throughout the flood regions of Pasig and Marikina to the northeast and Valenzuela and Caloocan to the northwest. Situated on either side of the Pasig and Marikina Rivers, in particularly low-lying zones, these lands tend to experience ongoing damage and a weakening of soil foundation due to the rivers' recurrent flooding. Unsurprisingly, these regions tend to be disproportionately occupied by the urban poor and informal settlements.

While various microlevel policies either stalled or failed, the larger interventions that Marcos made in the planning of the region were vastly more significant to the economic development of the Philippines. The massive consolidation and centralization of Marcos's authority led to implementations that defined the economic and political borders of what has largely become Metro Manila today. In addition, the regulation of land use and development directly precipitated the creation and industrialization of the CALABARZON (Cavite, Laguna, Batangas, Rizal, and Quezon) region, which provided for the expansion of economic activities like production, importation, and exportation. This produced a massive influx of internal migrants from the provinces, which continues to define the character of urban settlement in Luzon, the largest island within the archipelago, today.

The establishment of the CALABARZON economic zone is significant. The region, less a political subdivision than a geoeconomic site designated specifically as an agro-industrial growth zone, showcases the country's fundamentally neoliberal design. Early policies that had diverted industrial building projects away from Metro Manila were redirected toward the region. The following chapter will discuss how Marcos continued to rely on a strategy of "debt-driven growth," in which a large portion of the debt was reinvested in the industrial growth in CALABARZON. Ironically, even though Marcos's administration was directly responsible for leading the country into a prolonged economic crisis, subsequent administrations relied on the same strategies. The CALABARZON region continues to function as the country's base for industrial development and the focal point for launching many of the country's export-oriented economic policies.

The downfall of President Marcos and the inauguration of Corazon Aquino as the president of the Philippines in 1986 formally marked the restoration of democratic institutions in the country. This restoration was made official through the ratification of the Philippine Constitution in 1987 and the enactment of the "new" local government autonomy code in 1991. These laws effectively institutionalized political decentralization in the country. The Congress was restored, as were the regional levels of government—from the provinces to the *barangays*—and, with them, political autonomy was restored at each level. These changes had decisive effects on the management of urban planning in Metro Manila. While much of the Philippine populace, as well as various social movements that had been deeply influenced by the people power movement in 1986, had believed that the regime change and introduction of the Aquino administration would lead to a transformation of the oligarchic structure of Philippine politics, the enactment of the autonomy code essentially restored the governing power of the old guard of Filipino elites.

Beginning already during Aquino's administration, the state began to adopt a policy of economic liberalization, which was a drastic shift away from the state-centered governance of the Marcos regime. Under intense pressure from international lending corporations to make good on debt repayments, the Aquino administration decided against playing an active role in repairing and maintaining various sectors of Philippine society, which had been in dire need of attention (Bello 2005). One of these sectors was urban planning and the implementation of various improvements to the city's deteriorating urban fabric. Instead, Aquino hoped that privatizing the urban development of Metro Manila would cause foreign and domestic investors to jump at the opportunity to fund new projects for the sake of capital gain. Such an incentive would also allow local bureaucrats, property developers, and the landed elite to work together and support each other in building highly profitable developments.

Eventually, in order for the state to continue playing a pivotal role in the political economy of Metro Manila and the rest of the Philippines, the administration would continue to adhere to market-oriented policies that disproportionately benefited multinational conglomerates. The expansion of private property holdings throughout the region would play a key role in maintaining these public-private relationships (Ortega 2012). The development of property, which by now had become almost entirely directed by corporate interests, would take center stage within the country's economic policy. These strategies would slowly emerge as the foundation for the balikbayan economy, discussed in the next chapter.

The Modern Balikbayan Landscape

Today Metro Manila continues to "become modern." The most apparent traces are vividly conveyed by Metro Manila's ever-transforming landscape. In malls throughout Metro Manila, along with coffee products sold at Starbucks, Coffee Bean, and Seattle's Best, one can also find organically produced body soap at Lush or red velvet sweets at Tea Cake. Franchises that one would see in an upscale mall or neighborhood in the United States are finding their way into more and more commercial districts throughout Manila. At the same time, the traditional *sari-sari* stores or *karinderias* that once spilled out onto city sidewalks when I was child are becoming increasingly less visible. Commercial and mall developments have replaced most small businesses or pushed them into less frequented spaces on the fringes. Malls have also become intrinsic to the balikbayan landscape throughout Manila. With little public space left, malls have become not only a space of consumption but one of distinction as well. Here, the French flaneur strolling through the streets and plazas of Paris has been replaced by upper-class Filipinos, with shopping bags and *yayas*, or maids, in tow, strolling through malls and attracting the gazes of all those who can only afford to look and enjoy the air-conditioning.

Malls are fundamental to the daily life of Manileños in a way that is incomprehensible to those socialized in the nuclear and individualized ethics driving the disappearance of communal space in America. In the Philippines, the mall *is* the public. Family members "picnic" together in mall restaurants after a busy workday or on the weekends.[15] Malls throughout the Philippines contain churches, clinics, and even schools. And here, too, the working class is confined to separate minoritizing spaces within the mall, where they are forced to congregate and socialize in dimly lit stairwells. For locals and tourists alike, the mall is a destination rather than a pit stop. Commercial districts and giant malls sprouting around Manila have become not only conduits for foreign investment but also a circuit of cultural exchange that is transforming everyday life in the Philippines. The malls have also become the literal backyards of elite high-rise residential buildings. Consequently, Metro Manila has become a disparate patchwork of residential and business condominiums connected by these commercial districts and malls. Some developers have taken this type of enclave development to the extreme by physically attaching condominium buildings to Manila Rapid Transit (MRT) stations. Most MRT stations are already located adjacent to malls or include a type of swapmeet–mall amalgamation. To transfer from the MRT to the light rail transit line, for instance, one must wander through two separate malls. The acronym CBD, for central business district, a particular conglomeration of residential condominiums, corporate offices, and malls that share the same space, has even become integrated into the Manileño vernacular.

Gavin Shatkin (2008) utilizes the concept of "bypass-implant urbanism" to describe a particular component integral to producing this modernity. His concept conveys the increasing complicity between large developers and governmental partners through the privatization of urban planning. He argues that "in this context of unusually inert and indifferent government, private developers have been granted considerable power to reengineer cities to create new spaces for production and consumption, and to facilitate the flow of people and capital between these spaces, by 'bypassing' the congested arteries of the 'public city' and 'implanting' new spaces for capital accumulation that are designed for consumerism and export-oriented production" (384). Private investment and development facilitate the movement of capital without having to confront the lack of public infrastructure and the corrupt bureaucracy rampant throughout the Philippines; it not only bypasses it but directly depends on its inadequacy. Metro Manila's built environment is increasingly being produced by bypass-implant urbanism. As a result, not only are private corporations becoming more responsible for producing public spaces in the Philippines, but the ever-expanding multipurpose enclaves and malls they build, and the hypersegregation these elite developments create, are becoming the public.

These sites have become paradigmatic of the balikbayan landscape, not necessarily because they constitute the places where balikbayans actually resettle, but because these modes of elite lifestyle represent the mobility and affluence that is often assumed to adhere to balikbayans. Balikbayans do not often choose to reside in elite enclaves once they return to Manila. And yet these are being built with balikbayans in mind. The *balikbayan landscape*, I argue, should shift our attention away from individual figures and toward the *practices* producing the changes occurring throughout Metro Manila and other regions in the country. While appearing to exude a particular cosmopolitan modernity, these landscapes are actually emblematic of what Julie Chu (2010) calls the "oscillations between the one and the many of modernity, between its singularizing claims as ideology and its heterogeneous configurations as practice" (6).

Global property development attempts to fix a particular ideology of modernity in place by practicing a particular ideology. Yet, while the exterior and shape of these developments may appear to express a particular modern aesthetic, I take them to signal a much larger coherence between global capitalism and state formation. Likewise, I utilize the balikbayan landscape to conceive of return migration and the subsequent transformation of urban centers throughout the Global South as simultaneously signaling the ambivalence and precarity produced by the friction of this alignment.

This book brings together an interdisciplinary array of voices articulating a critique of the fraught connection between public and private enterprise that is patterning contemporary approaches to economic development throughout the Global South (Rofel 1999). The balikbayan economy, fusing return migration together with global property development, is a result of the convergence between the public and the private. The manner in which a particular cosmopolitan modernity appears to merge itself into the built environment of Manila is characteristic of this moment of urban expansion and becomes productive of the emergent aspirational class of Asians who are now (re)inhabiting intensely developing spaces throughout the globe. Yet, without the circulation of remittances, visits, purchases, and investments by balikbayans, the Philippines would lack a local consumer class to maintain this array of privileged economies. Rather than continuing to compete for foreign investment from Europe, Asia, and, of course, the United States, the Philippine government was able to turn to a new form of mobile capital, the transnational balikbayan. As such, an immense culmination of energy and capital has been drawn together to expand and even generate new investments from balikbayans. Those returning to the Philippines are also tasked with the responsibility for ensuring its future.

Mapping Returns

The complexity binding these tensions together represents the lived materiality of migration and home. Together, remittances, economic policies, public-private partnerships, and investments are the traces of the imaginative laboring produced by Filipinos living and working abroad and *not* merely the products of economic development. As Lieba Faier (2013, 2) argues, "If we can understand how migrants' experiences and dreams help articulate urban landscapes, we can better see the cultural resonances and gaps through which these landscapes materialize and attune ourselves to some of the ways that their development depends on the making of gendered transnational subjects." Mapping the routes of Filipino transnationalism and return *through* the development of real estate properties and the subsequent transformation of the country's landscape necessitates the study of not only physical traces of movement and change but also the imaginings, fantasies, anxieties, and dreams through which they take shape. The study of this mobility, both its material and affectual conditions, requires a deep attention to multiple geographies and positions.

By the time I began conducting preliminary research for this book in December 2007, the major platform for Filipino media outside of the Philippines, the Filipino Channel, or TFC as it is popularly known, began reporting on a growing number of home foreclosures affecting Filipino families in the United States. These reports mainly focused on families living in California. I focused my initial research on Filipinos residing in the predominantly Filipino-populated Daly City, just bordering San Francisco. At first, I located families affected by the housing crisis simply through the foreclosure signs dotting lawns throughout the city. In the following months, eager to understand where these families would relocate, I conducted interviews in churches, at family parties, in remittance centers, and, most often, in their homes. As my research expanded, family members, friends, and colleagues grew adamant about introducing me to more and more Filipinos who were struggling amid financial insecurity.

Not all of the Filipinos I spoke with were in the midst of losing their homes, but all were vexed by the question of whether they would continue living in America or move back to their homeland. The conversations happened to break down evenly between men and women, probably because my research focus lent itself to Filipino couples who were on the cusp of retirement, were married and had children, and felt at ease with the idea of moving back to the Philippines. As such, while some subjects were beset by financial insecurity exacerbated by the financial crisis, each fit the stereotypical profile of balikbayans. By the time I met them, each subject had sustained a living that allowed them to reside in America for several decades and had secured enough savings during this time to allow them to live comfortably in the Philippines for the majority of the year but to travel back to the United States periodically. Even though the suburbs adjacent to San Francisco were much more affordable during the late 1960s and early 1970s, the Filipinos who were capable of remaining in America and settling there were those who were fortunate enough to find jobs in economically stable industries like the postal service or other state employment sectors and, of course, nursing. Many more Filipinos were forced to return to the Philippines shortly after emigrating to the United States.

Concurrently, I had already noticed that a considerable number of Filipino Americans throughout the Bay Area were practicing real estate as an alternative source of income. While conducting research on real estate and homeownership among Filipino Americans (see Pido 2012), I noticed that several of the realtors I interviewed were consultants for and even contracted with real estate corporations in the Philippines, such as Ayala Land, Megaworld, and other major multinational land developers. Many of these realtors operated temporary booths at major Filipino events like the annual Pistahan festival in San Francisco, handing out flyers next to flat-screen monitors projecting dynamic and colorful images of new developments being built in the Philippines. During my conversations with these realtors, I identified a unique intersection between the housing crisis disproportionately affecting Filipinos in California and the upswing of property investments by Filipino Americans hoping to take advantage of a property boom in the Philippines in the years following the crisis that culminated in 2008. The housing crisis indirectly produced an impetus for many of these Filipinos to retire in the Philippines.

Thus, the research that culminated in this book eventually took place in cities in the United States and the Philippines between June 2008 and January 2011. I followed families moving out of their homes, mainly in Daly City, and met them again as they began the process of resettling throughout neighborhoods and subdivisions in different parts of the larger Metro Manila region. Over the course of living in Manila during this period, for months at a time, I also interviewed a host of Filipinos working for various real estate companies in the city. Their economic backgrounds were diverse. Some were executives for major real estate corporations, who were privileged enough to own units in the most elite and newly built neighborhoods in the city. Many more were poor and were obligated to finance their own expenses, including the costs for traveling each time a potential buyer was interested in seeing a property. Very few of these employees had an office; most floated from mall to mall, handing out glossy flyers with their name and cell phone number stapled to each handout. The economic diversity also determined how I communicated. Both executives and those realtors who were fortunate to work as full-time employees for a firm were often university graduates and preferred to speak to an American in English since it gave them the appearance of being more professional. In contrast, contracted employees, those who floated between multiple agencies without any guaranteed salary, preferred to speak in a mix of Tagalog and English, or Taglish.

The American intellectual preoccupation with and investment in perceiving the Philippines as endemic to U.S. imperialism is not lost on most

Filipinos. They are key to understanding the material impact of return migration to the Philippines in a tangible way and resisting the temptation to disembody processes within globalization and relegating the desires of immigrants purely to a logic of market capitalism.

Organization of the Book

By tracing the transnational flow of economic and affective labor between the United States and the Philippines, my aim is to intervene in the discourse on globalization and migration and to illustrate the instrumental role of the imagination and its centrality in dictating the continual reshaping of capitalist modernities. Part I utilizes the concept of the balikbayan economy as an analytical tool to conceptualize migration as a process of connectivity rather than a unidirectional movement. In this first part, I outline the architecture of the balikbayan economy and situate its emergence within the larger history of economic development in the Philippines.

Part II illustrates the affective production of imaginative laboring by embodying processes of return. Its starts with an examination of the contemporary transnational circulation of real estate development capital and the agents who facilitate these flows (chapter 3). Then my analysis shifts away from the political-economic relationship between the state and multinational corporations to examine the ambivalence and anxieties produced when migrants return to the Philippines (chapters 4 and 5). The final chapters discuss the economic and affective production of exceptional spaces through special retirement zones (chapter 6 and the conclusion), and the ways in which these various returns often sustain and intensify social inequalities within the Philippines (epilogue). This book examines how the logic of movement is not simply governed by attempts to capitalize on economic returns but equally through the active imagining constituted by those migrants who are *actually* returning as well.

PART I. DEPARTURES

1. The Balikbayan Economy » Filipino Americans and the Contemporary Transformation of Manila

Often, thinkers writing on international migration, even some employing a transnational lens, produce conceptualizations of movement that are fundamentally unidirectional. This envisioning of migration, travel, and economic trade subsequently creates a framework that perceives "receiving" countries as the sole beneficiaries of exploited "sending" countries. Scholars are beginning to develop a notion of transnational urbanism to trace the materiality of social change produced by patterns of transnationalism in order to offset this bifurcating framework (M. Smith 2001). The aim of this chapter is to map a particular economy produced by the multidirectional circulation of migration and financial investments, in this particular case, Filipinos visiting or resettling in the Philippines and the material capital that they bring and spend.

These "returns" are enabled by an assemblage of state-designed policies, international payment systems, and multinational corporate interests, which are together transforming the urban landscape of Manila and the everyday lives of those inhabiting it. The material and affectual transformations occurring throughout the National Capital Region (NCR) and other expanding regions throughout the globe complicate and unsettle the view that receiving countries are on the winning end of market interests and globalization. In many ways, the crises around economic development and local labor shortages are actually reproduced by the state governments that are sending multitudes of laborers abroad.

The *balikbayan economy*, in which the circulation of foreign investments and large-scale property developments play a key role, maps contemporary forms of transnationalism and globalization that intertwine Filipinos in the United States together with those living in the Philippines in material ways. This economy relies on the intensive exploitation of emigrant Filipino labor and capital to meet a demand for lifestyles of increased luxury supplied by multiple forms of foreign investment. Significantly, the foundational framework constituting this economy was set in motion more than three decades ago. Through the ingenuity of contemporary corporate investors and property developers, policies originally legislated in the 1970s have been reconfigured to enable flows of returning Filipinos, balikbayans who are increasingly becoming new investors in the country's real estate economy, to become crucial actors in the contemporary transformation of Metro Manila.

Investments made by balikbayans have been integral to creating a new market for property developers to lease or sell their real estate products in the emergent balikbayan economy. For example, 40 percent of the high-end properties in the Timberland Heights of San Mateo, Rizal, were purchased by Filipinos based in the United States (Salazar 2008). Furthermore, Philippine banks have started offering twenty-five-year mortgages for the first time. Several real estate agents even mentioned that balikbayans were seen as a particularly safe bet. "Alam mo [you know], banks prefer balikbayans. They are more eager to do business with balikbayans than even Filipinos here," one agent told me. A real estate agent who showed me a condominium in Fort Bonifacio Global City, one of the most elite residential neighborhoods in Metro Manila, explained, "Banks know that balikbayans want to return. Many of them have to return. When they return, banks think to themselves, where will they live? Of course they are going to want to make sure that they and their families have a good place to live. So banks will quickly give loans to balikbayans as long as they can prove that they can afford the amortization of their homes."

More recently, the country's remittance-fueled economy and subsequent rapid development have become cyclically propelled by a new imperative. Filipinos not only are simply visiting or sending remittances to the Philippines but for various reasons are now seriously entertaining the possibility of returning and staying. Seen by most property developers in the Philippines as the market with the highest buying potential and no longer simply a source of remittance income, balikbayans have become the target for an glut of high-priced residential and business investments emerging throughout and around Metro Manila. Understood through the context of Filipino migration since 1965, however, what appears to be a contemporary innovation is much more complicated, mirroring Luis Francia's (2001) observation of his own experience of transmigration as "the inevitable corollary to a theorem that had already been set" (184).

Integral to this process are the ways in which state institutions, and the policies they enact, coincide with the Filipinos living and working abroad, either permanently or temporarily. These Filipinos are increasingly encouraged in a myriad of ways to invest a portion of their wages, earnings that are substantially more than what Filipinos are making while working in the Philippines, in high-priced property throughout and around Metro Manila. In turn, a number of foreign corporate investors, who have been paying close attention to this growing trend, have chosen to take a calculated risk on these potential future streams of capital infusion and have continued to back the development of numerous retail and commercial centers. Such spaces are made possible through their interlinkage, both physical and ideological, with the residential property market and the balikbayan economy.

The dependency on foreign investment capital to drive urban development has subsequently led to the creation of a unique landscape: the entire NCR is now composed of highly segregated, multipurpose enclaves sewn together by an eroding transportation infrastructure and a vast network of informal settlements and economies. These property developments are perpetually being built, creating a world alongside the everyday people who continue to inhabit, service, and sustain them. Balikbayans return to a Metro Manila that has become extremely segregated, both economically and socially, and are continually reconciling themselves to a homeland whose transformation they have helped to produce.

Building Inequality

Metro Manila is more accurately a conglomeration of districts, cities, and municipalities rather than a single geographically distinct urban center. Originally four larger cities (Manila, Pasay, Caloocan, and Quezon City) and thirteen municipalities, eight of these municipalities have been chartered as cities in recent years, collectively occupying a total area of 63,600 hectares with a population just over 11.5 million (National Statistics Office 2007). By signing Presidential Decree 921 in 1976, Ferdinand Marcos attempted to capture the region's economic production by knitting together circulating networks of various industries and continual flows of internal and international migration within and around the region by formalizing the creation of the NCR. Since then, Metro Manila has consistently outperformed other regions in the archipelago from an economic perspective; its per capita gross domestic product (GDP) is twice the national average. Together with the CALABARZON (Cavite, Laguna, Batangas, Rizal, and Quezon) economic region, Metro Manila accounts for more than half of the country's total GDP (NSCB 2003). This disproportionately high rate of economic production perpetuates the persistent problem of overpopulation in the city. While Metro Manila constitutes only 0.2 percent of the country's total landmass, almost 13 percent of the country's total population, compounded each year by a growth rate of 2.8 percent, has come to situate itself in the region's densely compacted and dynamically structured space. Historical patterns of urbanization and concentrated economic activity have made the struggle for land and space an undeniable force driving urban transformation in Metro Manila.

Centuries of colonial occupation by several regimes and irreparable damage incurred during World War II in multiple waves of bombing by both the imperial Japanese and U.S. forces, followed by decades of financial mismanagement in state and private interventions into the implementation of urban plans, have shaped Metro Manila into the palimpsest of urbanization that exists today. Scattered remnants of its prewar architectural past are almost completely lost within the entanglement of gated industrial buildings, a variety of makeshift and fortified homes, and a vast landscape of protruding high-rises and malls. Taken as a whole, the city's geography is dizzying. To this day, the patterns of urbanization throughout the megacity are largely driven by the intensive stratification of economic production and the evolving social divisions already set in motion centuries earlier during Spanish rule.

Manila City did not become the center of cosmopolitan culture in the region until after the turn of the twentieth century. After the end of Spanish colonial rule, the walls of the fortress-city of Intramuros that separated Spanish colonials from both the ethnic Chinese entrepreneurial class, ensconced in what is today called Binondo, and the scattered indigenous Filipinos laboring class became irrelevant (Reed 1993; Doeppers 1984). Even before this transition, the vast majority of land was owned by an elite class of wealthy and educated Filipino mestizo families. Even after the Spanish colonial government and its ecclesiastical proxy had mostly disappeared, the legacies of feudal landownership and the societal hierarchies it created refused to dissipate. Much later, a census surveying the inhabitants of the Philippines in 1938 showed that only 4 percent of the entire population of Manila were landowners. In Makati this percentage was even lower, at 1 percent, while the more rural populations of Las Pinas, Taguig, and San Juan had a much higher rate of land ownership, at 20 percent (Magno-Ballesteros 2000a).

During the transition from Spanish colonial rule, a national design for the planning of towns and cities was largely absent. Rather, the implementation of city planning was left to the authority of smaller units: local councils or remaining Spanish friars who were capable of developing particular tracts of land. This energy was focused on building amenities for the colonial and business elite, such as the city's original suburban neighborhoods (Ocampo 1995). As such, far less attention was paid to expanding the infrastructure for sanitation, irrigation systems, or housing to serve the wider population. These early tendencies in land ownership and land use provided the primary sketches for the incongruous shape cast by the immense disparity in wealth in Metro Manila today.

The obstacles restricting the implementation of any city planning were due, in large part, to the deeply entrenched web of elite families who continue to control most of the politics around the city and beyond. Having so cleverly maneuvered themselves into the most elite strata during centuries of Spanish rule, these primarily agricultural elites refused to relinquish any of their wealth and property, or the control that these attainments imbued them with, under the newly fashioned American colonial banner. Realizing that the successful overthrow of the Spanish did not occur in Manila Bay but through waves of Filipino insurrections subsidized and sometimes led by these elite families, the American colonial government knew that its success would depend on its ability to compromise and work in concert with the interests of the mestizo elite (see McCoy 2009).

Cleverly, American colonials enacted a number of changes that effectively created new opportunities for the mestizo elite to expand their wealth and further consolidate their control. When the new American colonial government expropriated 400,000 acres of rich agricultural land once owned by the Catholic Church and the Spanish friars, it passed most of this land into the hands of the elite. Not only would the landholding families benefit from the labor and trade in goods and resources produced by these new properties, but Americans would also benefit from the consolidation in landownership (see Anderson 1998). The mutual benefits extending from this relationship were further enabled by the passage of the Payne–Aldrich Act in 1909. An early precedent to agreements liberalizing trade today, such as the North American Free Trade Agreement (NAFTA), this early legislation eased trading between the two countries by removing duties while increasing incentives, which once again chiefly benefited the Filipino elite (see Hawes 1987).

After the country was granted independence from the United States in 1946, favorable trade agreements between the Filipino landholding elite and American corporations continued. However, the unrestricted flow of trade came with a price. To pay off the debts accrued through the tax-free trade of exported and imported goods, elite Filipinos redirected the rehabilitation assistance funds. This aid was originally provided to the Philippines to repair the catastrophic losses suffered by the country's infrastructure during the Japanese occupation in World War II and, more specifically, the destruction caused by U.S. bombing during the war. Economic disparities throughout the rest of the country produced and deepened fissures within the larger state apparatus, paralyzing a number of attempts to promote governmental centralization and economic regulation. Another set of neo-colonial economic policies directed by the U.S. administration gave tax advantages and further subsidies to Filipino corporations and entrepreneurs who invested in expanding the domestic market for foreign investment. Therefore, the postwar years were marked by a clear focus on the development of industrial manufacturing in and around Metro Manila (see de Dios and Hutchcroft 2003).

During the same period, the Philippine Congress voted to make Quezon City, the municipality that former president Manuel Quezon had hoped would one day replace Manila as the country's new capital, the epicenter of government. An increasing flow of internal migration by middle- and lower-class Filipinos moving to Manila City and its surroundings led to the exodus of elite Filipino mestizos to Quezon City. During the 1950s the subsequent flight of these elite families led to the expansion of the Quezon City suburbs of Quezon and Makati. At the same time, outlying suburbs like the Parañaque (to the southwest), Mandaluyong (adjacent to Makati), and San Juan (just north of Mandaluyong) were developed for manufacturing and business use (see Caoili 1999). The development of these suburbs was further enabled by policies that sought a decentralization of planning authority, such as the Local Autonomy Act of 1959 (Republic Act No. 2264), which granted local and municipal governments great fiscal, planning, and regulatory powers. Predictably, this act tended to benefit the landholding elite since local governments were not vested with the powers to tax municipal residents, and the necessary finances were still under the authority of the state government. Thus, property development and the construction of urban infrastructure was left to the control of private developers (see Magno-Ballesteros 2000b).

Hoping to benefit from the growing political capital in Metro Manila, several families, such as the Ortigas and Aranetas, began establishing elite suburbs to the north of Manila City. Families who moved to these suburbs were within earshot of the political and business happenings in Quezon City but far enough away to escape the unsettling growth of the middle- and lower-class settlements mushrooming throughout the inner city of Manila. While the early trend of urbanization during this period began to move rapidly northward, the Ayala Corporation, possessing tremendous foresight, laid out plans to make the marshlands of Makati into the financial center of Metro Manila. Moving away from investments in agriculture or manufacturing, Ayala wanted Makati to capitalize on the emergence of the financial and service industries. By the 1950s the corporation had developed more than 2,200 acres of property holdings (more than 50 percent of Makati's land area) that it had been accumulating since the 1930s into a mixture of financial, commercial, and residential subdivisions. It was to be the first truly large-scale multipurpose real estate development in all of Southeast Asia. Eventually Makati became the core of this elite suburbanization.

The uneasy period marked by the transition between Marcos and his successors dramatically affected spatial change throughout Metro Manila. The former dictator's decades of political maneuvering and coercion had left the country near financial collapse. A number of external factors coincided with Marcos's obvious desire to maintain his presidency and wealth. These dynamics caused the president to adopt an aggressive policy of overseas borrowing, which left the country in the deepest recession it had experienced since the postwar period.

Development Banks and Debt Financing

Up until the late 1970s, the Philippine economy was growing at an exceptional pace. By virtue of its unique relationship with the United States, the Philippines continued to profit from the market of the world's largest economy until the expiration of the Laurel–Langley Agreement in 1974. The Philippines' relatively developed judiciary and legal system, and its disconnection from the threat of communism throughout China and several parts of Southeast Asia, created an environment of stability and confidence that compelled even the Asian Development Bank to locate its offices in Manila. However, by the late 1970s, various domestic political and economic troubles had brought the country's economic productivity to a halt. The nation's economy itself was being kept afloat only by various foreign loans.

During this period of economic decline and political instability, following the lead of a number of countries throughout the Global South, such as South Korea and India, the Philippines embarked on a path of economic development designed by the World Bank and approved by the Reagan administration. Around the same period, the World Bank and its partner institution, the International Monetary Fund (IMF), were confronting increasing pressures to tighten the terms they imposed on borrowing nations and to redirect their support to countries deemed strategically appropriate for aid. Of course, *appropriate* was usually a euphemism for those countries perceived to be seeking military aid for defense against communist threats. Under the auspices of funding counterrevolutionary efforts to stave off the growing rural-based revolutionary movements like the New People's Army, the Philippines thus became a focal point for U.S. aid. By 1974 the average amount of money loaned to the Philippines by the World Bank had increased more than fivefold, from $30 million to $165.1 million.

Postwar development strategies were largely driven by a rationale of accelerated industrial growth that would mainly be energized by trade policies grounded on a strategy of import substitution (Bello, Kinley, and Elinson 1982). Similar to other developing postwar nations, the Philippines adopted policies of economic development around importing foreign goods, which, coupled with an arcane system of renting properties through landlord-tenant agreements, resulted in a dramatic drop in cash crop production. Over just a short period, these practices made it impossible for the country's agricultural industry to meet basic local food needs. Strategies of import substitution became an ineffective solution to alleviating unemployment and, ultimately, were unsuccessful at sustaining a local economy that would enable the local population to purchase the consumer goods produced by local manufacturers, who were simultaneously becoming more industrialized. For example, the report noted that the number of Filipino workers employed in the manufacturing industry in 1969 (1.3 million) was virtually the same as it had been six years earlier in 1963. Similarly, the number of Filipinos employed in the agricultural industry in 1971 (6.4 million) had remained constant since 1963 (see World Bank report, cited in Bello 2005, 17).

Intense political unrest ensued, and appeals to the U.S. government by the Marcos administration were partly answered by the World Bank, which naively believed that a strategy of structural adjustment would resolve the fundamental discontent of the urban poor. The World Bank, the IMF, and other multilateral financial institutions, together with U.S. foreign policy makers and U.S.-educated Filipinos, viewed the Philippines as the perfect test case for economic development through "authoritarian modernization" (see Bello, Kinley, and Elinson 1982). While the World Bank and the IMF collaborated within the Philippines, each institution played a separate role. The World Bank was responsible for designing the development program within the Philippines, including its evaluation and goals. The IMF was charged with calculating the balance-of-payment systems for the development program and evaluating its ability to produce returns on its investments.

Marcos's Reelection and the Making of the National Crisis

The other important event setting the stage for the World Bank's intervention was the presidential election of November 1969. While Marcos won reelection, he had depleted the country's foreign exchange reserves and left the country with a colossal amount of debt in the process. Unable to cover the huge trade deficit and pay the interest accrued on earlier debts, he turned to the IMF and the World Bank. The Philippines became a very early test case for an international payment system regulated by both lending organizations. An agreement was reached between the administration and the lending institutions but at a devastating cost. Marcos agreed to a 60-percent devaluation of the peso in order to achieve larger exchange returns for the dollar.

The devaluation of local currency is a key strategy of development economics (see McMichael 2012). In the case of the Philippines, the financing institutions, including the IMF and World Bank, believed that devaluation would eventually bring the trade account into balance. By increasing foreign exchange earnings by decreasing the cost of Philippine exports, while simultaneously introducing more costly foreign imports into the local economy, the scheme appeared to work. The deficit in trade was initially reduced from $257 million in 1969 to $7 million in 1970. However, over time, borrowers realize that the cost of devaluation usually has a catastrophic effect on the local and, eventually, the national economies of participating countries. The case of the Philippines became a prototypical example. The sociologist and Philippine senator Walden Bello and colleagues (1980) explain that devaluation of the peso resulted in dramatic domestic inflation: the rate of inflation rose from 1.3 percent in 1969 to 14.8 percent in 1970. While only a handful of elites profited from the country's exports, the majority of Filipino entrepreneurs were faced with bankruptcy owing to the rising cost of goods.

The declaration of martial law on September 22, 1972, marked a seminal moment in the restructuring of the Philippine economy. Rather than educating Filipinos on the principles of market fundamentalism, authoritarian rule allowed Marcos to align himself with the liberal interests of U.S. investors. In a telegram sent to Marcos after the declaration, U.S. investors leaped to show their support, saying, "The American Chamber of Commerce wishes you every success in your endeavor to restore peace and order, business confidence, economic growth, and well-being of the Filipino people and nation. We assure you of our confidence and cooperation in achieving these objectives. We are communicating the feelings of our associates and affiliates in the United States" (Bayani 1976, 26, quoted in Bello, Kinley, and Elinson 1982, 21). Ironically, although the World Bank touted itself as a financing organization that encouraged democratization through liberal economic reform policies and lending, there was a sudden surge in financial commitments in the months following the institution of martial law in the Philippines. For example, between 1950 and 1972, the total amount of money lent by the World Bank was a meager $326 million. In contrast, between 1973 and 1981, more than $2.6 billion was designated by the World Bank to fund sixty-one separate projects. By 1980 the Philippines ranked eighth among the 113 countries approved for lending by the World Bank, in sharp contrast to its ranking before the institution of martial law, when the country was thirtieth among designated recipients (Bello, Kinley, and Elinson 1982, 24).

Philip McMichael (2012) compellingly argues that strategies of structural adjustment, driven by the necessity for states to compete within the emerging global economy, transformed the discourse of development in two ways. First, their ability to manage the terms of debt repayment allowed multilateral institutions, state managers, and the financial classes to reframe the goals of the state toward whatever means were necessary to guarantee repayment of debt. Second, the austerity measures applied to each borrowing nation were aimed at serving the global financial system rather than reviving individual national economies (see McMichael 2012, 35).

To completely satisfy the terms of structural adjustment, Marcos, like several other leaders of developing economies, was forced to submit to a strategy of export-oriented industrialization. Adhering to the parameters of structural adjustment successfully made the Philippines, like so many other developing economies, into what McMichael calls a "participant in the world market." This radical reorientation of the Philippine economy meant that its domestic markets would be virtually abandoned, and the growth of the country's economy would be entirely dependent on the capricious cycles of the larger global economy. As McMichael astutely observes, this participation did not mean that the Philippines and other developing economies suddenly became "global," or equal partners to the United States or other western European countries, for instance, but that "the global economy itself became consequential in reshaping the conditions under which states made economic policy" (2012, 35).

The country's economic shift toward export-oriented production was to the detriment of its few welfare programs. As a consequence, the capitalization of domestic resources for export often came at the expense of the local economy and resulted in a contraction in locally produced goods. In short, McMichael concludes that "the goals of the development project of nationally-managed economic growth with a view to enhancing national welfare yielded to a new principle: globally-managed economic growth with a view to sustaining the integrity of the global financial system and the conditions for transnational corporate capitalism" (2012, 35). The sudden influx of foreign investments created massive internal migrations to urban areas, where the increased competition for jobs depressed wages. The state was further weakened by the need for public enterprises to join with private firms in order to continue operating. This further compounded the state's inability to set the terms of these agreements and ultimately limited workers' ability to unionize and resist poor employment conditions.

However, the focus on export-oriented industry did not limit itself to the manufacturing industry. Around the same time as Marcos embarked on his colossal plan of national redevelopment through the mandates detailed in the plan for a "New Society," the vast majority of governmental resources were redirected toward and concentrated on the urban renewal of Metro Manila. Marcos's administration was particularly interested in shoring up the economic stability of the larger NCR and introducing new inputs that would draw fresh capital into the economy by attracting foreign investments into the urban core. Marcos engineered plans to develop commercial and residential property on the lands that the government had been reclaiming from the urban poor. By interlinking the property and tourism industries, the administration could capitalize on foreign investments in its newly industrializing region. This allowed the government to continue developing the country's economy without having to devote resources to improving the country's welfare infrastructure or alleviating local unemployment.

Property for (Economic) Development

Property markets compose a particular sector of the global economy that has become radically transformed by the deregulation of financial markets and strategically enhanced trade between nation-states sparked by globalization. Property investment and development has become a central conduit for increasing financial exchange. Various innovations in financial technologies—including the deregulation of international lending, international pension fund investing, the selling of mortgage debts through securitization (see Gotham 2009), the removal of barriers to foreign property investments, and the ability to access information on property through a limitless number of databases and other technologies—have combined to create a fundamental shift away from the more traditional forms of foreign direct investment toward more speculative forms of investing (Olds 2001; Haila 1997).[1]

The accelerated transformation of Manila's landscape over the past three decades is endemic of larger trends happening throughout the rest of Asia and in Southeast Asia in particular (Sajor 2003). According to urban scholars Peter Rimmer and Howard Dick (2009), what distinguishes transformations in Southeast Asian metropoles from those occurring throughout Europe and Japan is the "rapidity" and "scale" of these patterns of urban change. These transformations throughout the region are not simply made visible through the sheer number of foreign corporations and headquarters, retail outlets, international chain restaurants, and residential complexes emerging throughout their urban landscape; they are also characterized by the manner in which the environment is shaped by the logic of segregation (see Connell 1999).

In the context of Southeast Asian cities, Rimmer and Dick (2009) call this process "rebundling," a strategic investment initially started by Southeast Asian entrepreneurs during the 1980s to enhance the profitability of their returns by "bundling as many as possible of these discrete facilities into integrated completes. These complexes comprise hotels, restaurants, shopping malls and office towers. Such integrated projects enjoyed enhanced profitability because each facility fed the other, by attracting and circulating custom. The externalities were thereby internalized. These projects required the ability to mobilize huge sums of risk capital to buy up land and finance construction in anticipation of the market" (39). As such, property markets throughout Southeast Asia and other cities along the Pacific Rim are focused on the packaging and marketing of "high class ('Grade A') office space, 'trophy buildings,' luxury condominium housing, hotels, vacant suburban tracts of land, rental housing, and industrial land, with strategic planning for both development and marketing phases" (Olds 2001, 24).

Simply put, investing in property development provides individuals and corporations with a consistently flexible means of improving their returns and diversifying their portfolios (see Berry and McGreal 1999). The globalization of financial markets, particularly the various ways in which financial exchange became less and less restricted, created opportunities for investors to creatively reallocate funds and move capital. Most Asian countries, for instance, have traditionally restricted land ownership by foreigners, viewing such privileges as a fundamental breach of national security. More recently, policy changes regarding foreign ownership have become more common, easing restrictions that had blocked foreigners and, especially, foreign corporations from owning land.

For instance, in the Philippines, where the ownership of private lands has been restricted to Filipino citizens and to corporations where 60 percent of the capital stock belongs to Filipino citizens, two laws were passed in 1993 to allow foreign individuals and companies to invest in property. The Investor's Lease Act (Republic Act No. 7652), signed in 1993, allots portions of private land for the use of industrial estates, factories, assembly or processing plants, agro-industrial enterprises, and development for industrial or commercial use, tourism, and other similar productive business. Similarly, the Condominium Act (Republic Act No. 4726), signed in 1996, allows foreign individuals and corporations to own up to 40 percent of a condominium complex. Each of these acts is based on the pretext that the property will be owned in a shared agreement with a Filipino citizen or Filipino majority-owned corporation (see Cornelio-Pronove and Cheng 1999).

In a more complex way, state agents, financial and service firms, and, of course, global consumers, which collectively compose the international property market, act as a fundamental linkage integrating national economies with the larger global economy and the broader network of global cities (Sassen 2001). Property markets then become linked to forms of national economic development through financial lending and the strategic utilization of foreign exchange rates created through property speculation and development. Trends that were occurring in New York, Tokyo, and London during the 1980s were replicated throughout Southeast Asia. Investors from Japan, Korea, countries in western Europe, Australia, and the United States began lending money and financing massive property developments in Singapore, Kuala Lumpur, and Manila, to name just a few cities. These investments included freeways and toll roads, corporate and residential high-rises, and the expansion of central business districts. Here, newer financing techniques have become incorporated into economic development regimes in the form of property leasing and mortgages or securities.

Fundamental to the international property market's incorporation into the architecture of economic development is the emergence and proliferation of transnational corporations operating throughout Southeast Asia and other countries within the Global South. All of the Philippines' largest property developers, including Ayala Land, Megaworld Properties, and Robinsons Land, maintain offices in several parts of the world. All of these corporations have established sales and marketing offices throughout the rest of Asia, Australia, western Europe, and North America: organizing mobile presentations or "road shows," advertising in Filipino newspapers and websites abroad, and joining in contractual business agreements with realty agencies and realtors abroad. Smaller transnationally operating realtors have even organized a network of Filipino realtors called the Chamber of Real Estate and Builders' Associations Inc., to work as an interagency realty group in other countries.

Until recently, urban studies has neglected the role of real estate in understanding processes of urban change because of the immaterial level at which real estate corporations and agents tend to operate (see Haila 1997). Because realty often functions as an intermediary device and not always as an actual product of property development, the discipline tends to focus on financing institutions instead. However, transnational corporations have come to play a vital role within the international property market because they have adopted a wide range of expertise on multiple scales, both locally and globally. Increasing cooperation between financing institutions and political offices has opened the way for more and more corporations to own large tracts of land and maintain complete control over its development. The subsequent deregulation of trade agreements and corporate investment allows transnational corporations to manage the entire gamut of property development from beginning to end: the sale of property (e.g., the marketing and brokering) and its development (e.g., both the financing and planning).

Another reason urban studies has ignored the importance of real estate, according to the sociologist Anne Haila (1997), is because, unlike entrepreneurs, developers and real estate investors are perceived as being "individuals who are inclined to subjective desires and irrational whims, rather than rational and calculating individuals" (57). Transnational property developers are becoming increasingly proficient at providing background support for various projects. Kris Olds (2001), for instance, provides the example of First Pacific Davies Savills, Jones Lang LaSalle, and Colliers Jardine, who act as chartered surveyors, developing and evaluating corporate property strategies, conducting market analysis, and facilitating the necessary planning consents, leasing, and property management. Olds points out that "Jones Lang LaSalle, for example, has a highly integrated network operating in 34 countries around the world, and it maintains some of the largest private databases in the world, including the ability to model central business districts in key global cities. . . . The company provides wide-ranging integrated expertise on a local, regional, and global level to owners, occupiers and investors" (25). Transnationally operating property development firms, such as Jones Lang LaSalle or Ayala Land in the Philippines, enable and control the flows of speculative capital that have become integral to the contemporary global economy.

A single problem still remained to be solved: who could afford to purchase the luxury units being built within these large-scale property developments? Concurrent with the accumulation of building projects throughout the Philippines beginning in the 1970s, funded in large part by lending institutions like the IMF and World Bank, rates of local unemployment actually increased during the 1970s. While investors from Europe and Asia were ready to pounce on these opportunities, the Philippine government had to be very careful to maintain its key relationship with the United States. At the same time, even though corporate investments continued to pour in from Japan and Korea, political and economic planners needed to be sure that the Philippines would maintain a role in the global economy, particularly in the Asian region. The Marcos administration would pass a series of key measures during the 1970s that, he believed, would solve issues of local unemployment while also allowing the Philippines to benefit from foreign investment.

Reproducing Crisis: Sending Labor Abroad

As in numerous countries in Latin America, Africa, and Asia during the 1970s, structural adjustment to the Philippine economy involved moving away from its traditional economic bases: farming, fishing, and local manufacturing. As the economy pushed toward commercialization of agriculture and manufacturing, Filipinos were increasingly unable to earn a living wage or find employment at all in the Philippines (Bello 2005). Simultaneously, structural adjustment programs regulated by the IMF were shifting the country toward an import-based economy. To ensure that there would be a local economy capable of absorbing foreign imports and investments, the Philippine government legislated a strategy of labor exportation. Subsequent decades of consumer purchases of foreign products and contributions to larger-scale investments would be driven and sustained by a continuous stream of remittances and transnational investment, thus putting into place one of the final pieces of the balikbayan economy.

Marcos originally passed the Labor Code of 1974, institutionalizing the country's labor export policy as a temporary stopgap measure to solve the rapidly escalating unemployment and as a strategic response to the employment opportunities brought forth by the Middle East oil boom of the 1970s (Asis 1992). From 1973 on, oil-rich countries such as the United Arab Emirates, Kuwait, Saudi Arabia, Iran, Iraq, and Bahrain sought workers for various infrastructural and development projects. Between 1975 and 1977, Filipinos found employment in these countries as construction workers, doctors, nurses, engineers, and highly skilled mechanics, with Saudi Arabia a leading labor recruiter. While the overseas employment offered by the Middle East oil boom was open primarily to Filipino men, the demand for nursing and domestic work eventually paved the way for the feminization of the country's exportation of labor. The policy of exporting labor produced an infrastructure to support a flow of remittances back to the Philippines, and many believed that this infusion of "local capital" would guide the Philippine state away from economic crisis. However, the ever-increasing debt totals on loans from the IMF, World Bank, and other global lending arms would ensure the opposite.

The Philippines continues to be one of the leading senders of labor abroad and receivers of capital remitted by migrants both temporarily and permanently settled outside of their home country. The interlinking of capital production by permanent Filipino emigrants and the balikbayan economy was solidified in 1989 when President Corazon Aquino redefined the legal definition of *balikbayan*. Aquino's legislation broadened the term to encompass any Filipino who had lived abroad for at least one year regardless of citizenship. Furthermore, the memorandum order (no. 230) mandated that 50 percent of the total US$1,000 allowed for duty-free shopping go to the Philippine National Treasury for repayment of the national debt.

For a while, such mandates reconfiguring the legal definition of a balikbayan had the effect of conflating two very distinct groups. On the one hand, the term refers to the highly skilled and relatively affluent Filipinos living as citizens of other countries for a number of years. Then there are the temporary and flexible Filipino workers contracted to work for a limited duration in other countries, Filipinos who had gained naturalization while working in other countries initially on a temporary basis, and the descendants of Filipino citizens who were born in another place. Clearly, the invention of the balikbayan demonstrates how the Philippine state continues to respond to crises in the local economy and competition from the outside. The widening influence of the IMF and World Bank permeated the contemporary Philippine economy. These influences, specifically the movement toward a policy of exporting labor, were based on a pervasive form of neoliberal technique that cleverly aims to, in Michel Foucault's terms, "individualize" and "totalize" the diverse multitude of Filipinos living and working abroad into a unified body of mobilized labor for the global economy (see Lemke 2002).[2] By 2010, nearly a tenth of the Philippines' 100 million citizens were laboring outside of the country, either as Overseas Filipino Workers or as permanent residents.

Urban Dialectic

In 1973 Marcos had put in place the initial structure for the institutionalization of a balikbayan economy whereby Filipinos living abroad could more easily send money or material goods to the Philippines. The Balikbayan Program also encouraged Filipinos to return to their homeland through various financial and touristic incentives. The work of drawing Filipinos back home was accomplished in part by evoking a perception of balikbayans as beloved "saviors" and "heroes" who should be welcomed back to the Philippines with open arms. At the same time, Marcos was compelled to make balikbayans see themselves as patriots who, having left the Philippines, were now obligated, through the evocation of a profound sense of duty, *utang ng loob*, to send money home and/or to visit the land that they must not abandon. Decades later, the rhetoric around balikbayan patronage, endlessly communicated through a throng of Philippine media transmitted through U.S. cable television and newspapers, has not diminished in the least. Now confronted by these disconcerting images, many Filipinos feel perplexed: weren't the duties contributed by balikbayans doing anything to change the country for the better?

As apparent as the poverty and underdevelopment so vividly presented in towns like Parañaque everywhere are the newly built high-rises and malls emerging throughout Metro Manila. A sprawling landscape composed of concrete, glass, and cables only begins to allude to the economic and cultural transformations that are occurring throughout the city. In fact, changes have even been made to the Ninoy Aquino International Airport itself. After more than two decades of political controversy and fiscal mismanagement, the third terminal was finally added to the international airport in 2008 to meet the tremendous spike in transportation demand that had developed over the prior two decades. It was built to serve just over thirty-three thousand more passengers daily. And, in true Manila fashion, the terminal has a four-story mall built on top of it. For a country and region in which two-thirds of the economy is contributed by remittances sent from overseas Filipinos, even the airport itself was forced to expand to help further facilitate the transformation of the Philippine economy and accommodate changes attributable to the flow of capital created by the balikbayan economy. The transformation of the airport, as well as the overall visual landscape of Metro Manila, is just a sign of the larger ways an entire city, having been sustained by the formation of this economy, is dramatically changing.

At one point during the global real estate crisis in the late 1990s, vacancy rates for commercial spaces in Manila reached 50 percent. Ironically, this crisis created a unique opportunity for the first wave of business process outsourcing (BPO) to begin investing in office space throughout Manila. More recently, vacant office space in Manila has declined to 3 percent, and in Makati's central business district (CBD) the number was 5 percent. Thus, the growth of the BPO industry allows for greater occupancy of not only residential space but commercial space as well. Ayala Land, the property arm of the Ayala global conglomerate, has set aside US$338 million to build twenty-seven major residential development projects in the coming years, concentrating their efforts around the Metro Manila area as well as an entire BPO campus south of the capital city (Magno-Ballesteros 2000b). Some property executives believe that even these investments in building will fall short of meeting the enormous demand for commercial space in the near future.

Such projections have led to a massive increase in the production of space throughout the city. The city is abuzz with the incessant sounds of construction: the pounding and cracking of concrete, moving cranes, and drilling even persists through the night and into the early morning. At the same time, developers, realtors, and balikbayans alike are conscious that the entirety of their investments depends on the sustainability of the BPO industry in the Philippines and the ability of Manila to remain competitive within the network of global cities and megacities throughout the world. Like these cities, Metro Manila has become uneasily constituted by two opposing yet simultaneously interlinked images: poverty and wealth, deterioration and renewal, an ever-growing paradoxical unity.

Reflecting the dialectical dilemma of creative destruction articulated in Marshall Berman's (1988) eloquent critique of modernity, much of Metro Manila is shaped by a state of perpetual construction, with sleek new office buildings and towering condominiums protruding throughout Metro Manila's concrete landscape, one after another. At the same time, this development purposefully creates and is perpetuated by a kind of vertical segregation from other neighborhoods that are disinvested from and left to disintegrate, their communities forced to make do. In many ways, the investments made by balikbayans are actually exacerbating the dilemmas of Manila's urban poor.

2. The Foreign Local » Balikbayans, Overseas Filipino Workers, and the Return Economy

Can we imagine the U.S. as an extension of the Philippines?
—Catherine Ceniza Choy, "Towards Trans-Pacific Social Justice"

During the spring of 2008, while stepping outside to exit a ferry in the provincial capital of Iloilo, I was politely ushered aside as two deckhands carted a thirty-two-inch plasma screen television from within the boat's hull. It was attached to two almost equally gigantic cardboard boxes, strung efficiently together with a single pink plastic cord. As the men hauled the boxes in my direction, it was easy to distinguish the names and logos printed on each box: "Sony," "DVD player," "amplifier," and "speaker."

Just ahead of me, a voice shouted loudly from beneath a wide-brimmed hat, "Ingat! Ingat! [Be careful! Be careful!] Bring it down slowly. My husband will get the car to meet you." A diminutive Filipina stood at the edge of the landing, directing the two men and speaking with the characteristically balikbayan habit of interspersing broken Tagalog with perfect English phrases. Her hands moved so demonstratively that the gold bracelets wrapped around each of her wrists clanged together, ringing out sharp dissonant noises.

"How many of these do you think we'll carry this year?" grunted one of the men in Ilongo as he weaved beside me. "It's only September, so only God knows how many we will carry by the time this year's over," the other man laughed. I was captivated by the spectacle. My gaze fixed on the two deckhands as they gracefully made their way across the poorly built, three-piece wooden plank that bridged us to the port. Both men were careful not to drop the prize as the third member of the scene waited impatiently at the bottom of the steps, carefully directing each of the deckhands' movements with her hands and loud voice.

Discussing the intertwining linkages of transnational capital that web together nationalist sentiments within the Philippines, Vicente L. Rafael (2000, 204) eloquently suggests that the "labor of mourning . . . tends to bring forth the uncanny nature of capitalist development itself on which the nation-state depends. The moral economy of grieving is persistently haunted by the circulation of money." The juxtaposition of the wreckage left by Typhoon Fengshen in 2008, one of the most devastating storms to hit the provincial capital, Iloilo City, in recent years, with the image of the two young Filipino men hoisting the weight of that very expensive home entertainment system atop their slight frames became nonsensical to the point of absurdity. Yet regardless of the confounding nature of this conspicuous consumption that functioned as a means of relief from the havoc and devastation that Fengshen had wreaked, the basic necessities of money, food, and clothing were hardly the only items sent by concerned family members abroad.

Relief to ailing families left homeless by the storm, or for those mourning loved ones who had drowned during the flood, came in a myriad of forms. Family members living abroad dutifully and with tremendous compassion sent washing machines, microwaves, refrigerators, and, once in a while, even entire entertainment systems.

This chapter expands the scholarly gaze, which tends to be fixated on the role remittances play throughout the Philippines, by turning its lens toward those who send them, specifically balikbayans. The vast majority of the literature on remittances tends to focus on their impact on the local populations receiving them (see, for example, Eckstein and Najam 2013). This makes sense. Remittances have impacted every dimension of social and political life in the Philippines. Data imprecisely extrapolated from figures released by the Bangko Sentral ng Pilipinas (BSP 2014), or the Philippine

National Bank, suggest that over the past three decades remittances have constituted between 8 and 10 percent of the country's overall economy. When one makes one's way to the edges of Iloilo City, for example, the structural significance of remittances takes on a much larger scope. A year after Fengshen, the typhoon's impact vividly lingered in the numerous mud-filled roads yet to be repaved, the parks so devastated by flooding that they looked like unfurled sheets of tattered grass, and the shrubbery still left uncollected. Amid this destruction, one begins to make sense of plasma screen televisions and home entertainment systems beyond their consumptive façade. Remittances perform the labor of the state, rebuilding infrastructure and lives after moments of crisis.

Remittances provide a crucial means of understanding transnational ties for various reasons. These practices help elucidate the manner in which migrant communities continue to be threaded together by a common desire to maintain their connections with their homeland (see Glick Schiller, Basch, and Szanton Blanc 1995; Basch, Glick Schiller, and Szanton Blanc 2005). These flows also provide a framework for examining how the nation-state attempts to reincorporate citizens and nationals living abroad for the purpose of developing its national economy (Lessinger 1995). The transnational social field constituted by the material culture of obligation and kinship ties provides a conceptual tool to comprehend the sociohistorical circulation enabling return migration from cities like Daly City back to the Philippines.

Yet the impacts of remittances stretch far beyond the geographic boundaries of the Philippines. They also transform the communities and families of those sending them. This chapter focuses on how the institutionalization of remittance circulations over the course of multiple decades has reconfigured Filipinos who settle abroad as simultaneously foreign and local, or "foreign Filipinos." Furthermore, it articulates the physical coherency embodying the relationships that help facilitate the balikbayan economy. The ambivalent definition of balikbayans is historically rooted in the asymmetry that continues to characterize the relationship between Filipinos who successfully settle abroad and their homeland. The term is a direct result of former dictator of the Philippines Ferdinand Marcos's Balikbayan Program of 1973 and is sustained by the contemporary assemblage of policy makers, media corporations, and multinational property developers invested in maintaining Filipinos living abroad as foreigners in order to enable the transformation of the Philippines into a competitive global economy.

In the United States, regardless of how long most Filipinos have lived away from the Philippines, and whether or not they have family members who are living with them, or have made considerable investments within their host country, the generation of Filipino Americans who migrated after 1965 continues to uphold their obligations to family members and relatives in the Philippines through sending remittances (Menjivar et al. 1998). Furthermore, as first-generation Filipino immigrants in the United States wait to be reunited with their family members living in the Philippines, the financial support they send back home is the "repeated turning" described by Benito Manalo Vergara (2009).

According to data from the BSP (2014), Filipino Americans are the largest senders of financial remittances to the Philippines among overseas Filipinos. In 2005 their combined remittances reached almost $6.5 billion. By 2014, however, that figure jumped to a record-high $10.4 billion. Financial remittances sent by Filipinos living in the United States are indeed significant, their financial worth at least double that of remittances sent from the Middle East or other parts of Asia (Nikolits 2015). In order to make sense of the balikbayan's foreign-Filipino status, this chapter seeks to move beyond conceptualizing remittances as financial instruments of economic development. Rather, remittances directly reconfigure balikbayans into ambivalently regarded figures within the cultural fabric of everyday life in the Philippines.

Remittances, either the actual money or the gifts brought back by Filipinos living abroad, what are called *pasalubong*, provide the necessities and productive labor that the state relies on so that it can shirk its basic civic responsibilities. Most balikbayans see themselves as repaying their debt to their families and doing their duty by sending remittances and pasalubong to the Philippines, rather than enabling a kind of economy of excessive luxuries and conspicuous consumption. These reciprocal circulations, which are corporeally represented by Filipinos migrating abroad and sending remittances back to the Philippines, do not simply signify the desire of hundreds of thousands of Filipinos to leave the Philippines each year and live somewhere else, say, the United States. These circulations, which together structure and maintain the balikbayan economy, convey, in a very real sense, the Philippine nation-state's relinquishing of various responsibilities. They are evidence of the failure of the Philippine government to provide the most basic amenities that might allow its citizenry to experience success within the Philippines in the first place.

understand
the concept of charity giving back
taught to them by
their parents

The Balikbayan Program

Along with the decades of financial and material remittances sent by Filipinos living abroad, balikbayans returning to the Philippines to visit or resettle have themselves come to embody the balikbayan economy. Recent figures from the Department of Tourism in the Philippines show that, of the over three million tourists who visit the country each year, roughly one-fifth are Filipinos living and working abroad (Bernal 2014). These Filipinos are generally referred to as *balikbayans*. The official definition of a balikbayan, set forth by the Republic of the Philippines Bureau of Immigration (2016), is "Philippine nationals who are permanently residing abroad. . . . [It] also refers to those of Filipino descent who acquired foreign citizenship and permanent status abroad." Furthermore, Republic Act No. 9174 officially demarcates balikbayans into three separate categories:

1. *Returning Resident*: a Filipino citizen who has gone abroad for at least one year and is now returning.
2. *Overseas Filipino Worker (OFW)*: a Filipino citizen who has worked in a foreign country under an employment contract issued in the Philippines for more than six months and is now returning.
3. *Former Filipino*: a former or current Filipino citizen who has acquired foreign citizenship abroad, and has resided in that country for over six months, and is now returning to resettle.

These legal classifications contrast sharply with the local usage of the term, in which it commonly refers specifically to Filipinos who have settled in countries throughout the Global North, including Canada, the United Kingdom, Australia, and most especially the United States.

Balikbayans are unique owing to the manner in which they link the Philippine nation-state to flows of global capital and economic development. Filipinos visiting their homeland or attempting to repatriate to their homeland, along with their children, are entitled to a set of special benefits and privileges once they arrive in the Philippines. These legal privileges include exemptions from travel taxes, visa-free entry into the Philippines for a period of one year for Filipinos with foreign passports, and tax-free shopping at any duty-free shopping center for a limited quantity of goods. These incentives are designed to encourage Filipinos living abroad to visit or return to the Philippines and to invest money and capital in the tourism sector as well as in the local economies.

The term *balikbayan* was originally reengineered by Marcos as a means of enticing Filipinos living abroad to not only visit their homeland but also invest in the country's economy. As a result of Marcos's declaration of martial law in 1972, the status of the Philippines, once the benchmark for democratic rule and economic success in Asia during the 1960s, quickly declined in the eyes of the international community. And, with this, the number of Filipinos visiting or returning to the Philippines plummeted.

As a means of restoring the country's social and political reputation, and eventually restarting the country's tourist industry, the Philippine government adopted the Balikbayan Program in 1973. In 1970 there were already 343,060 Filipinos living in the United States. That number had increased dramatically by 1980, to 781,894, owing largely to changes in immigration policies, service in the U.S. Navy, and increased employment opportunities, particularly in medical fields. Marcos believed that these former and current Filipino citizens were the key to economic recovery in the Philippines. Government departments and local agencies worked together with foreign consulates and embassies to advertise to Filipinos living abroad and to encourage them to visit the Philippines during the Christmas season, which stretched from the Catholic holiday of All Saints' Day on November 1 to Epiphany on January 6.

The result was a massive advertising campaign that included the publication and distribution of hundreds of thousands of booklets titled "Invitation to a Traditional Philippine Christmas." Schoolteachers in the Philippines encouraged their students to write to their extended family members working abroad to entreat them to return during the holidays. Government departments assisted local agencies to host festivals to celebrate the success of Filipinos who returned to their home provinces. Most important, customs agents were mandated to provide balikbayans with tax exemptions, and the Philippine Airlines issued discounted rates for airfares to the Philippines.

As a result of the Balikbayan Program, nearly a million Filipinos and their families returned to the Philippines to visit and tour their homeland in the following decade. The increasing number of balikbayan visitors encouraged governmental officials to establish other related programs. For instance, the Balik-Scientist Program was adopted in 1975 to provide Filipinos skilled in scientific research with job placements, and the Balik-UP Program was created in 1978 to encourage alumni from the University of the Philippines, the most prestigious university in the Philippines, to visit the Philippines and share their achievements abroad with local schools and colleges. While these programs ended up costing the government, or, more specifically, the local population through taxes, the Philippine government achieved its original goal of raising its political profile internationally.

The success of the program led the government to issue special resident visas for balikbayans. The legal exemptions associated with these visas served to reinforce long-held notions that living and working in developed countries like the United States sets Filipino migrants apart from Filipinos living in the Philippines both economically and socially. By virtue of their working and even permanently settling abroad, there is a shift in their perceived status in the country where they were born. Consequently, balikbayans are neither compatriots nor foreigners in the eyes of local Filipinos living in the Philippines. In 1989 Corazon Aquino passed the Balikbayan Law (Republic Act No. 6768), which extended various exceptions for balikbayans. Along with tax exemptions at designated shopping centers and discounted fares for travel, balikbayans, as former citizens of the Philippines, were now allowed to purchase land.

This allowance is of particular significance since individuals with foreign passports have historically been restricted from buying land in the Philippines. This law allows balikbayans to buy up to fifty-four thousand square feet of property in designated urban areas and up to seven and a half acres of land in rural areas. Massive townships have been built over the past decade to cater to balikbayans, as well as other foreigners. Aided by the Special Resident Retiree's Visa (SRRV), balikbayans desiring to retire in their homeland not only can purchase property situated in luxurious, U.S.-modeled barangays (towns) but are also afforded special incentives that allow them to continue working and investing in the Philippines after they have officially retired.

By 1996 balikbayans were legally entitled to up to US$1,000 of duty-free goods (provided that these items were bought within the first forty-eight hours after their arrival); the privilege of visa-free entry into the country for up to one year; the ability to bring with them two balikbayan boxes (the limitations on size and weight varies, depending on the airline carrier), which are also completely duty-free; and various other travel tax exemptions and promotions.

Without exception, every subject who participated in my fieldwork in the United States maintained ties to the Philippines by sending remittances or by visiting their homeland. In addition to the three remittance centers devoted to sending money specifically to the Philippines that lay along Mission Street in Daly City alone, a number of banks and postal services offer expedited services for Filipinos to send money or boxes back to the Philippines owing to the high demand for such amenities. In 2000 the BSP reported that US$6 billion was sent through formal banking channels, making up 7.6 percent of the Philippines' gross national product (Matejowsky 2012, 316). In 2004 the BSP reported that Filipinos working in the United States sent the highest percentage of remittances to the Philippines, followed by those in the Kingdom of Saudi Arabia, Italy, Japan, the United Kingdom, Hong Kong, Singapore, Dubai, Germany, Kuwait, and Abu Dhabi. By 2010 the total amount of financial remittances being sent to the Philippines through the banking system or remittance centers represented approximately 13.5 percent of the country's gross national product (Matejowsky 2012, 316). Recently, remittance sending has increasingly been facilitated by various smartphone apps offered by traditional banks and money-sending services like Western Union. These apps allow users to send money more efficiently by foregoing in-person visits to banks and remittance centers.

Furthermore, foreign investment from Filipinos living abroad was facilitated by the passage of the Foreign Investments Act of 1991 (Republic Act No. 7042), which spelled out the procedures and conditions under which non-Philippine nationals, including former Filipino citizens, may invest and do business in the Philippines, and explicitly required paid-in capital of at least US$200,000. These investments were also carefully managed; state policy mandated that this capital would have to be invested in cooperatives, rural banks, thrift banks, private development banks, and financing companies in order for non-Philippine nationals to qualify for the same treatment as citizens.

Along with these investments, the Philippine state encourages the exchange of information, or the investment of knowledge, between Filipinos working and living abroad and Filipinos in the Philippines. According to the Commission on Filipinos Overseas *Handbook* (2005, 11), "various opportunities are available for Filipinos overseas to visit the Philippines and share expertise with local counterparts through lectures, workshops, and other volunteer work. These avenues include the Balik-Scientist Program of the Department of Science and Technology, Exchange Visitor Program of the Commission on Filipinos Overseas, and other exchange programs conducted by Filipino associations overseas in the Philippines. Aside from these activities, partnerships for research or special projects are being encouraged between Filipinos overseas and local counterparts to pass on new knowledge or develop indigenous technology."

Balikbayans provide the lubricating element that has enabled a distinct set of foreign investments—banking, telecommunications, and property markets—to become propelled into action. The returns produced by balikbayans have transformed them into key actors within the transformation of the Philippine economy, their presence marked in the transformation of major cities and provincial townships throughout the Philippines. Financial remittances, and the property investments they accompany, are driving these transformations.

The Labor of Remittance Sending

The imaginative labor propelling the balikbayan economy, what Neferti X. M. Tadiar (2004) describes as the generative force of "fantasy production," is driven by a deep ambivalence, held by most Filipinos in the United States, that returning to the Philippines will always be possible.[1] It lingers, stretched out like a lifeline, providing an unconscious sense of security while Filipinos journey together as strangers in the United States and other parts of the world. This sentiment materializes itself as waves of remittances, which have been propping up the Philippine economy for decades. Politicians and the media conspire to continually reanimate the circulation of remittances through a nationalist discourse that binds Filipinos in the diaspora to their homeland through contraptions of patronage tied together by feelings of intense indebtedness (utang ng loob).[2]

While the Philippine state concedes some of its sovereignty to the corporations that purchase the labor of its citizens working abroad, it also consolidates its sovereignty by producing migrants as "citizen-workers." According to Robyn Rodriguez (2010), the Philippine state "asks its citizens to live abroad and give themselves over to foreign employers. Simultaneously, the Philippine state attempts to secure migrants' sustained linkages with the Philippines as citizenship, because it is their continued linkages to the Philippines, especially in the form of remittances, that is vital to ensuring that migration remains profitable to the state" (19). Remittances have become integral to Philippine governmentality. In 1983 Marcos issued Executive Order 857, mandating that 50–80 percent of workers' salaries be remitted through Philippine banking systems and decreeing that OFWS would face punitive measures if they failed to remit their earnings through legitimate channels (Gibson and Graham 1986). Since then, the influx of capital through the export of labor and the remittances carefully infused into sectors of the country's economy has been so strong that it continues to be a major element of the Philippine economy.

Remittances sent by balikbayans, particularly temporary Filipino migrants, constitute the majority of foreign capital flows into the Philippines. These remittances function as a surrogate for much of the welfare that the state neglects or refuses to provide. The amount of capital contributed by Filipinos working abroad, through their remittances, is double the contributions of foreign direct investment. When combined with the role remittances play in augmenting the country's foreign-exchange requirements and paying off external debt, "these results indicate the Philippine state and economy is more dependent on the earnings of overseas workers than it is on foreign investments and foreign loans" (Ball 1997, 1615). By 2005, around 30 percent of households in the Philippines were subsisting on remittances sent by relatives working overseas (Bello 2005). Recent figures from the BSP (2009) convey the significance of financial remittances, reporting a sharp rise from $7.6 billion in 2003 to $17.3 billion in 2009. Over the past ten years, the flow of remittances has constituted 10–13 percent of the Philippines' total gross domestic product. The World Bank (2015) estimated that about $24.3 billion was being sent back to the Philippines each year throughout formal and informal channels.

These remittances, in their various forms, provide Filipinos in the Philippines with numerous everyday resources: funds for utilities, tuition, and food for family members, as well as for school uniforms or textbooks. Furthermore, in times of disaster, for example, the perennial destruction precipitated by typhoons or flooding, Filipinos in the diaspora often shoulder the responsibility for ensuring the welfare of their families and hometowns. Philippines news media are rife with tales of government incompetency when dealing with these events; stories of government corruption and the misuse of international aid abound.

Remittance money, clothing, and other goods assume the accountability for welfare, from which the state often shirks. When responding to the criticism that the government has come to rely on remittances, Vivian F. Tornea, a director at the Overseas Workers Welfare Administration, one of the arms sending Filipino labor abroad, casually responded that the financial contributions paid by remittance money to building public infrastructure "were simply 'payback' because [overseas workers] did not pay income taxes" (quoted in Onishi 2010b). Apart from functioning as a source of welfare for Philippine citizens, the flow of remittances also provides relief for domestic unemployment. This in turn releases government agents from the responsibility to provide jobs within the Philippines, particularly in rural regions where rates of unemployment are dire (Aguilar 1996).

For some privileged families, remittance money also drastically restructures elements of everyday living by offering greater security and upward mobility (Faier 2013). Describing observations of several rural communities throughout the northern provinces of the Philippines, Deirdre McKay (2006, 266) explains how remittances reshaped aspects of the landscape, labor patterns in the region, and local conceptualizations of progress, which, "in [the local Filipinos'] terms, was made visible through intensified patterns of consumption and enhanced local and national mobility, especially via transport and communications technologies." Other accounts describe more undesirable effects of remittances, including the dependency on care chains and rising costs, not only in the larger cities but in the provinces as well (Parreñas 2012). For example, in Mabini, a province of Batangas, the sending of remittances, which have subsidized many of the improvements to local homes, has also led to higher tuition fees for private schools, including Santa Fe Integrated School. According to the journalist Norimitsu Onishi (2010b), 80 percent of the 250 students studying at the private school are children of overseas workers, allowing school administrators to rationalize raising the tuition well above the average cost of other schools in the region.

Remittances also provide a buffer against the seemingly ever-increasing debt that fetters the Philippine economy to the whims of global interest rates. The annual level of remittances is roughly equivalent to the annual interest payable on the nation's sizable foreign debt (E. Rodriguez 1998). This source of perennial capital provides a crucial shelter for the country's economy, particularly in periods of economic crisis, such as that experienced in 1997. While state agents have veered away from making claims about the exact level of dependency that remittances enable, Labor Secretary Marianito Roque expressed the importance of the remittance system, explaining that "the flow of overseas worker money in an unstable global economy demonstrates the resiliency of the Filipino people." Roque continued, "Under the worst circumstances, our workers are getting jobs and sending home more money than ever. They are keeping the boat stable" (quoted in Glionna 2009). Again, remittances are viewed as the lifeline securing the financial economy against collapse during another period of massive economic crisis.

Aside from issues of governmental neglect and migrants' feelings of indebtedness, there are a number of concrete explanations for the increases in remittances sent by Filipinos working overseas over the past decade. The first involves the tremendous increase in Filipinos departing for employment outside of the Philippines. Currently, more than 7.75 million Filipinos are laboring outside of the Philippines in various sectors. This number has increased by more than a million since 1996. Another factor involves changes in skill levels among OFWs. Starting in 1995 and continuing well into 2015, the number of deployed Filipino workers rose significantly owing to increased opportunities in the service sector (e.g., medical services and health care, information technology, and food and hotel services). Finally, as already discussed, the BSP implemented several changes allowing for the efficient transfer of money from foreign countries to the Philippines.[3] The BSP improved access to financial services by establishing remittance centers across the globe. It also ensured the transferability of funds to Filipinos living in remote areas of the country by backing sending corporations like Western Union and MoneyGram. Overseen by the Philippines Overseas Employment Administration, the government arm in charge of organizing and supervising the export of Philippine labor abroad, various programs have been developed to assists OFWs and their families to increase their savings and investments.

In 2007 Metropolitan Bank and Trust Company (Metrobank), the largest bank in the Philippines, partnered with Xoom.com to allow Filipinos to send money electronically via the Internet and enable beneficiaries to claim the funds in a number of Philippine banks. Through a partnership between Banco de Oro and the SM group, the largest retailing conglomerate in the Philippines, Filipinos can not only exchange various currencies into pesos at any SM Supermall but also claim remittances there. The BSP has reacted positively to property investments by Filipinos living abroad. The BSP has partnered with real estate corporations to provide overseas Filipinos with an alternative to sending remittance money by directly managing their money through bank loans for condominiums or housing lots. Furthermore, the increase in government intervention appears to be having a positive effect on consumer confidence in the Philippine banking system. More than in the past, Filipinos remitting from various places abroad are sending their money directly through banks in the Philippines. The BSP (2014) claims that of the US$14.7 billion remitted by overseas Filipinos in 2014, 95 percent of the funds were sent directly through the country's banking system, in contrast with 72 percent in 2001.

The consensus among most economists and sociologists studying remittance flows into the Philippines is that while permanent Filipino migrants tend to lose their affinity with the home country and subsequently choose to focus their investments in their new countries, OFWs are compelled to continue to send money back to their immediate families who still reside in the Philippines. Furthermore, temporary Filipino migrants are also driven to send remittances because a major portion of these amounts is seen as an investment in their own security once they eventually make their way back to their homeland. Raul, the vice president of international marketing at one major real estate corporation operating in twelve different countries, was quick to respond to my question about the differences between selling to permanent Filipino emigrants and to OFWs. "It's simple. OFWs have to return. So you know that they will want to have something to return to. Whether it's sending money back to their family or making payments on their new property, OFWs provide a very dependable market."

It is imperative to contextualize the ideological labor sustaining the balikbayan economy within the historically constructed global system, which eventually allowed the contact zone between American imperialism and the disparate regions of the Philippines to take shape. In this context, the structure of feelings—the historical practices of patronage and indebtedness underpinning Philippine socioeconomic culture—produced the originating pathway for the waves of Filipino labor migrants to the United States to maintain and sustain their connection to their families and hometowns in the Philippines even though permanently settling in the United States remained their ultimate dream. Eventually, these pathways were reincorporated into neoliberal projects to create a vast assemblage: global labor brokers, remittance-sending corporations, communication and media technologies, multinational property developers, and the circulation of various consumer goods would merge, intersect, and form the contemporary balikbayan economy. For this reason, a significant portion of the profits that continue to be made by sending Filipino labor abroad is reaped by the Philippines or, more specifically, a very concentrated and elite portion of the population who decides what direction the rest of the country will take.

While Filipinos in the United States send money, microwaves, and entertainment systems back to take care of their families in the Philippines, the looming hope is that their imaginative/material labor is also securing an alternative future, not only for the families they support in the Philippines, but for themselves as well. Often, migration and its attendant consequences, like remittance sending, are assumed to take an asymmetrical shape. Historically, the United States has drawn out and exploited the brightest and most creative resources in the Philippines to tremendously benefit its militaristic, economic, and political endeavors. However, this conceptual emphasis, which privileges the unilateral transfer between the United States and the Philippines, does little to explain how an entire system of transnational circulation has persisted for over a century—and, more important, how Filipinos in the diaspora continue to envision return in a very real way.

Transnational Connectivities

Alongside popular Philippine *teleserye*, widely viewed television dramas similar to the Korean K-dramas or the *telenovelas* produced in Mexico, the transnational mediasphere linking Filipinos throughout the diaspora is regularly saturated by television commercials, print-media ads, and Internet pop-ups advertising remittance services and products. This transnationality reveals the contemporary shape of remittance-driven development mobilizing economies throughout the Global South, especially in the Philippines.

The cultural practices materializing obligation and reciprocity, central values for Filipinos, are made visible throughout Daly City in the United States. There are at least as many Philippine banks and remittance centers as Filipino-owned businesses in the city. These are examples of the proliferation and significance of these cultural commitments. Informal practices of remittance giving from Filipino business owners and church congregants to the Philippines through balikbayan boxes are just a few other examples. The entrepreneurship and investments produced by these transnational circulations of capital are shifting social relations and instigating transformation within sending nations (Levitt 2001).

Enhanced by technological innovations and more efficient modes of mobility, Filipinos are increasingly able to maintain connections to their homeland. Most important, these connections are sustained through the belief that the possibility of returning is quite real. The traces marking Daly City as a Filipino space, from the "meeting halls" of restaurants and bowling alleys to the slew of remittance centers, underscore how ethnoburban landscapes operate as hubs within the larger global economy.[4] In addition, these tracings allude to another question altogether: what might an American city look like if America is no longer the focal point anchoring everyday life but rather, as Catherine Ceniza Choy (2005) has it, an "extension of the Philippines"?

Carla Jimenez, a nurse who migrated to Daly City in 1982 from a small town in the province of Laguna, explains the unrelenting presence of familial obligations vividly tying her to her community back home.

> When I first arrived, I would send at least half of my paycheck to my parents [in Laguna] each month. If I had a little bit more, I would send my younger brother and sisters some as well. But most of the time, I expected my parents to distribute it equally. . . . There was no contract. There was no one to tell me that I had to do this, to give half of my paycheck. I just knew that it was expected. Yet even now, twenty years later, even though I was able to bring my whole family to the States, my parents, brother, sisters, and they were able to bring their families here because [my husband] and I came here first, I still receive phone calls from family members in the Philippines. Nephews will call asking for a lot of money to start a business. Distant relatives will ask for help to pay hospital bills. You know there isn't affordable health insurance for poor people in the Philippines, right? So [Filipinos in the United States] have to help with that a lot. I'm not complaining, I'm not saying that it's bad. It's just that sometimes my family does not realize that I'm not made out of money.

Carla's ambivalence points to the complexities of familial obligation and the ties perpetuating the uneven relationship between Filipinos in the United States and those in the Philippines. Carla's experiences help to make sense of how, over decades of migration from the Philippines, the circulation of financial resources between Daly City and the Philippines has transformed the built environment of Daly City and the social life of the Filipinos living there.

Throughout Daly City a host of remittance services are inconspicuously marked by exchange rates between the peso and dollar posted on their store windows or on makeshift signs on the sidewalk outside. Philippine banks, like the Philippine National Bank and Metrobank and their subsidiaries, compete with one another to garner a percentage of the remittances sent by Filipinos, whose household incomes are, on average, substantially higher than the median household income of other Americans in the United States. Remittance centers also seek to take advantage of the number of new Filipino immigrants who consistently filter through the neighborhood.

There are no concrete data tracking the real total of remittances sent to the Philippines because many of these remittances are transacted informally. Filipino grocery stores and small businesses sometimes informally send remittances. Emilio Manalapit, for example, one of the respondents I interviewed who arrived in the United States and struggled to find a full-time job for almost two years even though he held a engineering degree, explained how informal transactions provided by friends who owned a neighboring grocery store were essential to providing money to his family back home. "My friends had family in the same town where my family lived. I didn't have a good job for a long time. I couldn't send very much money back home. It was shameful. So my friends said, 'Help us with the store. You know, just small accounting things. Nothing really big. And we'll just send money for you because you're working here too.' So a portion of the money that they gave to their family was given to my family too." Other times, owners of Filipino businesses will do the work of remittance centers and, for an informal fee, "do favors" for their clients by transacting money themselves. Then there are the formal contracts that business owners will make with banks in the Philippines in order to provide remittance services along with selling their goods.

Along with the remittance centers, cargo-shipping companies like Johnny Air Cargo in St. Francis Square or the Philippine-owned LBC Express are scattered throughout Daly City. These international shipping companies specifically cater to a Filipino clientele and specialize in guaranteeing daily shipments of gifts and other material goods to the Philippines. Marisha Maas (2008, 136) describes how these "door-to-door" services, prevalent within cities even in the Netherlands, and the "diffused forms of solidarity and generalized forms of reciprocity that they encourage, are integral to the formation of the Filipino transnational community."

Respondents consistently mentioned that most of the remittances they send are not actually processed through remittance centers but conveniently transacted over the Internet through websites run by Western

Union, MoneyGram, Xoom.com, and others. Rather than making their way to remittance centers, provided they are able to offer a limited amount of personal information and are willing to pay larger transaction fees, individuals can simply use their credit or debit cards to send money to Philippine banks or designated remittance centers almost anywhere in the Philippines. Roberto Cardenas describes his responsibility to his family in the Philippines by saying, "I'm the oldest in the family. That means that I'm the first person that my brothers, my sisters, and my parents call if they need money. I send one of them money at least every other month. Sometimes just fifty dollars, sometimes more. Not always a lot of money, but all of that builds up." Roberto and his wife, Rosemarie, met in the United States through friends. After Roberto found a permanent position working for the City of San Francisco as a civil engineer, he and Rosemarie bought a home in what was then the newer part of Daly City in 1986 and raised three children there. "We've had financial difficulties before. Maybe not as bad as now," Roberto explained while discussing the financial predicament that has forced them to sell their home. "But it never mattered. We've always sent money back to the Philippines."

At times, the obligation to send money can lead to friction between spouses, who may also be struggling to save money for their children's college tuition or to manage daily expenses. "I'm going to tell you something," Roberto whispers, directing his voice away from Rosemarie. "[Rosemarie] doesn't get along with my family. She doesn't like that I'm always sending money to them. But you know what, she sends as much money to her family." Rosemarie later told me that Roberto's family, most of whom still reside in Antipolo City just outside of Metro Manila in the province of Rizal, have consistently found it difficult to work over the years owing to an array of health problems and financial misdealing. Unlike Rosemarie's family, who have enjoyed a relatively higher level of affluence, Roberto's siblings have been forced to rely on their oldest sibling's success in the United States.

Similarly, Efren Padilla, a once hugely successful realtor who at one time owned two homes in California and one in Las Vegas, until he began falling deeper and deeper into debt as the larger economic crisis began to take shape in 2007, found remittances and the intertwining obligations around them extremely burdensome. For Padilla, familial obligations not only take the form of remittances but also involve the implications that come with sending money back to the Philippines.

It begins with sending money home. But what you are telling your family is that I am the caretaker of the family. I am the one who is responsible for their welfare. My younger brother and sisters did not bother to work in the Philippines. It's not because they were lazy. It's because they were just waiting to come here. So they never developed any skills while they were [in the Philippines]. They knew that once they came here, they would live with me and my family until they found a job. It's eleven years later, and they are all still living with us! I don't need them to give me the respect. To respect me even though I was the one who helped them to come [to the United States]. I would have liked it if they would contribute to the house by getting married or getting a job. But my wife is always reminding me, "This is your family. You're the oldest. You're the one with the means." So even though they don't know how bad things are right now, it still makes me happy to provide for them.

The significance that obligation entails remains vital within the lives of Filipinos throughout the diaspora, who see remittances as not only an obligation to their family members but one of the few ways they can have a tangible presence in the everyday lives of their family and community while living away from the Philippines. The Philippine banks and remittance centers inconspicuously located within the landscape of Daly City are vital clues that provide evidence of these commitments and struggles.

Locating Balikbayans

The homes, furniture, clothing, and electronics provided by the balikbayan economy are often referred to as *katas* or *gatas* among local Filipinos in the Philippines. They are the "juice" or "milk" produced by the "fruits" of overseas labor. When a teenager arrives at school and presents an iPhone to a growing number of gawking onlookers gathering around them, their friends might pose the question, "Gatas ng U.S. ba yan?" (That [juice] comes from the United States, right?). This query tends to be accompanied by a jumble of emotions: curiosity, jealousy, excitement, and resentment. The ambivalence behind these colloquial terms directly reflects the complexity of how balikbayans and OFWs are regarded in the Philippines. Just as kinship ties between Filipinos in the United States and their relatives in the Philippines are delicate, held together by the continuous stream of remittances, and precisely the much-coveted goods acquired through them, the national image of balikbayans in their homeland is similarly fragile. Diasporic Filipinos, particularly balikbayans, are tethered to the Philippines through a complicated system of financial dependency and imaginative labor.

Rick Bonus (2000, 90), explains that "articulating the articulations" of immigrant identities demands a deep attention to the ways in which immigrants vacillate between producing spaces of belonging and being shaped by their attempt to gain access to social, material, and political resources. By virtue of the mobility that characterizes them, migrant identities are continually in flux and contingent on their everyday representations throughout the spaces they occupy. Their sheer presence challenges static notions delimiting national identities. The identities they fashion are shaped by pressures to conform and assimilate, compunctions to react and adhere to the standards delimited by the nations where they settle. At the same time, immigrant identities are also defined by the overt and subtle ways in which they confront and contest particular social norms and subsequently create new identities through their resistance.

Conversely, return migrants are challenged by an opposing force. They have already encountered the "immigrant moment." And through years and decades of settlement in a foreign world, the foreign has become familiar. In the midst of return, they must reconcile memories of the homeland to which they used to belong with the ways it has changed. Thus, while return migrants may, to differing degrees, cling to their old identities, they are now continually confronted by a homeland that recognizes them in a very different way. Because of this disjuncture, balikbayans resist definition, regardless of the legal and political discourse continuously seeking to fix them to a system of financial obligation and cultural indebtedness. Their identities, in both law and practice, are contingent on an ever-changing matrix of economic, geographic, and social conditions. Instead, balikbayans are often defined by their differences from OFWs.

While balikbayans are often conflated with OFWs in both legal and vernacular discourse, there are clear demarcations between the two groups. The primary distinguishing characteristics relate to how each group settled abroad and the time they have lived away from the Philippines. Whereas OFWs are defined by the temporary conditions set forth in labor contracts, balikbayans leave the Philippines without a due date for return. Filipinos keenly recognize how balikbayans are integral to the economy structuring

FIGURE 2.1
Advertisement for
Amaia Land in
Balikbayan, 2013.

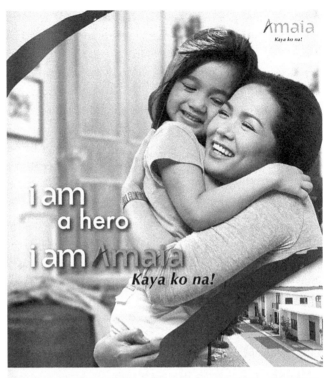

everyday life in the Philippines. Yet, unlike OFWs, who often toil abroad in grueling conditions, balikbayans are not perceived as "new heroes" struggling in the places where they settle. Along with employment in advanced economies, balikbayans often obtain citizenship in the countries where they settle. Therefore, since balikbayans do not fit within easily definable categories or political agendas, they have generally escaped scholarly examination. And when they are written about, they are often misrepresented.

One of the major reasons that balikbayans are often depicted as "ugly" or "vain" is that the literature indirectly juxtaposes them with the figure of the OFW. Unlike their balikbayan counterparts, who are capable of claiming the rights granted through the citizenship they gained from other countries, albeit in a contingent and differentiated fashion, OFWs cannot easily claim or assert their rights when working abroad (R. Rodriguez 2002; Parreñas

2001b). By the very nature of their temporary status, the livelihood and safety of OFWS are intensely dependent on the arbitrary arrangements of the Philippine political system. The harrowing consequences produced by this liminality are further perpetuated by the Philippine state, which encodes Filipinos working abroad through the rhetoric of the *bagong bayani*, or modern-day hero.[5] The official language of migration transmitted by the Philippine state championing OFWS as "new heroes" functions to conceal the perpetual nature of this whimsicality, which continually endangers the general image of prosperity the state hopes to evoke. Likewise, by selecting OFWS as the symbol of Philippine migration, an array of critics are able to identify how the neoliberal state often chooses to safeguard its economic relationship with other countries rather than defending the rights of citizens who encounter human or labor rights violations in their country of employment (Ong 2006).[6] Although, on the surface, the Philippine state has espoused a rhetoric of protecting the rights of OFWS around the world, even passing Migrant Workers and Overseas Filipinos Act or Republic Act No. 8042 in June 7, 1995, which would apparently concretize the government's commitment to protecting the rights and promoting the welfare of migrant workers, their families, and other overseas Filipinos in distress, numerous cases of assault and murder of OFWS have been met with few repercussions on the side of the Philippine government (Guevarra 2010).

These highly publicized cases involving abuse of domestic workers, especially those working in Asia and the Middle East, have become crucial cases to thrust these debates into the political and intellectual arena. The OFWS, who are often cast as acutely vulnerable "victims" and a highly exploitable group of "low-skilled" laborers regardless of their diverse backgrounds, function as a prototypical case for the prevailing discourses on globalization, transnationalism, and global connectivity. The political and economic significance represented by their laboring bodies acts as a tool to champion and distinguish the Philippine state within the global market and, likewise, to pose critical interventions necessary for disrupting the dominant logic of global capitalism. These cases and the vast assemblages of government and corporate agencies responsible for regulating and financing this "brain drain" have had a significantly gendered effect on the labor market produced by OFWS. Rhacel Salazar Parreñas (2008) argues that practices and policies around Philippine migration generally operate through the "force of domesticity," a persistent ideology that continually relegates women to forms of reproductive labor within the global economy.

FIGURE 2.2
Customs declaration form
completed by visitors to the
Philippines, which includes six
categories for purpose of visit,
including "Balikbayan" and
"Overseas Filipino Worker,"
2011.

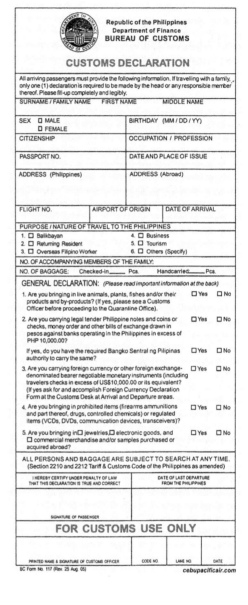

The juxtaposition of OFWS and balikbayans is further complicated by the gendered exploitation of Filipino women, who constitute a disproportionate percentage of contracted overseas Filipino laborers. Just as the gendered effects of labor production and migration often relegate both women and men to particular gendered roles and compel individuals to discipline themselves and those around them according to the larger logic of domesticity, projects of nation-state building often attempt to replicate this logic in an expanded form and refashion the boundaries around citizenship through the same logic.[7] The nation-building project constituted by the logic of domesticity is often transmitted through the future-oriented language of parenting and responsibility. Kathleen Weekley (2004), for example, discusses how migrant workers in Hong Kong are induced through a logic of domesticizing governmentality to envision themselves as entrepreneurs and "stakeholders" rather than simply workers who are providing for their families back in the Philippines. The Philippines Overseas Employment Administration has instituted policies that force OFWs to pay percentages of their remittances to the Philippine government and labor brokers. Subsequently, "training programs" have been initiated to educate OFWs on how to manage their finances and act "responsibly."

At the same time, there are no political or legal regulations obligating Filipinos who settle abroad to pay taxes or contribute portions of their income to the Philippine government. Along with the normal rights assumed by any citizen of the Philippines, there are critical incentives for balikbayans to claim dual citizenship, including the ability to purchase property and establish a business in their homeland or pay taxes to the Philippine government unless the income is derived from business in the Philippines. And while the Philippine Supreme Court recently upheld its decision to deny dual citizens the ability to run for elected office in 2003, balikbayans are still capable of directly impacting the political sphere in the Philippines through their right to vote. For these reasons, apart from a handful of mechanisms including the SRRV (discussed further in chapter 6), tourism programs specifically catering to balikbayans, and the Philippine customs declaration form haphazardly collected by agents at Ninoy Aquino International Airport (see figure 2.2), there remains no institutionalized system for calculating the number of balikbayans who enter the country each year and, more important, remain in the Philippines. This inability to track the mobility of balikbayans also contributes to their lack of attention in scholarship. Yet balikbayans are indeed integral to the economy of the Philippines.

3. Transnational Real Estate » Selling the American Dream in the Philippines

For those who are living on modest Social Security pensions, a better option is to come back to the Philippines. Here, they can live comfortable lives, with household help, plus what people need most in their old age: relatives and friends. There should be opportunities in this dire situation for the Philippine Retirement Authority and for mid-priced real estate developments. —Greg B. Macabenta, "Hard Times in America"

From Crisis to Crisis

Eleanor gently tugged at one side of the ornately woven tablecloth tightly hugging the surface of her oak dining table. She gave it one more pass to smoothen out the remaining wrinkles, perhaps thinking to herself that they might somehow deter her guests from savoring the fresh *lechon* (pork) or one of her painstakingly made *lumpia shanghai* (fried eggrolls). The tablecloth was just one of various ornaments decorating her small dining room, a milieu of treasures that she had accumulated while working in Jidda. The second-largest city in Saudi Arabia, the coastal metropolis had been home to Eleanor for three years while she worked as a nurse. Afterward, she picked up once again and achieved her dream of living and working in the United States.

A shiny brass coffeepot rested awkwardly atop an Islamic prayer rug in one corner of the room. With its long, protruding spout pointing toward a set of matching cups resting on the sacred cover, it evoked an image of prostrated acolytes praying toward the Aladdin lamp–like pot. In a metaphorical sense, the assortment of Arabic decor merged seamlessly with the typically "Filipino" dishes, devoured by guests as each floated in and out of the room. Together, the room fused into a snapshot of a particular moment in Filipino migration, when variously skilled Filipino migrants traveled far from their homes in the Philippines after the oil crisis of the 1970s to make momentary pit stops in the Middle East before arriving at their final destinations in western Europe and North America.

Such interstitial moments exhibit the contrasting spatial practices of Filipinos as they traverse different continents while being pulled or pulling themselves from the Philippines. The bricolage of nomadic tracings sprawled across Eleanor's elaborately decorated dining room is reenacted across Filipino homes throughout Daly City. These practices, which attempt to re-create a sense of home in the diaspora while simultaneously expanding a network of community, distinctly contrast with the vibrant and colorful fiestas they once hosted in their cities, provinces, and homes in the Philippines.

However, this was not exactly a fiesta. Eleanor Acupang, a resident of Daly City for twenty-two years, was hosting a pair of realtors from Manila who had come to the San Francisco Bay Area to sell property to Filipinos who had been settled in the United States for many years. Both realtors were employees of Eton Properties Philippines Inc., the real estate branch of a much larger international conglomerate, the Lucio Tan Group. Eleanor, who recently began supplementing her income from nursing by becoming an independently operating realtor selling properties on both sides of the bay, came into contact with Eton Properties during one of her many return trips to Manila. While inquiring about a particular property advertisement just outside of Metro Manila, Eleanor was directed to the corporate office of Eton, located in the central business district (CBD) of Makati. She said, "I told them that there are a lot of Filipinos like me who are thinking about retiring in the Philippines. Many Filipinos are thinking about returning. After I convinced them that I could be a helpful contact in the United States, we organized a time for them to come and speak to my friends and neighbors here."

Eleanor once adamantly believed that she had finally found a home in Daly City and that she would never return to the Philippines, thus ending her journey as a diasporic nomad. But as was the case for many of her relatives and Filipino friends who had migrated and settled throughout cities along the American West Coast after 1965 and were now approaching retirement, the current ailing economy had forced her to reconsider the sustainability of her lifestyle and residence in the United States.

The emerging trend of Filipino Americans investing in property in the Philippines is a fairly recent one; it began picking up steam only during the early 1990s. Once the interest in property investments around the Philippines had been identified by a handful of opportunistic Filipino American realtors and entrepreneurs, global real estate firms operating mainly from Metro Manila began testing the market in the United States. Philippine corporations began by sending out "road shows" and connecting with a network of "bird dogs" like Eleanor to target large concentrations of Filipino Americans. Once these communities were identified, real estate corporations would take advantage of local Filipino newspapers to advertise openings for new property developments.

In 1997, however, the entire region of Asia experienced a sudden financial crisis beginning in Thailand. Described as a "contagion" or the "Asian flu," to use the predictably racialized term, by several economists and policy makers, the crisis quickly spread throughout the majority of Asia, particularly Malaysia, Indonesia, Singapore, South Korea, and the Philippines. The real estate economy, which had been booming during the late 1980s and early 1990s, driven by international speculation and the potential for opening new markets in the region, came to a quick halt. While other Asian countries struggled desperately to stay afloat after the crisis swelled, the Philippine economy remarkably rebounded in a relatively short time (Balisacan and Hill 2008; Krinks 2002). While there are a number of reasons that the Philippines experienced a relatively mild recession compared with its neighbors, the focus of this chapter is on a particular sector of the country's economy that has continually sustained its financial system in the face of repeated crisis.

This chapter examines the transnational processes circulating among real estate agents and brokers operating between the United States and the Philippines, and the subjectivities produced by these practices. In recent years, buoyed by a continuous stream of remittance capital, business outsourcing, and the exportation of labor produced by the balikbayan economy, the Philippine real estate market has been able to maintain upward growth. Now, corporate interest in potential capital investments from Filipinos living abroad, especially in the United States, has led to an aggressive campaign of transnational real estate advertisement and intensive property development on the part of global real estate firms in Metro Manila.

As an entire generation of Philippine immigrants who arrived after 1965 finds itself on the precipice of retiring from various sectors of the U.S. labor force, global real estate firms are designing elaborate projects and developing sophisticated techniques to attract many of these retirees back to the Philippines. This wave of property development has made real estate agents and brokers operating in both the United States and the Philippines central to the balikbayan economy and the transformation of Metro Manila. Their communication with clients in the United States and developers in the Philippines has created a transnational circuit that materializes in massive global ad campaigns and multisite real estate megaprojects. Subsequently, agents and brokers act as intermediaries and conduits for Filipinos in the United States to transform the physical and cultural landscape of Metro Manila. This chapter will focus on the transnational circulation of real estate development capital that knits together the aspirations of Filipinos living in the United States with the interests of state agents and corporate developers in the Philippines. It provides glimpses of how nation-states' governments utilize neoliberal practices to generate streams of transnational capital. While these practices might appear to diminish nation-state boundaries and the sovereignty of the Philippine government, they are, in fact, helping to solidify the country's place in the global economy in the face of intense competition and transnational connectivity.

Beginning in 2007, the financial crisis had precipitated a series of mortgage defaults, home foreclosures, and tremendous losses of personal assets for a number of Filipino families. One opportunistic realty entrepreneur, writing from the perspective of Filipinos in California in the Philippine newspaper *BusinessWorld*, urged corporations in the Philippines to continue targeting Filipinos in the United States, eagerly suggesting that "for those who are living on modest Social Security pensions, a better option is to come back to the Philippines. Here, they can live comfortable lives, with household help, plus what people need most in their old age: relatives and friends" (Macabenta 2008).

This chapter captures the various ways real estate agents working between the United States and the Philippines are attempting to lure Filipinos in the United States back to the Philippines. Interweaving this discussion is Anna Lowenhaupt Tsing's (2005) notion of an "economy of appearances," particularly through the manner in which the aspirations of Filipinos living abroad have created a source of both fictional and material capital to subsidize property developments in the Philippines. I will explain how the "performance" of this speculative capital produces the context in which many Filipino families are now confronting the possibility of traveling back to the Philippines and remaining there permanently.

As discussed in the previous chapter, the vested attempts to attract investments from Filipino Americans slowly evolved out of decades of economic and cultural reliance on remittance money sent by Filipinos working abroad. This web of remittances threads together the transnational and transhistorical veil beneath which Filipinos find themselves tied to both the United States and the Philippines. Today, potential returnees like Eleanor slowly turn their investments into property developments in the Philippines, while multinational property developers prepare for their impending return through the construction of massive megaproject developments throughout Metro Manila. On the other side of this pathway lies a much longer historical trajectory. The various developments and the web of foreign and domestic investments needed to secure these properties and construct the built environment into which Filipinos living abroad will eventually move have been subsidized by an accumulation of decades of exported Philippine labor, both high and low skilled, both flexible and permanent. Both the historical and contemporary material accumulations of these investments have produced a circuit of transnational real estate binding Filipinos in the United States with much larger processes of transformation in the Philippines.

Selling Appearances: Speculative Capital and the Transnational Real Estate Market

We've put our house in order. . . . There are attractive investment packages for you if you want to explore, develop and process mineral resources. . . . Easy entry for expatriate staff. . . . Doesn't that sound like an offer you can't refuse? We like multinationals. Manila's natural charms as a regional business center have been enhanced by a special incentive package. . . . [Y]our expatriate-managers will enjoy Asia's lowest living costs among the most outgoing people in the Pacific. . . . Accountants come for $67, executive secretaries for $148. Move your Asian headquarters to Manila and make your cost accountants happy. . . . The country is lovely. And loaded. Beneath the tropical landscapes of our 7,000 islands lies a wealth of natural resources. — advertisement in *New York Times*, quoted in Tadiar 2004, 43

The advertisement above, bought by the Philippine government and printed in the *New York Times* on July 28, 1974, conveys how for almost a century policy makers and entrepreneurs, from early pro-expansionists in the United States to contemporary multinational corporate executives in East Asia, have sought to turn the speculative gaze of prospective investors onto the archipelago with a confidence inspired by the *potential* for economic expansion and wealth acquisition rather than its actual presence.[1] Whether it was its serendipitous geographic location that made the archipelago significant to trade relations with other Asian countries, the promise of its natural and human resources, or simply the undeniable beauty of its paradigmatically tropical landscape, foreign entities, state administrators, and business entrepreneurs (the latter two often being one and the same) have sold the Philippines to international investors based on a promise and a particular performance of this promise. The interaction between promise and performance in the Philippines reflects Tsing's (2005) notion of an "economy of appearances," where the production and accumulation of finance capital are based on the performance of the country's potential rather than its current political shape or the present reality of its congested urban landscapes and glaring lack of integrative infrastructure.[2]

In the case of foreign direct investment, the Philippines remains competitive with other Asian countries by devoting a significant portion of government spending to increasing tourism and encouraging trade through the liberalization and deregulation of the Philippine economy. Integral to the expansion of industries and trade are those speculators who risked investing speculative capital in the Philippines during various moments of economic crisis and political transition. In a reciprocal fashion, the elaborate labor-brokering industry that sends millions of Filipinos abroad as Overseas Filipino Workers (OFWs) each year operates by encouraging migrant workers to aspire to work outside of the Philippines. Images of economic security and self-fulfillment produced by movies, commercials, songs, and phone calls linger in the imaginations of Filipinos who either cannot find suitable employment in the Philippines or are incapable of earning wages commensurate with their education or status. The continual performance of such appearances compels 10 percent of the country's labor force to work abroad. As previously discussed, state administrators, together with private entrepreneurial groups, have absorbed a relatively high amount of risk in order to establish the Philippines as one of the leading nations in exporting labor by sustaining an infrastructure that both allows

OFWs to continue to work abroad and redirects a portion of their income back to the state.

Fundamentally, these divergent yet functionally interlinking processes, generated and maintained by flows of speculative capital (one drawing foreign capital into the Philippines, the other searching for it abroad), compose the productive force turning the machinery of the balikbayan economy. As speculative investors, various entities attempt to win profits by absorbing the risk, literally purchasing it, in order to stabilize a particular market, determine the price for a given commodity, and eventually accrue an enormous financial return and even the majority of the commodity's market. In both cases, for the initial investors in the balikbayan economy, there were relatively few safeguards that would ensure a profit for their transactions or labor. As such, the economy of appearances is always principled on the promise of what could be rather than what is already there.

International property speculation and real estate development, particularly in the case of transnational real estate in the Philippines, are preeminent examples of Tsing's economy of appearances. In their endeavor to discover emerging sources of financial capital, transnational real estate entrepreneurs are compelled to exaggerate the potential for capital wealth accumulation in the Philippines in order to attract the investments they need to pursue their business plans in full. The rest of this chapter describes how transnational real estate corporations look to the economy of appearances as a means of compelling Filipinos in the United States to invest in real estate in the Philippines.

In Tsing's (2005) formulation, "performance here is simultaneously economic performance and dramatic performance" (57). Whether the aspiration toward profit might entail marketing a new clothing line or introducing an innovation within the food industry, the "economy of appearances . . . the self-conscious making of a spectacle is a necessary aid to gathering investment funds. . . . It is a regular feature of the search for financial capital" (57). Whether the attraction is real or imagined, capital investments rely on the dramatization and exaggeration of possibilities in order to begin operating or expanding their industries. "The more spectacular the conjuring, the more possible an investment frenzy" (57). Tsing's notion is particularly relevant to transnational real estate, where more often the intended property or township is still in the model phase, and finance capital is integral to beginning to build and achieve these various development projects. This is especially the case in Metro Manila, where properties are commonly funded by "preselling" up to 40 percent of the development.[3] "In order to attract companies, countries, regions, and towns must dramatize their potential as places for investment. Dramatic performance is the prerequisite of their economic performance" (Cornelio-Pronove and Cheng 1999, 118).

Tsing's framework is instructive for comprehending the processes producing the circulations of capital investment between the United States and the Philippines within the transnational real estate industry. Through a far-reaching and oftentimes disjunctive network of transnationally operating realtors and developers and the various modes of strategic advertising they produce, Philippine real estate corporations attempt to lure capital investments from Filipinos living in the United States by making the potential for financial gain appear as real as possible. They induce investments by kindling nostalgic aspirations of Filipinos desiring to return to the Philippines while promising them a life similar to the one they would be leaving behind in the United States. Real estate agents conjure images of vast, elegantly constructed townships and depict the Philippines without the overcrowding and insecurity that have historically kept balikbayans from staying there. At the same time, agents carefully meld these images with ones reminiscent of childhood and with compelling allusions to the comfort of living alongside one's compatriots, in contrast to the alienation brought on by being an immigrant.

Before the performance of these appearances is described, it is imperative to discuss the current predicament of speculative capital within the transnational real estate industry. It should be clear that the transnational real estate market between the United States and the Philippines, particularly where fueled by financial investments made by Filipinos looking to return to the Philippines, is burgeoning. A number of Filipino business owners in the United States, for instance, have been following property market trends outside of Metro Manila, particularly throughout their home provinces, and are eager to invest in building in their hometowns. Belen Butay is the owner of Loulen Hawaii Sports Wear as well as the co-owner of Crown Court Restaurant in Hawaii. He admits that he is paying close attention to the real estate market in provinces like Ilocos Norte. "I've seen the economy improve every year," Butay said. "The middle class is starting to grow. My friends are rich. The shopping centers are much better here than in Hawaii and the mainland" (Kreifels 2009). Like other Filipino investors who have chosen to purchase property outside of Metro Manila,

Butay acquired properties in the provinces of Batangas and Quezon southeast of Manila. While he is away, his family watches over his farms, where they raise poultry.

Filipino investors like Butay are conscious that in order to begin seeing larger returns it is paramount that they devote a significant amount of their financial capital to building an infrastructure that will support the expansion of provincial economies, just as it did in Manila during its early period of growth. Previously, the small number of state and privately owned banks could not manage to finance individual homeowners. However, over the last two decades, the state has aggressively pursued an agenda of deregulation, opening the door for foreign banks to provide more residential loans at lower interest rates. Along with the introduction of foreign banking capital, other government incentives targeting the increase in real estate investments have created a window of opportunity for balikbayans to begin investing heavily in the residential market.

At the current moment, however, the majority of Filipinos who have lived in the United States since the 1970s and 1980s, those who arrived as highly educated immigrants and have integrated themselves into the skilled sector of the U.S. labor market, remain content to reside in their adopted country. For the moment, Filipinos in the United States have not chosen to return to the Philippines en masse, nor are the majority of the real estate developments built to accommodate this return complete. For the transnational real estate market to draw Filipinos from the United States and greet these returnees with real estate developments, a foundation of speculative capital investment must be introduced and the first round of massive infrastructure and real estate has to be built.

Over the past decade, imaginative entrepreneurs have increasingly invested enormous amounts of speculative capital into multiscaled property developments and global advertising of these developments. Investors have looked to the housing market, already subsidized in many ways by the office property market boom of the 1980s and 1990s, to diversify their portfolios (Cornelio-Pronove and Cheng, 1999). By the end of the 1990s, investors became increasingly convinced that returning Filipinos would be willing to purchase upscale housing properties, particularly Filipinos working abroad in the white-collar sector. Within the residential sector alone, for example, in Quezon City, a traditionally upper-class section of Metro Manila where the first wave of suburbanization had begun in the first half of the twentieth century, there were about twenty-four different private residential subdivisions, with a total of six thousand homes in the early 1990s. Most of the homes were single detached houses, and each subdivision occupied about five square kilometers of urban space (Nierras et al. 1992). In less than a decade, developers expanded the number of subdivisions to five hundred, housing over a million residents and drastically transforming the residential core of urbanism in Metro Manila toward suburbanized dwellings (Connell 1999). Multinational corporations based in the Philippines began building properties—not only high-rise condominiums in the CBD of Makati but also western bungalows and multipurpose townships around the periphery of Metro Manila. "Eventually the wave of Filipino retirees will make their way back to the Philippines. Soon the trickle will become a river," claimed Norman Reyes, an executive of international sales at Ayala Land.

As these developments slowly reconfigure the social world of Filipinos in the Philippines through the transformation of the built landscape and the redirection of labor, real estate corporations are increasingly encouraged to invest more finance capital as more and more Filipinos return to the Philippines, witness these evolutions, and, in turn, look to invest their finances in their future back in the homeland.

Edgar T. Pascual (2003) has served the Filipino immigrant community in Southern California for over twenty years. He has also been one of the pioneering figures in transnational real estate between the two countries; at the end of the 1980s, he forecasted the potential purchasing power of returning Filipinos. Pascual observes that "other countries have seen an influx of retirees simply because they have developed means to keep these retirees in their paternal abode. I believe that the Philippines can find ways and means to do the same for the thousands of Filipino Americans retirees" (13–14). Pascual's book, *How to Profit from the $27 Billion Filipino American Market,* describes his early partnership with real estate corporations in the Philippines in selling Philippine property to Filipinos living in the United States. Based on buyer profiles and insights he gained while dealing with Filipinos in both countries, Pascual argues that Filipino Americans should be the primary target for financial investments, particularly in the real estate sector.

More broadly, his handbook illustrates the dual "performance" of speculative capital that is necessary to entice *both* real estate developers in the Philippines and potential property buyers in the United States to invest in the Philippine real estate economy. As such, Tsing's economy of appearances operates on two simultaneous fronts within the transnational real estate industry: (1) garnering speculative capital for development projects in the Philippines and (2) eliciting initial investments from Filipinos in the United States as they purchase preselling properties.

Carlos Estel, an international agent working for Robinsons Land Corporation, a global real estate corporation, explained, "Most of the properties that we are selling in the U.S. market have yet to be completed. Our clients have to take a leap of faith and buy properties that they will not move into for several years. Sure, it's an investment, but we also know that it's very different than how you buy homes in the States." Robinsons Land Corporation is the parent company to Robinsons Malls, the second-largest shopping mall and retail operator in the Philippines and just one of various corporations devoting substantial resources to selling property to Filipinos in the United States. Estel noted, "The biggest obstacle to selling property to Filipinos is assuring them that they'll get what they buy. For most companies, it's an even bigger problem because they cannot build until they secure enough investments from buyers abroad. Especially in Manila [where property is more expensive]. This is because they do not own the land they are developing on. This is not a problem for Robinsons since we own many properties throughout the Philippines." This sentiment was mirrored by another international real estate agent, who was operating through Eton Properties:

> We are under the Lucio Tan Corporations. The corporation already owns two banks, and there are many nonperforming assets. Instead of idle lands, we'd rather develop it. If we are not the biggest developer in the Philippines, we are certainly the biggest land bank. For some developers, their problem is, where to buy land for them to develop. Our problem is we have so many lands, which one should we develop first. Right? Just imagine we have a thousand hectares, it will take you twenty or thirty years to develop that. For just one project. Well, we have thirteen projects right now.

Yet most real estate developers do not have the luxury of owning the property they are attempting to build on. Unlike large landowning conglomerates like Ayala Land, Robinsons, and Lucio Tan, smaller real estate companies not only are forced to attract speculative capital investments to purchase land and commence building but must invest more funds to advertise and attract buyers to complete their projects. For this reason, and others that will be discussed in the following chapter, the vast majority of property in the Philippines is owned by a handful of corporations, which not only operate as large land banks but also, as part of their diverse business portfolios, own a number of banks to finance loans, real estate firms that are in charge of selling various commercial and residential properties, and even media shares in order to advertise their properties through television commercials and print media.

The introduction of the balikbayan retiree property market in recent years has made the selling of properties more complicated. Much of the confidence maintained by real estate corporations selling retirement property to Filipinos living in the United States is sustained by decades of migrations back and forth between the countries. For instance, when asked why corporations are willing to invest billions of pesos to develop massive amounts of land and build grand and ornate home for Filipinos who may or may not be able to afford them, Reyes laughed and quickly responded, "Well, sure, those Filipinos who work in Hong Kong or Saudi Arabia as household helpers, of course they cannot afford these high-class projects. But if we're talking about Filipinos working in the United States, well, so many of them are working in the medical field, right? Nurses and those kinds. These Filipinos are the ones who can afford to live in our high-class developments." Idealizations of the lifestyles of Filipinos settling in the United States and their financial success are by now depicted in every form of Philippine media, described in popular literature and labor-brokering manuals, and relayed in conversations at the dinner table (see Tadiar 2004). Oftentimes Filipino migrants themselves are guilty of perpetuating the myths about life in the United States, glossing over their hardships, as a way of communicating their successes and bringing honor to their families in the Philippines. Even statistics taken from the U.S. Census and other data paint a picture of Filipino Americans as "model minorities" whose achievements as an ethnic minority in the United States even outweigh those of their white American counterparts (see Bonus 2000).

Even as a resident of the United States for over two decades, Pascual himself, for instance, employs data on employment statistics and educational attainment as evidence to convince developers in the Philippines that Filipinos are ideal candidates for property investments. Asserting that "the average annual family income of Filipino Americans is $50,000, which is almost twice as much as the family income of the total American income of $34,400," Pascual argues that Filipinos in the United States "generally enjoy stable livelihood and, in most cases, hold more than one job" (19). Pascual fails to mention that oftentimes the high cost of living in the United States compels Filipinos to look for multiple jobs. The author's claim also conceals the disparities of income among Filipinos who are employed within various levels of the U.S. labor market. Then there is the more recent problem of overconsumption and credit dilemmas, as evidenced by the number of home foreclosures experienced by Filipinos throughout California and the Southwest, discussed earlier. Pascual's views, shared by a number of real estate executives, perpetuate a commonly held perception that the mere fact that a Filipino lives in the United States equates to them somehow being financially secure.

Such idealizations are intrinsic to the performance of appearance needed to compel real estate corporations to invest in large-scale property developments. Estel exclaimed, punctuating his statements with his fingers as he tapped on the large keys of his scientific calculator, "Everyone here knows that a domestic worker in the U.S. can make ten times more than what they would make here. How much more nurses, doctors, and engineers? They make their homes in the U.S. The goal for us is to now convince them that they can make their home here in the Philippines too." Estel, who, like Pascual, had traveled back and forth between the countries for over two decades, was adept at calculations. He lowered his head and ushered me closer to his tiny desk, which was crammed in a small office together with those of four of his coworkers. The eager agent, who exuded the excitement of a youthful upstart, proceeded to calculate the earnings of a typical Filipino nurse working in the United States and their ability to make payments on particular properties owned by Robinsons. After that, he moved on to breaking down the purchasing capabilities of a retiring engineer. "Anyone else?" Estel asked, smiling broadly. Most of the real estate executives I spoke with were far too reluctant to calculate such figures in hard numbers. Having participated in a number of trade shows throughout the United States over the years, Carlos felt extremely confident that, according to the numbers at least, most Filipinos living in the United States could afford some type of retirement property in the Philippines.

Carlos was one of a handful of real estate executives who were privy to the daily plight of most Americans, let alone Filipino immigrants, who experience difficulties in paying for their homes in the United States and making a living in the intensely competitive U.S. labor market. The speculation over property investments and capital gains that could be made

TABLE 3.1 Philippine Real Estate Corporations Specifically Targeting
Filipino American Buyers

Developer	Main location(s)	Main category	% Filipino American buyers
Robinsons Land	Metro Manila	Condominiums	50
Starland Properties Inc.	Subic	Retirement villas	80
Brittany Corp.	Nationwide	Lots, houses and lots, condos	50
D. O. Plaza Estates	Parañaque	Houses and lots	30
Megaworld	Metro Manila	Condominiums	10

Adapted from Tan 2007, 18.

through the supposed "$27 billion Filipino American market" becomes much more attractive in the minds of property executives, however, when compared with the limited financial investments that might be made through the modest incomes of Filipinos in the Philippines. It was the performance of these appearances, coupled with the increasing number of property purchases made by balikbayans, that eventually led to a surge of property development targeting Filipino American retirees in the last decade. Ayala Land Inc. launched Ayala Land International Sales Inc. in early 2005 to cater exclusively to OFWs and permanent emigrants, particularly professionals and retirees based in the United States and Europe.

Similarly, the Brittany Corporation devoted substantial resources to working with U.S.-based realty firms and financial planners to gain a deeper grasp of the Filipino American market. The by-product of these collaborations was a corporate focus on "patriotic investments." This strategy focuses on exploiting national sentiments and the longing for return that might be felt by Filipinos living in the United States. In fact, all of the major real estate corporations in the Philippines have a development sector devoted to balikbayans or Filipino American retirees (table 3.1).

Home Foreclosures and the Multifaceted Roles of Filipino Realtors

The language of return for most Filipinos lingers in ambivalence. The longing for "simpler" and "easier" times casually expressed by Filipino immigrants while recounting their days growing up in the Philippines is tethered to an extraordinarily complex set of sentiments, choices, and compromises. While the idea of return continuously looms like tantalizing fruits hanging from the stems of a vivid nostalgia, decades of material and emotional investments and the memories accompanying these experiences resign most permanent emigrants to the belief that they will probably never return and settle back in their homeland. Framed high school graduation pictures hanging above stairwells, gold and silver trophies from various sports competitions and blue ribbons from elementary school awards stacked on shelves and displayed in glass cases, pristinely remodeled kitchens, and well-worn karaoke machines are together the sparse remnants of decades of investments and memories that can be seen throughout the homes of Filipinos.

Transnational real estate agents and brokers are not faced simply with the task of convincing Filipinos to move to the Philippines, tempting their compatriots with modern conveniences, familiar comforts, and the optimistic fervor exuded by image after image of the transforming landscape of their homeland depicted in brochures and PowerPoint presentations. The more difficult challenge is to convince Filipinos in the United States that the life they had built for themselves in the United States—their friends and community, potential professional opportunities, and homes—are worth leaving behind.

Selling and leaving one's home is perhaps the most vivid example of the complexities tied to the decision of return. During the early part of the economic crisis (2006–2007), however, beset with compounding debt and recent layoffs, and often lacking knowledge of alternatives, many Filipinos had little choice but to leave their homes. Some found refuge in temporary living situations with other relatives or friends. Others abruptly returned to the Philippines. In the midst of the crisis, local Filipino realtors were uniquely positioned to assist Filipinos who were struggling to keep hold of their homes and who lacked knowledge around their basic property rights, ways to implement these rights, and various ways to navigate around the loss of their homes and other assets. As such, Filipino realtors served various functions and fulfilled several capacities: real estate agents and brokers, legal advisors and advocates, and emotional counselors.

Edna Mendoza, a particularly proactive Filipina realtor who had been working throughout the Bay Area for four years, explained, "I have two types of clients on both ends. I have good clients who are the doctors, lawyers, and who are professionals. I have also Filipino clients who don't know what to do with their homes and don't know how to deal with the lenders." She continued, "Most of my work over the last few years has been with those clients who cannot deal with losing their homes. Who don't know how to handle the banks and so forth." A host of Filipino families were confronted with these issues, particularly in Daly City. In fact, Daly City experienced the highest rate of foreclosures within San Mateo County, at about 30 percent, and homes owned by Filipinos composed a large portion of this percentage (Rodis 2008; Vasilyuk 2009). High rates of foreclosures were found in three other cities that had large concentrations of Filipino Americans. Along with Daly City, Stockton, and Vallejo (all cities in California), Las Vegas had the highest number of home foreclosures from 2007 till the end of 2009.[4]

The real estate crisis and subsequent home foreclosures created a small window of opportunity for a small number of realtors who were capable of weathering the crash of the larger real estate industry. During 2007 property prices began to plummet to the point that the value of most homes dropped to one-half to one-third of the price the homeowners had originally paid for them. Realtors, both those working in larger firms and those working independently, found it nearly impossible to sell the homes of their clients. Between 2007 and 2008, the housing market was in such a fragile state that potential home buyers, hoping to seize the opportunity of the downward-spiraling prices, remained tentative.

Edna, who arrived in the United States as a biochemist and worked at a lab in Palo Alto for almost two decades, had only recently begun working as a realtor and had been a full-time agent for an even briefer period. Yet she found that her gregarious disposition and her knack for finances easily complemented a profession in sales, particularly in the sale of property. Rather than throwing in the towel on her newfound passion, Edna invested more money in traveling to realty conferences in Las Vegas, Palm Springs, and as far away as Florida. Eventually, when Edna realized that her connections in the Filipino community provided her with a particular niche, she integrated new strategies to marketing herself. After she successfully sold a friend's home in Union City, other friends and distant relatives in the Filipino community began asking her for advice and soliciting her services. It became apparent that more and more Filipinos were experiencing similar housing problems. Edna told me, "In the first quarter of 2008, I was so excited to do this. Because we have clients who come in [who] are so distressed [that they] are going home to the Philippines. And these clients are so paranoid. They don't know what to do. They have banks who are constantly calling them, and they don't know what to do."

As Edna began recounting a series of stories, detailing the experiences of Filipinos who were on the brink of losing their homes, it became clear to me why she was capable of persisting while the real estate industry around her was falling to pieces. Her eyes glistened with sincerity, and her voice cracked beneath her words as she spoke to me about her clients. It was apparent that Edna felt compelled to protect and guide those Filipinos who were most vulnerable during this crisis.

EDNA: I had one client who stands out. She had come to me one day. I didn't even know she was coming to see me because she didn't call. They thought they're going to go to jail. Even the husband left to go to the Philippines [while the rest of the family stayed behind]. They just left their home. I had to counsel them. I told them over and over again, don't just leave your home. There is a process that the bank has to go through before they take your home.

INTERVIEWER: If you're not there, why don't these Filipinos look for information?

EDNA: The thing is, if you are going to go to an attorney, you're going to pay. And a lot of them didn't even know that there is a process. Because of the letters they received; the letters are so threatening. I know of a client in Daly City, when she got foreclosed [on], she really didn't know what to say. She didn't know how to communicate for herself. If you talk to someone and nothing happens, I know you have to keep going to the second level. You have to go to the next level if nothing happens on the first level. I know how to do these things, that's why so many Filipinos come to me.

Indeed, not all Filipino realtors possessed the same level of altruism. Predatory lenders worked together with a number of opportunistic Filipino realtors to take advantage of Filipinos who were in danger of losing their homes because of subprime mortgages or job losses. For a price, these Filipino realtors promised their clients help with adjusting mortgages or legal assistance with their home foreclosure.

This dire situation escalated to the point that TFC (the Filipino Channel) began hosting a special series on the "Filipino foreclosure crisis." The series, titled "Payong Kapamilya sa Foreclosure," was hosted by the channel's news show, *Balitang America*, in 2009. In a characteristically over-the-top and sensationalized manner, the news show begins with music intended to evoke a sense of panic and hysteria. For no explicable reason, a camouflaged voice states, "Fact: Six of the top cities worst hit by foreclosures are in California, followed by Las Vegas, Reno, Nevada, Phoenix Area in Arizona and Cape Coral Area in Florida." Faith Bautista, the president of Mabuhay Alliance, along with agents representing lending agencies, was asked a number of questions regarding possible alternatives viewers might have in the midst of losing their homes to foreclosure.

Developing support, beginning with a number of "foreclosure clinics" in various cities throughout the United States, the Mabuhay Alliance had successfully advocated for residents living in the city of Vallejo, a city that boasted the tenth-highest foreclosure rate in the country at the time. By organizing town hall meetings and circulating petitions, the organization helped convince the city's administration to place a moratorium on foreclosures (Ehrenreich 2009). The Mabuhay Alliance was capable of garnering much political attention to the plight of minorities, particularly Filipinos, experiencing home foreclosures, so that in early 2009, together with the National Federation of Filipino American Associations, members of the Mabuhay Alliance met with the leading financial advisors of the Obama administration, including Federal Reserve Chairman Ben Bernanke, Federal Deposit Insurance Chairwoman Sheila Bair, Secretary of the Treasury Timothy Geithner, and House Financial Services Committee Chairman Barney Frank (*Asian Journal* 2009). Both organizations met with administration members to suggest solutions to the foreclosure crisis through their collective experiences as advocates for homeowners and as real estate professionals.

Utilization of short sales was another reason Edna was capable of surviving as a realtor. In a short sale, the bank or mortgage lender agrees to discount a loan balance owing to economic or financial hardships experienced by the borrower. During the short-sale process, the homeowner sells the mortgaged property for less than the outstanding balance of the loan, and the proceeds of the sale go to the lender. In the climate surrounding the U.S. real estate crisis, short sales became one of the most economically prudent solutions. Banks opt to incur a limited financial loss rather than suffer greater losses from foreclosures or nonpayment of mortgages.[5]

Other Filipino realtors have adopted more creative strategies to supplement their sales or transform their marketing strategy entirely. Like Eleanor Acupang, who hosted the party in Daly City, other Filipino realtors in the United States have taken more transnational approaches to the selling of real estate. Road shows have become a common facet of the transnational real estate industry. Each Philippine real estate corporation targeting Filipinos in the United States devotes a significant amount of its budget to advertising. One advertising practice is to send real estate representatives to the United States to present models of preselling developments around the Philippines, particularly in the provinces around Metro Manila. Filipino realtors in the United States are valuable barometers measuring interest within their communities, and if a realty organization determines that there is a critical mass of interest, it will send one or two representatives to meet with a local realtor. Depending on the amount of down payments received after the presentation, the realtor will receive a commission on the sales.

As I sat listening to the representative of Brittany begin her presentation at a home in Union City, just east of Daly City on the other side of the bay, I was immediately struck by the cover on the brochure. It depicted a man resting contentedly with his son draped over his chest, both sleeping together on a hammock. As I was staring at the picture of the father and son sleeping peacefully in an open grassy field, the lights dimmed, and immediately similar images of people enjoying or resting in grassy fields began to fade in and out of the PowerPoint presentation. Leisure is a common theme in Philippine real estate ads. Accustomed to hearing about the demanding pace of life in the United States, the realtor from Brittany continually evoked intimate and romantic images of family members finally able to spend time together. Pictures of tire swings and three-story wooden mansions created an environment reminiscent of the places for which the development, the Georgia Club in Santa Rosa, was named. The presentation emphasized the central location of the soon-to-be-built development: "Georgia Club is a central development in the fast-emerging industrial hub of the South. It is close to premier recreational destinations—from the top golf course to the cool mountain retreats of Tagaytay and the inviting beaches of Batangas. The country's foremost academic institutions are also close by, including the forty-five-hectare campus of the University of Sainto Tomas. Right nearby, Paseo de Santa Rosa, the commercial center, brings together restaurants, bars, shops, and other lifestyle establishments."

Emma Araneta, the realtor giving the presentation to an audience of thirty-two Filipinos and a handful of non-Filipinos, repeated the descriptions of the development as if having memorized the brochure in my hands. Later, Emma told me that she comes to the United States at least once a year but always to the same place because she has family members who live just northeast of San Francisco in Vallejo. "I come here each year, but the company doesn't pay for all of my expenses. They pay for my plane ticket, but if I didn't have family here, I wouldn't be able to come. The trip has too much expenses, *diba*?" Each year, Emma's goal is to sell at least ten lots during her road shows. "I rely on my family members a lot to keep in touch with interested buyers," Emma expressed with genuine gratefulness. "They actually do a lot of the convincing for me because it's too hard to convince someone to just give me all of their savings when I'm living in the Philippines [and not in the United States]." The quasi-professional relationship that Emma has with her family members is indicative of an increasingly creative network of Filipino realtors who continually collaborate among each other between the United States and the Philippines.

This growing network of realtors and real estate corporations is devoted to connecting buyers in the United States with property investments in the Philippines. Along with developers who operate with as many as twenty international sales offices focused on selling to OFWs, Philippine corporations are increasing their presence in the United States and developing elaborate strategies to grab hold of the transnational realty market in the United States. Edward L. Tan (2005) lists the common activities of transnational realty networks:

> Having sales and marketing offices abroad with regular activities there, having their own regular road show presentations in selected countries, coordinating and having connections with Filipino realty organizations abroad, advertising in the main broadsheets both in the physical newspaper and the Internet, placing ads in specialized OFW newspapers and/or Filipino newspapers abroad, quoting dollar amounts to sell their projects in their webpage, placing ads in various OFW webpages, having their own call centers, exhibits at the duty free shops and joining regular international real estate fairs organized by the Chamber of Real Estate and Builders' Associations, Inc. (CREBA). (49)

Joining realty associations like CREBA provides real estate corporations with the opportunity to participate in annual road shows in cities like Tokyo, London, and Los Angeles, particularly for larger corporations. Such associations provide a speculative edge to larger corporations since their

membership fees are too often beyond the budgets of smaller developers. Larger corporations are capable of writing off the risk of losing prospects or being unable to gain financial commitments from buyers. Smaller developers, eager to find a position within the transnational real estate market, are limited to joining local real estate exhibits or placing ads in Filipino American newspapers. While local shows in the Philippines cost ₱35,000– ₱50,000 (US$760–$1,090), participating in road shows abroad can cost each realtor more than twice that amount. According to CREBA, membership fees for the West Coast, USA, road show from September 16 to

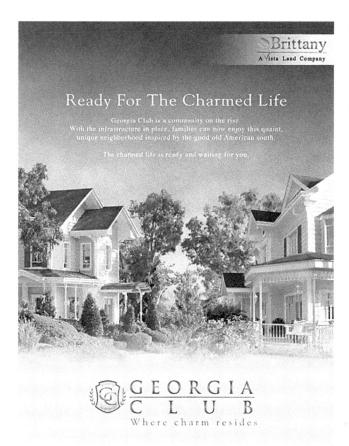

FIGURE 3.2
Advertisement flyer for the Georgia Club gated community, a Brittany property located in Santa Rosa, Laguna, 2009.

October 1, 2006, cost each member about ₱92,000 (US$2,000) for food, taxes, booth fees, posters, and flyers (Tan 2005). As Emma already noted, this price did not include the plane fare or visa fees for travel to the United States.

Bird Dogs and Transnational Realty Network

Unlike some Filipino families who lost their homes early on during the real estate crisis, the Cardenas, through a mixture of foresight and fortune, placed their two-story bungalow in Daly City up for a short sale rather than risking greater financial losses by eventually having their home foreclosed on. Upon making my way to the entrance and stepping into their foyer, I noticed that apart from a few boxes stashed to the side of the living

FIGURE 3.3
Advertisement flyer
for Laguna BelAir,
located in Santa
Rosa, Laguna, 2009.

room and the dull white sheets draped over much of the furniture, the majority of the Cardenas's packing had been left for the last days before they would move out. One box in particular, partially filled with their children's elementary-school yearbooks and old beat-up textbooks, created an image of a family who was not yet completely ready to leave a life they had struggled so hard to build.

Rosemarie Cardenas unwrapped the foil from a plate and placed fried *tapsilog* and eggs in front of me. The smell of the freshly cooked rice wafted into my nose, and as the yolk of the eggs dripped along one side of the scorched edges of the beef cutlets, Rosemarie burst out, "*Sige, sige,* go ahead," insisting that I eat before I commenced the interview. Her and her husband Roberto's jovial affect and warm generosity concealed the slight shame they felt at losing their home and their pain in deciding to sell their home and return to the Philippines, as they had originally planned over two decades ago. "Robert was the one who really wanted to return. He had always wanted to open a business back home. But I wasn't convinced, really," Rosemarie admitted, looking affectionately at her husband.

A number of health complications had taken a toll on the couple, both physically and financially. With both of their children about to finish college and Rosemarie having lost her job as an office administrator at the University of California San Francisco Medical Center more than two years ago, Roberto began looking into the real estate market in the Philippines. In a serendipitous encounter, Roberto found himself in a conversation with an old friend during one of the many family parties that the couple hosted. Jeffrey Abella was a childhood friend who grew up with Roberto in Antipolo, one of the various cities composing the province of Rizal, bordering on Metro Manila. Jeffrey had moved with his family to the East Bay of California and had been working as a realtor in Union City since the 1990s. Realty came fairly easily to Jeffrey since several of his family members had worked in the real estate industry in the Philippines. In the early part of his career as a real estate agent, Jeffrey would occasionally refer Filipino American clients to family members who could broker property deals around Manila.

"This is the key to buying property in the Philippines. You have to know your agent very well. It helps if they are a family member or a friend," Roberto said sternly. It was one of the few comments he made in such a serious tone. His comment made enormous sense in the context of the real estate profession in the Philippines, particularly in Metro Manila, where real estate agencies are still capable of operating without a license and where their armies of realtors can easily be found passing out flyers in *any* bustling area in the city, including street corners, MTA escalators, and of course the malls. And while licensed Philippine real estate agents and brokers have lobbied hard to enforce the licensure of the profession and are the first to inform potential buyers about the importance of working with a licensed agent, ill-informed and easily convinced Filipinos who are eager to make investments in Philippine properties continue to fall prey to false advertisers over the Internet or elsewhere.

FIGURE 3.4 Mall kiosk for Manhattan Garden City development, 2009. Photo by author.

Jeffrey had proposed that Roberto look into purchasing a home and lot from a member of his family who sold properties in Rizal. "Buying the property was simple. Making sure the house was built to spec was another thing entirely," Roberto continued.[6] "Not only were Jeff's family responsible for the sale, but they were responsible for looking over the construction of the home. It was harder to do that [supervise Jeff's family in the Philippines] than to take care of selling our home here. Can you imagine that? With the way that the market is here? We were lucky to get rid of our home even if it was at such a low price, but it was nothing compared to dealing with the problems of building our home over there. Poor Jeff was in the middle of all of that." Indeed, not only did Jeffrey help to sell property in Rizal to the Cardenas, but he oversaw the short sale of their home in Daly City. Roberto explained:

> He was good. I did not want to approach him with our problems at the party so I arranged to meet with him at his house later in the week. He had no idea that I wanted to talk business with him, but he was really happy to help us. Not just for the money, you know; he knew a lot of Filipinos were going through this and didn't know how to handle this problem. He was the one who arranged the short sale of our home here. He did such a good job that I trusted him to help us find a good property in the Philippines as well.

The versatile real estate dealing conducted by Jeffrey points to the interwoven web of transnational labor produced in the global real estate industry. Having prospective clients desiring to purchase property in the Philippines, Jeffrey occasionally provided leads to his family members in the Philippines and connected them with his clients in the United States. Although Jeffrey would never call himself such, he is *essentially* what Pascual (2003) refers to as a real estate "bird dog." Like the majority of Filipino realtors operating throughout California, Pascual originally worked under a large firm, Century 21, and sold properties throughout the greater Los Angeles area during the 1980s and 1990s. It was the manner in which Pascual aggressively targeted properties in adjoining areas that set him apart from other Filipinos. Integral to this strategy was his recruitment and implementation of "bird dogs," whom he encouraged to work with other agents and expand their sales beyond their particular office listings.

"From 1988 to 1994," Pascual says, "I recruited, trained and managed a robust sales group that was predominantly Filipino Americans. Most of them are now a part of our growing network that dedicate their efforts in promoting and selling Philippine properties to Filipino Americans in the U.S." (2003, 24). Like those hunting dogs who fetch pheasants after they have been plucked from the sky, realty bird dogs scour for real estate deals and earmark them for investors for an agreed fee. Pascual's method of employing a widely spread network of realtors is not unique within the rest of the real estate industry but is, in fact, a common component to creative property sales made increasingly necessary by the current dire state of the industry.

Recognizing a potential market niche in the early 1990s, Pascual devoted his work to selling Philippine property to Filipino Americans while working as a certified public accountant to supplement his income. He and his staff became adept in the most minute rules and procedures regarding escrow laws in the Philippines, knowing full well that any hint of incompetence or malfeasance would drive potential clients, who are already hesitant, away completely.

> Birddogs in the Philippines focused their efforts by prospecting for Filipino American buyers. . . . A big chunk of Filipino American prospects prefer to buy beach lots and farm properties located in their home provinces. This is because they are so knowledgeable of what is happening almost daily in their home provinces. If a new McDonald outfit is opened there, the news is passed along to him in a matter of just days. Strangely, they are not versed with the massive development that is transpiring in the metropolitan districts like Metro Manila, unlike the minutest happening in his home province. [It is] because birddogs are aware of this, they know what to offer, what type of financing deal is ideal and when will the visit to the Philippines be done. Thus, these birddogs apparently will then notify their counterpart Philippine birddog to complete the rest of the sales process. (2003, 58–59)

Transnational realtors like Pascual and Jeffrey have become key figures within the transnational real estate industry, soliciting and selling properties for a wide range of realty corporations, independent property holders, and individual homeowners. Their ability to physically meet and speak with clients throughout the entire transaction provides an important safeguard against the potential scams that might occur via the plethora of other realtors who solicit international sales primarily through the Internet.

"Balikbayans can realize 100 percent profit in one year," claims Reynaldo Duterte, a real estate agent with RP Duterte Realty in Manila. Duterte adamantly believes that real estate throughout the Philippines will experience at least a 20–30 percent annual growth rate over the next five years. "Filipino Americans should look here to invest and retire" (Duterte quoted in Kreifels 2009). Given the projections of growth in Philippine real estate and the opportunity for a new bubble of transnational real estate investments to emerge, particularly in the residential sector, networks of transnationally operating realtors have begun aggressively targeting Filipinos in the United States. Through the practice of bird-dogging and road shows, Filipino realtors have adopted creative strategies to convince Filipinos in the United

States to invest in Philippine property. These strategies have become ever present in the transnational advertising of Philippine real estate.

"Own a Piece of the Philippines While Taking America with You":
Transnational Advertising

"A new city is about to breathe life into Metro Manila's south: Eton City," announces an elegantly designed brochure produced by Eton Properties. The master plan of Eton City is an exemplar of the most recent type of mega-township projects that are being built throughout the periphery of Metro Manila. Being constructed in mostly rural and industrial zones like Cavite, Santa Rosa, and Tagaytay, these townships are slightly different from the commercial or suburban districts that have been modeled after Makati's CBD or the extremely affluent Forbes Park. Unlike the continuously growing Global City in Fort Bonifacio, the township of Eton City will include every amenity typically provided within a tourism district, like golf courses and nature preserves, along with the malls, business districts, and schools that one would find attached to any of the residential developments sprouting up in Metro Manila. What also makes Eton City different is that it almost entirely caters to Filipino retirees, particularly those coming from the United States.

"Inspired by famous lakeside communities overseas such as . . . Lake Las Vegas in Nevada and Foster City in California, to name a few, South Lake Village at Eton City has made cosmopolitan island living in the Philippines a reality," boasts one page in the brochure. The West Wing Residences, immediately signaling the title of the popular television show *The West Wing* from the 1990s, is one of the suburban developments being built within Eton City and was specifically modeled after various neighborhoods in California. Raquel de Guzman, an international real estate agent with Eton, explained, "We designed this after the western United States. It's basically designed to be a typical western house. In fact, our model houses were all named after U.S. presidents. The house models are called Jefferson, Eisenhower, McKinley . . . Those are the different kinds of house models. We designed these residences to make Filipino Americans feel like they will be owning a piece of the Philippines while taking America with them." More accurately, Eton City is being modeled after the contemporary, massive, enclave-style residences currently being built in Brazil, India, Korea, China, and other countries throughout the Global South.[7] These large-scale developments, while inspired by the architecture and city planning of traditional "American" or "Western" designs and tastes, are focused on merging these tastes with the specific familiarities that make these countries and cities feel like "home" to repatriating emigrants. The West Wing Residences is one element within what Eton is calling the first "island-lot" development in the Philippines.

The master plan is actually inspired by the artificial Palm Islands in Dubai. In contrast to the 200-square-mile beaches constructed alongside the Palm Islands, Eton City will include an artificially built 135-square-mile lake. Island villas will be named after island countries in the Pacific Ocean, like Maui, Guam, Fiji, and Bali, or other centers of tourism, like Ibiza, Bermuda, the Maldives, and Macau. The model of Eton City, however, still stands on the shoulders of the Philippines' first commercial metropole, Makati's CBD. At the top of the first page of the brochure are three pictures depicting "Makati before," "Makati now," and "Eton City" now, while one can only image what the *future* "Eton City now" is supposed to look like.

It is the work of transnational realtors to project the future of Filipinos and perform the appearance of safety, security, and happiness. Eton City is both the material and metaphorical construction of these aspirations, which expand on earlier imaginings of class status and wealth made physically visible by the construction of previous suburban subdivisions. These ideals are clearly felt in walking past elite communities like Forbes Park adjacent to Makati. John Connell (1999) discusses this earlier model of gated communities that quickly emerged throughout Metro Manila during the 1980s and 1990s. Connell discusses how these "fortress enclaves," which reflected urbanization trends in a number of places throughout the Global South like São Paulo, Brazil, were the physical manifestation of social divisions created by anxiety and paranoia related to insecurity and crime.[8] In his study of real estate advertising in Manila, Connell argues that each advertisement evoked five common themes: value, security, exclusivity, escape, and community. Megadevelopments like Eton City are a hyperrealization of these ideals; in the next chapter, I will discuss how contemporary transformations in Metro Manila are marked by a process of bypassing various social infrastructures entirely, thus dividing the world of the elite into nodes of cosmopolitanism while the lower classes are continually neglected and forgotten.

Tucked away in the Eton City brochure, one can find a list of "Frequently Asked Questions" posed to Eton employees by balikbayans considering whether to purchase property in the South Lake Village, the subdivision

TABLE 3.2 "Frequently Asked Questions" in Brochure for Eton City Real Estate Development

1. Will the water be breeding ground for mosquitoes?	9. How will you ensure aeration of the lake?
2. Will the development be prone to flooding, especially during typhoons?	10. Where will the water in the lake come from?
3. How will the possibility of an overflow be addressed?	11. How will the water discharge system for the lake work?
4. Won't the river water be a source of pollution?	12. Where will the village water supply come from?
5. How will the accumulation of too much algae be prevented?	13. How will the noise and pollution from the South Luzon Expressway be addressed?
6. How will you ensure that the water in the lake will be flowing?	14. Will lot owners be allowed to have swimming pools in their backyard?
7. Will there be a garbage disposal policy?	15. How will the water be treated? Will the water in the rivers be treated also?
8. Will erosion of the island and lakeside lots occur?	16. What will be found in the center island?

closest to the South Luzon Expressway and adjacent to the southern part of the lake. On the list are concerns common to most Filipinos who have lived in Metro Manila regarding flooding, the water supply, and even noise pollution from the freeway.

There are also questions that are more particular to the concerns of balikbayans who have grown accustomed to their homes in nontropical environments. While concerns around mosquitoes, garbage disposal, aeration, and swimming pools appear obvious to some, they speak to a number of obstacles that transnational realtors confront when attempting to convince Filipinos in the United States to return to the Philippines.

The logic informing these concerns will be discussed more thoroughly in the following chapter; however, it is important to point out that the ever-present ambivalence surrounding immigrant return is always perpetuated by a lingering desire to keep one foot firmly planted in each world at the same time. When one physically places oneself in the Philippines, whether in the rural setting of the provinces surrounding Manila or deep within its urban core, the intense polarity between one's life in the United States and

FIGURE 3.5 Community swimming pool in Eton City, 2012. Photo by author.

that of the Philippines is nothing short of staggering. The expectation of being able to escape mosquitoes, refuse, the enveloping humidity, smells, and noises, elements that are inextricable from everyday life in the Philippines, speaks to the transformation of the immigrant's own subjectivity while living abroad. Transnational realtors who attempt to sell property in the Philippines do so by conveying a built environment, an entire world in fact, that, while literally placing Filipinos back in the Philippines, is entirely separate from it at the same time. Architecture and design exuding American sensibilities become intrinsic to this paradoxical process and signal in many ways the impossibilities of modernity itself.

In the brochure for the Georgia Club, for instance, the description overtly communicates the desire of Philippine corporations to specifically attract Filipinos living in the United States: "It's time to call this charming community your home. A 30-hectare community designed to reflect the gracious, classic architecture of the American south. With its naturally lush landscape of sprawling trees, its intertwined parkways and pedestrian pathways that link that neighborhood, Georgia Club evokes an idyllic, suburban lifestyle." "Charming," "American south," "sprawling trees," "idyllic," and "suburban lifestyle" evoke ideas and sentiments that are almost antithetical to the visual landscape of Metro Manila. The invocation of this unthinkable world, the Georgian countryside in Manila, allows Filipinos to begin imagining a Philippines completely unlike the one they left behind decades ago. The captions describing the "Mansions of Georgia Club" are just as provocative. "With wrought iron fences, colorful shutters on French windows, brightly colored doors, inviting front porches, and open floor plans, The Mansion of Georgia Club is a perfect combination of architecture set amidst nature's beauty." Invoking a television-like image of the American South, suspending the reader in time with "wrought iron fences" and "inviting front porches," the real estate advertisement creates a world that is nothing like the Philippine environment surrounding it.

The brightly colored designs depicted in the brochure advertising Augusta Santa Rosa and the Georgia Club are part and parcel of Brittany's new marketing campaign to sell property to Filipinos in the United States. Brittany is the real estate development arm of Vista Land and Lifescapes Inc., a multinational corporation that touts itself as the leading seller of upscale and luxury properties in the Philippines. Currently, the Georgia Club, located in Santa Rosa, Laguna, is just one of four large-scale property developments currently being built in provinces around Metro Manila. All of these are being actively marketed to various international communities, particularly Filipinos in the United States.

Along with inundating the Internet with advertisements, transnational realtors focus much of their advertising on an array of Filipino American newspapers. Take one newspaper article advertising another of Brittany's real estate developments, printed in the popular Filipino American newspaper the *Philippine News* (September 18, 2007). Brittany Bay, a multipurpose condominium development, claims to afford its residents "San Francisco Living in Metro Manila" (figure 3.6). The author advertising the yet-unbuilt residential complex claims that, along with facilities for busi-

Brittany Bay:
San Francisco Living in Metro Manila

BY LORENZO G. ABELLERA

PASSING through the busy stretch of the South Su-per Highway in Paranaque City, a vibrantly colored structure -- now gaining recognition as the commer-cial center with quaint shops and dining establishments called The Wharf -- never fails to rouse the curiosity of the public. It's neo-Victorian architecture, marked by bright hues as well as fine details such as arches and pre-cast curves on windows, steers interest of mere passers by, more so of those who are acquainted with such style.
  But upon learning that The Wharf is only a fraction of a bigger development, one will definitely be amused

FIGURE 3.6 Advertisement for Brittany Bay real estate development in Metro Ma-nila, printed in *Philippine News*, 2007.

nesses, Brittany Bay provides its residents with "retail, clubhouses, serviced apartments and the like, creating a live-play lifestyle." While the Georgia Club caters to the idyllic rural sensibilities of Filipinos desiring to resettle in the provinces, the Brittany Bay advertisement replicates common urban themes, which draw on images of San Francisco, a major immigration hub for Filipinos, in order to convince Filipinos that they will not have to leave the United States at all.

The real estate conglomerate Philtown uses similar imagery to promote its developments. In a single-page layout (figure 3.7) in the *Philippine News* (November 23, 2007), Philtown advertises its condominiums against the backdrop of the White House, Mount Rushmore, the Hollywood sign, and other paradigmatic icons of American architecture and landscape. This ad-vertisement avoids any subterfuge that might conceal its motive. Accord-ing to the ad, "each project of Philtown *transcends* mere address into new realms of architecture" (my emphasis). Advertisers are openly marketing the trend of contemporary urban transformation in Metro Manila and the attempt that developers are making to create nodes of urbanism that give upscale property owners the *choice* to bypass Metro Manila almost entirely.

FIGURE 3.7
Philtown Proper-
ties advertisement,
printed in *Philippine
News*, 2007.

Finally, another advertisement in the *Philippine News* sells the Lake-
shore developments by claiming that "today, ordinary folks can now take
pleasure in extraordinary perks in a very family-friendly environment
that espouses natural beauty, open space, and life-enhancing amenities."
Through the language of leisure and ordinary space that the advertisement
utilizes, it once again reconstructs the familiarity of American suburban
lifestyles, a learned sensibility, which is completely opposed to the distinctly
stratified world of the Philippines. "Ordinary folks," "extraordinary perks,"
"family-friendly," "natural beauty," and "open space" together directly signal
the transcendence of class difference reflected in the ideals of American
suburbia.

Like many other Asian metropoles, Manila is reconstituting itself
through global migration and trade. Americanization, embodied by the

imagining of transnational Filipinos who are embedded within these types of suburban neighborhoods, has indelibly influenced the architecture and built environment of Metro Manila and other urban hubs within the Global South (Leichenko and Solecki 2005). These ideals of social division through suburbanization certainly mirror the history of suburbanization and suburban sprawl in the United States and the evolution of the "American dream."[9]

What becomes apparent, however, when viewing the layouts of the contemporary wave of condominiums and houses being built in Metro Manila is that there is a particular convergence between desires for "American" and "Filipino" tastes. Together, the cultural meanings exuded by these designs create an idea of the "global" by signaling tastes and ideals that cannot be understood as either purely "Filipino" or purely "American." This formation of a paradoxical hybridity has emerged as the trademark of transnational urbanism and the material traces of postcolonial geographies in the making.[10] As Philippine real estate corporations hire American architects and urban planners to ensure that the contemporary built environment will reflect an "American style," or as a host of Filipinos return and infuse a sense of self and taste brought with them from their life abroad, these ideals are easily subsumed within a culture and environment that is by now accustomed to transformation and hybridity. What becomes vividly etched into the landscape, however, are not the "American" ideals intended by designers, corporate executives, or even the buyers. What continues to remain and emanate from the built environment is the hybridity so characteristic of the Philippines and the metropolitan core of Manila.

One way to examine this particular hybridity is through the domestic space created for maids in each of these developments. Like homes throughout Latin America, contemporary homes built in the Philippines are almost always equipped with a room and even a separate bathroom for a domestic servant. It is almost unthinkable within a U.S. context to allocate a room and bathroom in a suburban household for a domestic servant—not only because it is unaffordable to house a domestic servant within a suburban household but also because it defies the classless ideal espoused by suburban lifestyles. In all of the floor plans for the Phoenix Grenada developments, each household is equipped with space for a domestic servant, regardless of the model. In the Philippines, employing domestic help has been a requisite mark of class separation and visible wealth for centuries, dating back to Spanish colonization. What might appear unthinkable in a sector of American society has become indispensable in Philippine society.

The hybridity of contemporary Philippine urban designs is reflective of the complicated ambivalence among repatriating Filipinos, who desire to return to the comforts of their formative years and the memories of adolescence and yet simultaneously remain in the United States.

Impossible Returns

I waited patiently with Ernesto Calderon at Los Angeles International Airport as he eagerly waited to board his flight for the Philippines. As he carefully folded the yellow McDonald's Quarter Pounder wrapper into an unrecognizable origami shape, I could see the anxiety written on his face transferring itself to his fingers, which nervously searched for something to occupy them. Ernesto is a retired postal service inspector who worked at the South San Francisco branch for almost thirty-two years. Recently separated from his wife, Ernesto decided that it was the right time for him to return to the Philippines. While I was visiting my mother in Southern California, Ernesto told me that he had found a deal on a ticket to Manila but had to fly out of Los Angeles rather than San Francisco. Knowing that I was in Southern California, he told me that he would just meet me at the airport to discuss his trip to the Philippines and his plan to look for a retirement home for himself and his younger brother's family.

"I don't know whether it will be close to Manila or in Dumaguete." Dumaguete City, on the southern coast of the Island of Negros Oriental, has become a thriving hub. Ernesto had grown up there and graduated from Silliman University years before the city became an attraction for tourists, non-Filipino and Filipino alike. More than a decade ago, he loaned his younger brother $5,000 to open a business there. For several years the fish stand his brother ran had done well, but more recently competition from larger businesses had slowed the profits. Rather than running a fish stand, Ernesto was fairly confident that he and his brother could open a restaurant with the money that Ernesto had saved.

However, Ernesto also had friends, returning Filipinos like himself whom he had known in San Francisco, who had opened a pizza parlor in Tagaytay. The lakeside city is just about thirty-five miles away from Manila and had been for many years a vibrant tourist destination for Manileños; according to Ernesto's friends, the city was slowly accumulating more business as developments were continuing to be built in the area. He didn't seem to mind that Tagatay sits adjacent to Taal Lake, where the still-active

Taal volcano is situated. For Ernesto, the value of moving to either place depended more on the business opportunities each offered rather than the climate or conveniences. His trip to the Philippines was more of an exploratory visit, but Ernesto agreed that he would certainly buy a new home if he found the right situation.

Filipinos choose to return to the Philippines for a host of reasons. According to Ernesto, his reasons for returning were principally a matter of finances and security. "I've become unaccustomed to the weather. People say that I can move to Baguio [where the climate is cooler], but who do I know there? I want to go where I can put my savings to use and hopefully make enough money where I can hire somebody to do the day-to-day tasks after a few years. I'm already old, you know," he says while laughing loudly. Ernesto is actually sixty-seven, having arrived in California when he was twenty-three. He worked as an auto mechanic for a garage in Excelsior before finding stable employment at the post office. Listening to Ernesto discuss his plans for when he arrived in the Philippines, I got the sense that he had been planning this next stage in his life for a long time. His desire to become financially secure in the Philippines was more of a desire to fulfill certain aspirations that he could not achieve in the United States. "I always wanted to own a business. It gets old to go to your same job and have the same boss for years. But then I married Nancy, and we had kids," Ernesto explained.

For most of the Filipinos I interviewed, their desire to return was primarily an issue of security. Having seen many of their friends struggle with paying medical bills after being diagnosed with severe health disorders, most Filipinos did not feel that their government benefits would be enough to cover any unforeseeable trauma. It's a common sentiment that although one has to pay for health care out of pocket in the Philippines, most health care services cost considerably less than they do in the United States. And considering that most of their physicians and nurses have been Filipino and received their education in the Philippines, it makes sense that Filipinos are quite confident about receiving proper health care back home.

Then there is the idea of household help. As already mentioned, most households in the Philippines have at least one household helper. Returning Filipinos are eager to relinquish their household duties to domestic help. For instance, Alex Caday, a retired real estate agent who had lived in Hawai'i for twenty years, collects about $1,500 a month in Social Security and in retirement benefits. According to him, it did not cover his expenditures in Hawai'i, but in the Philippines, where he retired in 1989, he can afford two maids to help him and his wife, who also receives Social Security and retirement benefits. "I'm more secure here financially and socially," said Caday (quoted in Kreifels 2009), who had retired in Ilocos Norte, his home province. "My roots are here. My old friends are here. I have property."

Based on a survey that Pascual (2003) and his colleagues conducted on interested Filipino American buyers in 1997 and 2002, he provided the following sample responses regarding why his clientele actively pursued buying property in the Philippines and have chosen to return (13–14):

1. "Because of the tremendous infrastructure and building boom near the economic districts of Metro Manila, buying near these locations is a win-win proposition."

2. "Availability of dollar financing."

3. "Belief that the Philippine resurgent economy is moving steadily towards progress and stability."

4. "The stable and working democracy in the Philippines. Unlike in most parts of Asia where the stability of governments is continually threatened, coup d'états, while often staged in the Philippines, are considered healthy expressions of democracy."

5. "Wants to put up a business in the Philippines and therefore needs a residence and an office."

6. "Will stay on the property as a retiree while doing business on the side."

7. "Wants an extra source of income on the side."

8. "Wants children and grandchildren to establish roots."

9. "The apparent trend now is for Filipino Americans to send their college bound kids to the Philippines for studies. Tuitions are not only low, but the quality of education is excellent."

10. "Market value increases faster in Philippine investment property vis-à-vis in the U.S."

11. "Good resale value seems present since prospective taker-buyers are plenty, including foreigners."

12. "Wants to take advantage of the best terms extended by developers such as favorable off-plan (pre-sell) prices and non-qualifying finance terms."

13. "Wants to buy properties with markdown prices because of over-supply of residential properties."

14. "Loves the Philippines and its people. Invest in the Philippines first rather than in other countries."

15. "They can leave the care and maintenance of their properties to *katiwalas* [relatives you can trust]. Many abhor these arrangements though, as they become counter-productive for both parties."

16. "As a second residence, they can enjoy tremendous tax breaks in their US 1040 taxes. As a rental income property, it may bring extra income while deductions are allowed in their US 1040 taxes."

17. "Retiree's pension and Social Security dollars can be sent freely in the Philippines. Similar to several other countries without the objection of the U.S. government. Likewise, medical coverage for Filipino Americans can easily be made to extend to cover their medical needs while in the Philippines. Blue Shield does this now, but hopefully others will follow soon."

18. "Many have found out that even big private corporations and giant pension funds like the CalPERS [California Public Employees' Retirement System] funds that has billions of dollars in portfolios have strongly considered several investments in the Philippines."

19. "Becoming a dual-citizen has advantages."

20. "As a retiree, in the Philippines would spend less money and time traveling."

All of these reasons convey the sense of optimism that has energized the transformation of Metro Manila's landscape. After decades of remitting money and material goods back to the Philippines and raising the standard of living of many of their family members, Filipinos have elevated their expectations of what their home country might offer back to them. Like the paradoxical real estate advertisements promising America in the Philippines, repatriating Filipinos have come to expect the impossible. Their idealism—a consciousness forged through centuries of hybridity and transformation and signaled by the notions of political stability and economic affordability expressed above—tends to overcome the contradictions and uncertainties enveloping their return.

Networks of transnational realtors navigate around these ambivalences and enable Filipino Americans' expectations by generating a host of real estate advertisements promising Filipinos that they will never have to leave the United States while they are in the Philippines. As such, the contradictions of hybridity become perpetuated and built into the disjointed landscape of the Philippines. This process is particularly dramatic in Metro Manila, where contemporary real estate developments create self-contained nodes of urban life that bypass the rest of the city. Metro Manila has become a trope for globalization: such global megacities are "connected externally to global networks and to segments of their own countries, while internally disconnecting local populations that are either functionally unnecessary or socially disruptive" (Castells 1996, 404).

However, this dynamic energy reconstituting Manila has not been propelled by the balikbayan economy alone. Economic policies aimed at opening and deregulating markets in the Philippines have created a new surge in and a diversification of exported labor. Beginning with the administration of Fidel Ramos (1992–1998), motivated by trends in the global market and the success of its Asian counterparts, the Philippines aggressively adopted a policy of liberal economic reform. With an inspired confidence made necessary partly by the departure of the U.S. bases, Ramos's administration resurrected the Bangko Sentral ng Pilipinas in 1993 and opened the telecommunications industry to foreign and domestic competition. And unlike in previous administrations, which allowed the country's economy to be driven largely on debt and foreign aid, Ramos's economic policies were principled on foreign and domestic investments (de Dios and Hutchcroft 2003).

These reforms paved the way for two congruent inflows of financial capital to reinvigorate the country's economy and transform the real estate market over the last decade. First, the Philippines has become a global leader in business process outsourcing with over 780 operational call centers, which provide salaries that are considerably higher than the average incomes of most Filipinos. Second, perennial waves of returning OFWs have brought in increased income and have been particularly eager to invest in residential property throughout the Philippines. This dual flow of capital created by exported labor, combined with investments made by returning Filipinos like Ernesto, has enabled a newfound momentum within the real estate market throughout Metro Manila and its surroundings.

PART II. RETURNS

4. The Balikbayan Hotel » Touristic Performance in Manila and the Anxiety of Return

Tourism, if it is nothing else, is the kind of travel, the kind of geocultural movement, that specifically leaves the place of the traveler's home behind. . . . The minute tourists begin to believe they have "come home," their identity as tourists falls into question, or, as with the Balikbayan, becomes plausibly deniable. —Shelly Ann Ness, *Where Asia Smiles*

The Balikbayan Hotel

The advertisements for the Mabuhay Manor hotel, played repeatedly on TFC (the Filipino Channel), avoid mentioning the hotel's immediate surroundings. Upon entering Manila's disjointed landscape of highways, searching for the hotel's location, one quickly realizes that the Mabuhay Manor is nestled discreetly among Pasay City's inconspicuous street paths. Unlike more prominent tourist hotels, it is impossible to identify the Manor from Epifanio de los Santos Avenue (often referred to as EDSA) or Taft Avenue, the two major thoroughfares located on opposite sides of the hotel. Instead, the relatively small 150-room lodge is situated along a dingy alleyway, hidden among a row of concrete-walled apartments and bustling markets spilling out in front of the hotel's orange-granite driveway. Regardless, the hotel has become somewhat of a popular destination for tourists traveling from the United States, not because of its accommodations but rather because of its target clientele: balikbayans, Filipinos returning to the Philippines.

This chapter examines the ways in which balikbayans, through their participation in the country's tourism economy, have come to play a central role in the development of the Philippines, their negotiation around this new role, and the ambivalence produced by it. Particular spaces like the Mabuhay Manor represent, in a clear way, the unique and complex approaches that the state utilizes to exploit these ambivalences, which are experienced in different ways, and the complex subjectivity that continuously sews these anxieties together with an imagination of a once safer home.

Apart from the vibrant pastel colors that seem to accentuate the contours of the hotel's diminutive shape, few elements distinguish the Mabuhay Manor's three-story structure as a place where Filipino American tourists would prefer to stay. The hotel's outward style, with its flat, adobe-like façade and green-tinted windows, reflects an American suburban aesthetic, in contrast to the modern skyscraper hotels that tend to be associated with world travel. Furthermore, at one end of the narrow road where the hotel is located is the cluttered parking lot of the Pagcor Casino Club. Local residents rather than tourists tend to visit the club to try their hands at some baccarat or partake in a small game of poker. Toward the other end is one of the many Victoria Court motels scattered throughout Manila, a well-frequented hub within the city's sex-industry circuit. The narrative of globalized accommodation and luxury becomes askew. It becomes readily apparent that the Mabuhay Manor, whose advertisements tout it as the "first balikbayan hotel in the Philippines," is far from being "world-class for the world market," as the establishment is depicted on TFC. Something else is obviously more attractive to the sensibilities of balikbayans.

The challenges posed by navigating through the hotel's surrounding geography are a jarring metaphor for how the routes of global tourism in the Philippines are continually hindered by sectors in the economy that are less mobile. The fractured and disjointed nature of Metro Manila continues to present a formidable challenge for a tourism industry scrabbling to draw foreign capital into the Philippines, particularly to the National Capital Region. As the Asian market evolves and expands at a quickening pace, the Philippine government looks to tourism as a fundamental strategy to ensure that the country's economy keeps up with its regional neighbors. State administrators have charged the Department of Tourism

(DOT) with the immense task of synchronizing a complex and disjointed network of tourist agencies, hotels and motels, vacation resorts, and food retailers to help develop the struggling economy of the Philippines. To do this, the Philippine tourism industry has targeted one of its most unique assets—balikbayans—as a means of maintaining the country's foothold in the larger global economy.

Once Neighbors, Now Visitors

Over the course of six years, beginning in 2005, I examined narratives of return by recording the experiences of Filipinos who, having settled in the United States after 1965, were now coming back to their homeland to re-settle. For many of these immigrants, during the decades they spent away from home, the idea of the Philippines has become encircled, simultaneously, by longing and apprehension, familiarity and angst. For instance, Lorenz, now in his early fifties, was the first of his family to move to the United States, in 1969, along with his wife, who was recruited as part of one of the first major waves of nurses to work in what was then the Mary's Help Hospital in Daly City, California. Both retired recently and are now returning to live in their home province of Bacolod. "As much as you want to say that this is home, everything is different in a way. Mostly in how Filipinos see [balikbayans]. They hear the way I speak in Ilongo, how I speak in English, and immediately I'm different. I want to have a drink with old friends or go out to eat, and they're the ones who say, 'Pare, you're American now.' Maybe they see it as a compliment, but it's not really. Because now the drinks are on me," Lorenz jokes, but his discomfort is obvious. Notions of bounded nationality and belonging become distorted in the context of return. Filipinos who have settled abroad, especially in the United States, may continue to express feelings of connection toward their homeland, but in the eyes of their compatriots they are balikbayans.

Much of the literature on tourism, both globally and in the Philippines, focuses on the effects of globalization through the impacts that foreign bodies and capital are having on local economies and the consequences for local communities.[1] And what constitutes the "local" often remains uninterrogated. However, the issue of what is local comes into question when it confronts contemporary forms of return migration or periodic returns to one's home country.[2] The term *balikbayan* is officially defined by the DOT in the Philippines as "Philippine nationals who are permanently residing abroad. . . . [It] also refers to those of Filipino descent who acquired foreign citizenship and permanent status abroad." As former Filipino citizens, balikbayans operate, as the Philippine historian Vicente L. Rafael (2000) says, "neither inside nor wholly outside the nation-state[;] they hover on the edges of its consciousness" (205).

Rafael was one of the first scholars to articulate the significance of distinguishing those Filipinos who live abroad as Overseas Filipino Workers and maintain their Philippine citizenship from those who have acquired citizenship elsewhere. While both groups reside outside of the Philippines, Rafael astutely observes that the latter are often viewed by Filipinos in the Philippines as "ugly" and "steeped in their own sense of superiority, serving only to fill others with a sense of envy" (207). It is this group of former Philippine citizens that functions as the focal point of this chapter. Rarely are these individuals or families the transnational corporate agents who jet between countries as a matter of business.

Framed above the concierge's desk at the Mabuhay Manor, the title of an article reads, "Welcoming Living Heroes at the Mabuhay Manor." The news article continues: "Time and again, the Philippines has hailed their Balikbayans as modern day heroes of the country. With over millions of dollars worth of remittances each year, Filipinos living abroad continue to help their families in the Philippines in particular and the nation in a general way. The Mabuhay Manor, the first Balikbayan Hotel in the Philippines[,] has geared all their efforts and best intentions to welcome the Philippine balikbayan in a most special way by no less than giving their guests genuine Filipino hospitality evident of our timeless and valued traditions." As alluded to by Rafael, within the fantasy of the Philippine nation-state, the conventional balikbayans are not the exploited laboring bodies sent abroad to work in Europe or the Middle East as domestic labor or construction workers. They are those fortunate few who are imagined as having achieved the "American dream," owning a home and earning a sizable income abroad.

Balikbayans have come to be viewed by local Filipinos, paradoxically, as both "traitors" who have abandoned their home country and "heroes" who have found success abroad and continue to support the Philippines by returning. As such, the subjectivity produced by these overlapping and seemingly paradoxical imaginaries has reconstructed the homeland as a place of danger and threat for the Filipino Americans who have now become tourists in their own homeland. As these newly formed tourists seek to come to terms with the ambivalence around their return, dealing with their nostalgia for a childhood that no longer exists, the state mobilizes these aspirations and the fear produced around their homecoming in complex ways.

Balikbayan Paranoia

As the "first balikbayan hotel," the Mabuhay Manor functions as a poignant example demonstrating how the contemporary Philippine tourism industry steers through political corruption and seeks out overseas capital. The relatively small resort is one of four newly built hospitality centers owned by Legend Hotels International Corporation, which caters specifically to balikbayans. As a means of competing with larger and more widely recognized hotel chains, the Mabuhay Manor sells itself, according to its previous website, as an "alternative to the country's major-corporate hotel chains, which lack the personal and cultural charm many Filipino's seek out when traveling back to their homeland." It does this by establishing a reputation based on providing Christian service and running a hotel owned and managed by Filipinos. Given the myriad of inconveniences and difficulties that travel in Manila poses for balikbayans, hospitality centers like the Mabuhay Manor provide a unique respite from the city before returning Filipinos embark on the journey back to their home provinces. Much like the multipurpose enclaves in Manila discussed elsewhere, balikbayan hotels like the Mabuhay Manor enable returning Filipinos to imagine themselves as circumventing the immense emotional anxiety accompanying their return.

Tales of thievery and kidnapping—or, to use Teresa Caldeira's (2000, 19) phrase, talk of crime—prevail throughout narratives of return, cutting across each of my interviews, and it usually required no prodding whatsoever to elicit them. As Caldeira observes of her interviews, the "talk of crime . . . is contagious"; it insinuates itself into the most mundane exchanges: conversations, discussions, jokes, reporting, and, of course, narratives.[3] One might assume that every single Filipino across the globe can easily recount experiences of thievery, assault, or worse while living in the Philippines. Widely viewed *teleserye* (soap operas) and news reports continually devote episodes to these tales, and balikbayans living in the United States are thus subjected to them when watching TFC. For balikbayans, as transformed Filipinos privileged by a lifestyle imaginable to Filipinos in the Philippines only through the media and the Internet and capable of freely transporting themselves between the countries, these tales of thievery and other forms of violence are internalized and shape how they imagine their return.

Balikbayans conduct exhaustive research on banking and credit card companies to ensure that they will never be forced to rely on the Philippine banking system, maintain U.S. postal addresses for fear that Filipinos will steal their mail and it will fail to reach them, and spend substantial amounts of money on security upon their return. In spite of the fear and anxiety induced by these tales, balikbayans are almost obliged to recount them as warnings to each other. "Did you hear . . . ?" usually prefaces each tale of misfortune. Each joke, anecdote, or warning produces the very reality that balikbayans experience when they return; as Caldeira (2000) says, "the talk of crime is not only expressive but productive" (19).

While in its everyday usage *paranoia* tends to refer to feelings of persecution or threat that are unjustified in reality, these feelings, whether based in reality or fiction, "produce real effects in the present," as Victor Burgin (1996, 118) explains.[4] Whether or not these fears and anxieties are grounded in reality, that is, based on material evidence, what becomes critical are the ways in which the tensions resulting from these feelings are projected onto others regardless of whether or not these projections are true. Burgin's analysis points the way to imagining how paranoia becomes mobilized by fears and anxieties as a structure of feeling.[5]

In using the phrase *balikbayan paranoia*, I am *not* attempting to argue that crime and violence are nonexistent in the Philippines, nor to say that these occurrences are not prevalent. My concept of balikbayan paranoia seeks to illuminate how returning Filipinos have, like other elite and privileged communities, created a world for themselves, built around these fears and anxieties, that governs in many ways how they act in relation to Filipinos in the Philippines. Talk of crime is common among balikbayans because it serves to reinforce their dissimilarity from their compatriots: they are Filipinos by citizenship and birth but also different. Having settled in the United States, balikbayans are also models of success, "modern-day heroes."

Coupled with this discursive turn is the way in which the talk of crime also reproduces the built environment around balikbayans. The phrase *balikbayan paranoia* allows me to emphasize the rationalizations and behaviors exhibited by returning Filipinos and the exploitation of this logic by a litany of businesses in the Philippines. These together make the paranoia a very real thing regardless of the *actual* violence that exists throughout the Philippines. The Mabuhay Manor was purposefully created to exploit this paranoia.

While the hotel's modern interior layout and decor is clearly overstated, a nascent subtext of American colonialism permeates the hotel's nostalgic surroundings, illuviating like clay into wet sand. At the front desk, for example, the concierges differentiate themselves from other staff by communicating in impeccably constructed American accents. Employees communicate with guests in sophisticated American colloquialisms. One also quickly discerns the sound of *kundiman* music, so characteristic of popular music during the 1940s and 1950s, playing throughout the hotel lobby and restaurant.[6] From the paintings depicting Filipino farmers to the jars of evaporated milk served beside the restaurant's coffee dispenser, it becomes clear that the hotel is expressing not only an ideal depiction of traditional Philippine history but also a particular moment in time when American colonialism still openly ran the country's affairs. All of these elements reflect a very particular moment in Philippine history. For returning Filipinos who left the country after 1965, the Mabuhay Manor's surroundings are reminiscent of a time in their childhoods before the dictator Ferdinand Marcos's rule left many Filipinos feeling jaded and fearful about the country's future.

Visitors are transported even further into their childhoods when they enter the hotel's restaurant, where, in addition to the buffet of typically Filipino breakfast fare, is the hotel's very own *naglalako*, who waits on each table with freshly prepared traditional desserts. Like little children, patrons light up at the sight of *bibingka*, *puto*, *kutsinta*, and cassava nestled inside an aluminum *bañera* lined with banana leaves.[7] I heard whispers as parents fondly recounted memories of their childhoods while the chef folded each banana leaf and carefully sliced baked coconut indulgences as children listened impatiently. This imaginary space, suspended in time, illustrates how the DOT is attempting to harness the values of leisure, economic opportunity, and patronage by providing services that allow visitors to transcend the immediate environs of Manila, with its dizzying tempo and vexing geography, in order to return to an idealized homeland.

The Mabuhay Manor provides a poignant case study conveying emerging trends in Philippine tourism that emphasize return migration as a means of propelling economic restructuring, particularly through the broader tourism industry. As repatriating Filipinos are transformed into "retirees," balikbayans see themselves as patrons of the state who, because of their decades of overseas labor, patronage, and performance of their duties to the Philippines, are now entitled to enjoy various luxuries they could not partake of in the United States. This chapter examines the production of illusory memories through which returning Filipinos are able to straddle the space between their new and former lives as they make the choice to re-patriate into Philippine society. The construction of nostalgic space within the Mabuhay Manor reflects techniques employed throughout the tour-ism industry that seek to attenuate balikbayan paranoia. I argue that this complexly felt type of anxiety and ambivalence represents a major obstacle that the DOT and its partners ironically exploits in developing strategies to entice Filipinos to return, and ultimately repatriate, back to their homeland.

State Development and the Performance of Tourism

One of the major campaigns implemented by the DOT centers on portray-ing the Philippines through the "spirit" of *mabuhay* (welcome). Executives operating within and around the DOT have taken to the idea of transform-ing the practice of mabuhay and formalizing it into a "culture of tourism," which is being taught to local governments and even barangay leaders in cities and provinces where tourists are prominent. For instance, many ho-tels and restaurants in the past offered two separate sets of rates for local Filipinos and foreign tourists. The DOT and its partner agencies have at-tempted to organize training programs in the culture of tourism to encour-age hotels and restaurants to provide all guests with a single standard rate.

The term *mabuhay*, similar to the Hawaiian word *aloha*, has several meanings. The literal meaning of *mabuhay* is "long live." Yet while the cele-bratory term is occasionally used for toasts, like the word *cheers*, it is more often used to welcome guests and as such has been adopted by the DOT to embody a larger cultural attitude toward visitors to the Philippines, not only non-Filipinos but balikbayans as well. Hotel managers at the Mabu-hay Manor have confronted this dilemma, for instance, by reconfiguring the practice of mabuhay into a concept of *bisita sa bahay*, or "visit home," to stabilize the paradox of overseas Filipino tourism. Bisita sa bahay rep-resents the contemporary configuration of processes that began three de-cades earlier and have led to a tourism industry that is becoming more and more inextricable from its interest in drawing balikbayans back home.

When one examines the concept of mabuhay more deeply, one begins to see the intense complexity and ambivalently experienced cultural nuances embedded within it. As Ness's quote in the epigraph carefully points out, the culture of tourism is complicated by returning balikbayans. The tourism campaign around mabuhay immediately enables balikbayans to simultaneously feel like tourists and celebrated guests who are returning to their own homeland. It seemingly counteracts balikbayan paranoia by giving balikbayans the sense that they are at once "at home" and abroad. However, the result is quite the opposite. As "retirees," balikbayans are paradoxically transformed into guests in their own homeland and are forced to face their ambivalence toward living in a society that is rapidly changing but that is, in many ways, still the same.

Amid stunning levels of visible poverty and the perceived omnipresence of everyday violence, the Philippine government has continuously sought out innovative means to "welcome" Filipinos back and encourage them to "visit home." While these inequities remain vividly clear and the threat of violence continues to haunt, the touristic performances implicit within mabuhay and bisita sa bahay function together to conceal or even dispel the risks involved in visiting and investing in the Philippines. What results is a glaring paradox: while only a miniscule fraction of the country's local Filipino population is capable of experiencing the world of leisure promised by the tourism industry, balikbayans, Filipinos returning to the Philippines, are welcomed to enjoy the country's unique offerings and elite privileges when they visit home.

Attempts to assuage negative perceptions about traveling to the Philippines began much earlier. Marcos, the former president and dictator of the Philippines, was confronted by the challenge of attracting foreign investment in the face of a bankrupt economy and the recent establishment of martial law. As discussed in chapter 2, in order to resurrect the country's tourism industry, Marcos established the Balikbayan Program in 1973. The program subsidized visits to the Philippines by Filipinos living abroad through a number of travel incentives and customs concessions; it was originally implemented by Marcos to provide preferential treatment to balikbayans. Because the Marcos administration, through all manner of financial mismanagement and political corruption, had built an economy that was entirely dependent on debt accumulation, he strategically implemented the program as a secondary means of securing a flow of foreign aid and remittance money.[8] It was at this moment that balikbayans became integrally linked to the country's tourist economy.

The true value of the Balikbayan Program rested not in the material financial capital drawn from individual balikbayans who returned to the Philippines but in the performance of various state and local agents whose labor depicted the country as politically and economically stable. As with his political use of tourism, Marcos was more interested in making certain that the Philippines appeared economically viable to investors than in addressing the inequalities that had been sparking violence throughout the country, thus perpetuating the lack of confidence that others in the international community had in his ability to bring stability to the Philippines. For these reasons, it is difficult to assess the early successes of the program. According to key figures in the establishment of the program, the economic losses caused by the program were insignificant compared with the political role the program had played. Echoing the economic fiasco of hotel financing during the World Bank Conference, figures sympathetic to Marcos's program acknowledged its heavy burden on taxpayers but found consolation in its ability to inspire positive public sentiment. As a fervent supporter of Marcos's project, the assistant director of the DOT's Research and Statistics Division claimed that "the government[,] of course, has lost and is losing a rather substantial amount of revenue from the program. But the benefits derived by the country are not only from the foreign currency spent here. . . . [I]t is also an effective means of rebutting through actual experience the lies they have spread about this country in foreign lands" (quoted in Richter 1982, 193).

The role performed by the economy of appearances within the DOT clearly illustrates how development schemes rely on the manufacturing and regulating of public perceptions as a means of drawing speculative capital that will hopefully turn into larger economic returns. For example, the ideology implicit within these performative techniques was made patently clear by the country's "Reunion for Peace," launched in early 1977. Inspired by similar initiatives implemented by the authoritarian government in South Korea to inspire favorable reviews among compatriots living abroad, the program specifically subsidized the return of former World War II servicemen and their families who were living abroad. By funneling them into nostalgic tours of old battlegrounds and memorials such as those in Corregidor and Bataan, the administration hoped to present the country as an independent and democratic nation-state committed to peaceful reconciliation. By 1978 alone, nearly a million Filipinos had utilized the government program, and, more important, the positive reviews of various balikbayans were successfully transmitted to Filipinos residing in North America, Europe, and Australia (Richter 1982, 60).

In the face of ever-present poverty, pollution, and shortages of energy, water, and housing, along with the public shame around the country's thriving sex industry and the ongoing fiscal mismanagement by the Marcos administration, subsequent presidents have been challenged by the task of propping up tourism in the Philippines and maintaining the façade of prosperity that led the country into enormous debt. One of President Corazon Aquino's primary tourism policy agendas was to cut the budget of the DOT and ensure that the management of its finances was focused on national development rather than perpetuating a structure that had spent exorbitant amounts of taxpayer money and shifted economic gains toward private corporations and individuals.

In particular, state administrators were keenly aware of the perception created by the country's historical complacency toward foreign sex tourism in the Philippines. State-directed policies and publicly endorsed initiatives focused on transforming the face of Philippine tourism by ridding the nation's capital of the majority of its most visible sex establishments while simultaneously refusing to allow the industry to function on the margins.[9] From 1991 to 1994, under the direction of Aquino and her successor, Fidel Ramos, city governments closed sex establishments around Manila's tourist belt, particularly in Ermita and Malate. For example, the first secretary of tourism appointed by Aquino, Jose "Speedy" Antonio Gonzalez, quickly implemented a tour program that brought upper-class Japanese women to visit the Philippines and partake in its thriving import economy. Gonzalez hoped that such tours would project an image of the country as a wholesome destination rather than a major node for sex tourism (Baguioro 2002). As such, Manila's municipal government transformed previously bustling commercial sex districts, spaces that were deemed integral to the urban economy of the National Capital Region, into vibrant commercial leisure districts that fell seamlessly into the emerging infrastructure of malls and high-rise projects already being built throughout Metro Manila. At the same time, the sex industry did not disappear but was relegated to cities and districts less significant to the core economy of Manila.

Along with visitors from around the globe, balikbayans continue to play an integral role within the economic plans of the Philippine tourism industry. In 2009, during a meeting between the Philippine Retirement Authority (PRA) and executives from Philippine Retirement, Incorporated, the representative to the private sector, leaders discussed the significant role that balikbayans had played in improving the tourism industry and developing the larger Philippine economy. The PRA's chief, Edgardo Aglipay, explained that the entrepreneurial vision behind the creation of a retirement industry is to "become a large organization composed of multi-sectoral members from different lines of business relating to the housing, health, and lifestyle needs of retirees in the Philippines" (quoted in Alave 2007).

The unease created by fears of crime and insecurity continues to impact the tourism industry and acts as a major impediment to balikbayans returning to live in the Philippines permanently, particularly in Manila. Ironically, one of the dominant responses adopted by the Philippine administration to counter these negative perceptions and anxieties around travel in the Philippines is to exploit them.

Returning Costs

Balikbayans are often convinced that their status as privileged returnees makes them targets for con artists and thieves. As such, the price that balikbayans will pay for security represents both the financial commitment *and* the emotional duties that many balikbayans justify having to pay in order to return and live in the Philippines. It is one of the hidden costs that deter many Filipinos from visiting their homeland and returning to live in the Philippines permanently. Even television shows played on TFC and Philippine newspapers marketed toward Filipino Americans constantly perpetuate these fears. For instance, the *Philippine News* (March 1989) printed a list of "tips" for balikbayans returning to Ninoy Aquino International Airport and suggested, "In Manila, minimize advertising yourself as balikbayan. Those boxes with the balikbayan letters emblazoned on them can be your discomfort or death."

Tales of airport dangers are widespread. Ezmeralda, who admits she is not immune to the paranoia, remembers feeling startled when her brother jokingly passed along a warning to her for when she arrived in Manila. Having just reached the retirement age of sixty-five, it came time for her to leave the United States and her adult children and make her way back home to the Philippines. While saying good-bye to her family members and making her way to the airport's security gate, her brother pulled her by her shoulder and joked, "You know there are only two things that you need to watch out for, Ate, dengue and *dengoy*." "I slapped him when he said that," she laughed. Periodically, the Philippines experiences outbreaks of dengue fever, and tourists are advised to take precautions for it before flying to the Philippines (Tenorio et al. 1998). *Dengoy*, on the other hand, is the colloquial term for swindling. Exemplifying the characteristic fondness that Filipinos have for puns and other forms of word play, Ezmeralda's brother was comparing the threat of dengue with the ongoing threat of local Filipinos cheating balikbayans of their money—dengoy.

The balikbayan paranoia that drives visiting Filipinos to continually seek guarantees against criminal malfeasance, corruption, extortion, and violence has long been characteristic of the Filipino journey back to the Philippines. This intense anxiety around the possibility that poor Filipinos will take advantage of or harm balikbayans, predicated on and deeply enmeshed within very old notions of class difference, has been a continuous hurdle that the Philippine state and the country's tourism industry have been vexed by. And when balikbayans arrive in the Philippines and witness the ever-present security economy, with its legion of security guards, poorly crafted shotguns and handguns, and guard dogs, the apparent paranoia around returning to the Philippines might appear, at first, well founded.

In addition, cautions like "watch out for your valuables" posted on the walls of public restrooms, or the ominous warning to "beware of pickpockets" clearly marked throughout the city's Metro stations, heighten the anxiety and fears of tourists and locals alike. Even the flyers encouraging passengers to "call this number to report erring taxi drivers," handed out at the taxi stands common in any thriving metropolis, signal the particular culture of fear exuded throughout the Philippines. Balikbayan paranoia is ironically perpetuated by both balikbayans and local Filipinos. While this specter of danger is enhanced by a host of media outlets in the United States, including Filipino American newspapers, television shows, and movies, it especially finds its way into a host of media broadcasts *in* the Philippines. Each day, television shows sensationalize violent events and make it appear as if they are happening everywhere and every day around the country.[10]

"It's become so bad that I never take a taxi without my husband," Ezmeralda explained, pointing out the particularly gendered nature of these anxieties. At the moment, Ezmeralda was staying in a two-bedroom condominium near Quezon City that she had purchased with her husband, Rosario. She told me:

I don't go anywhere without him. I don't know how any woman would make the decision to come back here and retire without their husband. I don't trust the people here. Without my husband, they would easily take advantage of me. You hear about it all the time on the news [in the Philippines]. My brothers and sisters in the Philippines call me all the time. Yes, *in the Philippines*. Even they are worried about how I am here. So I wonder if this was the right choice for me to come back. But I would never do it without my husband.

She freely admits that the transition to living in the Philippines has been difficult. Still without a car, she rarely travels at night. It is a glaring compromise and stark contrast to her life in California, where she would frequently take evening dance classes without her husband or occasionally venture to the casino and play blackjack with friends till early in the morning.

Ezmeralda is hopeful, however, that the retirement villa in Tagaytay that she and her husband purchased will bring back some of the familiarity that she lost when returning to Manila. "Before we moved here, we thought we made a good plan. Now I see it's more difficult to start a business here than I thought. Now that I might be able to open a store here, well, we're banking on our new home [in Tagaytay]." Even though they have another year to wait before they can move into their new residence, the all-inclusive amenities, constant security, and "good neighbors" are all elements that compelled Ezmeralda and Rosario to invest the majority of their savings in the development. "I just want to have the life we had in the States back. But we can't go back there so we just hope we can have it here," Ezmeralda expressed, her voice sinking beneath the weight of her uncertainty.

The emotional toll precipitated by returning home is extraordinary. Filled with uncertainty, the journey home is fraught with enormous unseen costs. Difficult to capture in their entirety, these anxieties are manifested differently across the differentiated class lines of balikbayans and returning Overseas Filipino Workers, and also between Filipino men and women who are returning. What had begun for Ezmeralda as a bright new business venture was complicated by a very real sense of anxiety and fear of failure, thus ironically instilling in her a new desire to go back—not back home in the Philippines, but back to the United States.

There is an irony attached to conversations about crime. The talk of crime among my interviewees in the Philippines always conjured a faceless culprit. Unlike similar narratives in conversations with my interviewees while they were still living in the United States, when interviewees shared encounters where these faces might be "black," "Mexican," or "Vietnamese," there was no "face" to criminalize or racialize. Almost always, such talk attributed crimes to the faceless poor who might come from the squatters in the historically depressed and crime-laden district of Tondo or simply "another town." The irony is that, according to the National Statistic Office of the Philippines, about a third of Manila's 12 million residents live in slums, and a third of the 94 million Filipinos live below the poverty line, earning only $1.25 a day. "The poor," whom balikbayans fear, could be just about anyone in Manila.

Sinking back against the plastic back of his patio chair, Adrian Banal resorted to laughter when probed about the conundrum:

> It's backwards. When I think about it, Filipinos are like their own worst enemies, especially us coming from the United States. We're probably the most guilty when it comes to keeping tourists from coming to the Philippines. And yet we get so angry when some negative about the Philippines comes up on CNN or the Internet. When there's some travel advisory, we get all riled up because we feel so insulted. But what happens when my boy wants to go out, even very close. The very same Filipinos tell us not to go to town by yourself, because it is not safe. The people in that town will kidnap or rob you, they say.

Adrian's comments are poignant not simply because of the ambivalence and reflexivity around "us coming from the U.S." His words also convey the almost schizophrenic shifting between "us" and "them." One moment, "us" is Adrian and his cohort of balikbayans, and just a moment later, it's the Filipinos who tell him and his son that "the people in that town will kidnap or rob" them.

At first, it would appear that enabling balikbayan paranoia would be counterproductive to luring balikbayans to visit on holidays or even return to the Philippines permanently. Contrary to Adrian's perception, the talk of crime and the paranoia and anxiety it creates become productive for the development scheme of the Philippine state. These same fears also serve to arouse sentiments of obligation and indebtedness, compelling balikbayans to continue to return to their homeland to ensure the welfare of their families and communities. The economy produced by what Rafael (2000) calls the "labor of mourning" also maintains and regulates the flow of goods and Filipinos to and from the Philippines.

The circulation of these physical and financial remittances, fundamental to the Philippine economy, is sustained and perpetuated by a culture of anxiety and paranoia. Not only are Filipinos in the United States, compelled by these innumerable fears, moved to ensure the basic safety of their family members by giving them money to pay for the construction of huge metal gates and other security services, but the balikbayans who do return easily rationalize their enormous expenditures for various services and goods to ensure their own safety. Balikbayans continually fear the corruption of police officers and taxi drivers, the probability of having to bribe a public servant, or even the chance that they will be kidnapped.

If they can afford it, Filipinos who are forced or make the choice to return will gladly pay high prices for luxurious hotel and resort accommodations, private drivers, and bodyguards to ensure their safety. At the same time, developers, private investors, and state agencies are actively exploiting these compulsions, literally banking on balikbayans' paranoia and desire for security. Various agencies and programs have been developed to ensure the security of balikbayans who desire to return to the Philippines and enjoy various amenities without the fear of being robbed or swindled. The DOT and its partner agencies have gone to great lengths, establishing international booths and ad campaigns aimed at luring financially attractive Filipinos living abroad to invest a substantial amount of money and retire in the Philippines. Built on promises of security and world-class service, selling retirement to those who are capable of affording it has, over the last ten years, become an entire industry that functions specifically to develop the larger Philippine economy.

5. The Balikbayan House » The Precarity of Return Migrant Homes

Because migration is often conceptualized through fixed trajectories, perceptions of migrant homes, much like the discourse around their homelands, also remain static. The home is a structure produced by nostalgia, constantly remaining within a state of future-past, reconstructed in narratives, memoirs, and oral histories. By the same token, others conceive of migrant homes as a mobile attachment, strapped onto the migrant like an Anzalduan turtle shell: wherever the migrant may be, they bring their home with them. The home is merely an extension of their nomadism. Migration, of which return is but a single facet, is constituted by bodies, objects, practices, and ideas *in motion*. This chapter reconceptualizes migrant homes in the context of return. In the same way that this book conveys how migrant homelands shift and transform along the tangled circuitry of globalization and economic development, migrant homes also absorb and express their own disorienting modernity.

Return fundamentally challenges the ontology of modernity. As such, *actual* return complicates how we understand the life cycle of migration. When migrants do return, the home is no longer a fixed end point to this cycle. Return disorients perceptions and assumptions around home, even as governments and state policies aim to normalize these migration patterns (Xiang et al. 2013). And for migrants who return, either to visit or to resettle, their experiences are just as discomfiting. Their experiences are simultaneously perfused with ambivalence and unease but also relief and assurance. Nothing is the same, yet nothing has changed. If the home is then, as Pierre Bourdieu (1977, 89) describes it, "the principal locus for the objectification of generative schemes" mirroring social structures within larger society throughout its intimate spaces, how does the balikbayan home reflect patterns of mobility, disjuncture, and absence, which are intensified by the constant mobilizing circuitry of transnationalism?

This chapter examines the spaces produced by Filipinos returning to the Philippines, specifically the balikbayans' homes, where specific memories of being Filipino during their childhoods must be reconciled with the habitus balikbayans have adopted while living in the United States. The neighborhoods where balikbayans invest, rebuild, and resettle are often unremarkable in contrast to the "remittance landscapes" transformed by money sent home by transnational migrants. Likewise, they appear humble and simple in comparison to ultraplanned, hyperglobalized cities like Eton City and Fort Bonafacio Global City. Unlike remittance landscapes, perennially uninhabited by Overseas Filipino Workers (OFWs), the provincial neighborhoods where balikbayans make their new homes are distinctly indistinct from those of their immediate neighbors who dwell beside them. Balikbayans remake their homes and lives from a particular nostalgia of their childhoods lived in the Philippines. At the same time, they merge these lifestyles with customs, beliefs, and traditions fabricated and innovated while acculturating to life in the United States. The results of this merging are homes that are in constant flux: irregularly inhabited, continually modified, and with familial proximity at the center of their function. They are material artifacts of a precarious modernity.

Precarious Modernity

There is an increasing fascination around the changes taking hold in the cities and rural towns from where transnational migrants originate. Much like the massive developments transforming urban centers throughout cities in Asia or creating entirely new cities where none existed before, the manner in which newly constructed homes are reshaping rural towns and villages in the region has drawn much interest. The *New York Times* published photographs depicting these vibrantly colorful transformations as traditional Filipino architecture is replaced by the "Mediterranean-inspired, pastel-colored houses" beginning to surface in smaller towns throughout the Philippines (Onishi 2010b). As previous chapters have shown, decades of remittances sent by both OFWs and balikbayans have not only filled local households with kitchen appliances and flat-screen TVs but also financed the building of schools and clinics and provided the capital to start small businesses. These remittances have also paid for the building of new homes and expanded single attached dwellings into multilevel bungalows.

In these accounts, homes financed by remittances are typically distinguished from traditional Filipino homes by their "Western" features, which tend to feel functionally out of place. They are identified by the newly planted greenery, more suitable for desert climates, and peaked roof designs fabricated with ceramic tiling, which quickly deteriorate in the humid tropical climate. They contain gold- or brass-plated fixtures that are eventually corroded by untreated water. These images, which together constitute an imagination of the "remittance landscape" in the Philippines, present return migrant homes as not fitting into their surroundings, in both style and function.[1]

When it comes to the built environment, it becomes difficult to discern where and when this particular aesthetic originates. In writing about the Philippines, scholars tend to assume that these styles and designs originate from decades of transmigration, both formal and irregular, brought "back home" by returning migrants.[2] However, American influences on architectural design have percolated into and melded together with Filipino designs since 1905 (see Cody 2002, 22–25). Likewise, it is often assumed that returning migrants consciously utilize investments in real estate and employ "modern" designs to distinguish themselves from their neighbors.[3] This emphasis on modern design directly implicates a particular notion of modernity with migration that implies a distinction from that which is not modern: the traditional.

Both Filomeno V. Aguilar Jr. and Lieba Faier argue that homes cannot be understood primarily as markers of class distinction. Aguilar (2009) provides an important intervention, arguing that there is much to learn from returning migrants and their investments beyond the brightly colored exteriors of the "diasporic homes" they are building. These OFWs are not simply "'forcibly' inscribing globalization and modernity onto their remote villages" (89). Rather, Aguilar argues that diasporic homes are "a tangible prize, a trophy of sorts that the migrant earns by persevering through" what he calls the "double liminality" of being simultaneously marginalized as a noncitizen in the countries where they are employed, while also living in near poverty in the Philippines (106). Similarly, Faier (2013) explains that because of the complex stigma that comes from working as bar hostesses in Japan, returning Filipina migrants make an array of "affective investments" in homes as a means of providing security for their families and themselves. Return migrants' reasons for choosing to differentiate themselves from their compatriots are complex and serve multiple functions. Diasporic homes provide few financial returns since local Filipinos cannot afford to purchase them or would rather buy an entirely new home. Homes do indeed function as markers of class distinctions and remain a fundamental strategy for shaping the habitus of individuals in society. Relying on economic rationales, however, as the sole explanation for why and how return migrants re-create their homes ignores the intensely ambivalent subjectivities produced by return and ultimately negates the possibilities for which the Philippine state might attempt to exploit this ambivalence.

Bourdieu's (1970) description in "The Berber House or the World Reversed" opened the way for sociologists and theorists of culture in general to think about the ways in which the dwelling—its design, decor, and function—structures not only the everyday life of those who inhabit its particular space but also the ways in which such a space provides symbolic significance for larger, macroprocesses of the economy, politics, and social relations, which project themselves through various practices of domesticity and intimacy. In this way, the home provides a guide to trace the social imagination of those who dwell in this space: their intimacies, their production of desires, and the enactment of the norms shaping their societies. The everyday habits and exchanges that occur within the home provide a glimpse of not only systems of kinships and communal life but also these systems' interactions with external forms of legal authority and their relationships to surrounding communities.

Bourdieu's (1970) ethnography of the Kabyle home remains a pinnacle reference for understanding the home as a synecdoche for the "world inversed." However, his depiction of Berber culture remains static. The inertia is created by his representation of Berber culture as a direct consequence of the uprootedness spawned by French colonial violence, rather than a singularly evolved culture.[4] This penchant to contrast migrant homes with classical Western aesthetics locates the inherent problem of "structural nostalgia," or the tendency to read modernity as an intrusion and corruption of tradition.[5] The innate ambivalence derived from return, infused within balikbayan homes, complicates the structural nostalgia that views practices of migrant homemaking as a unsettling consequence of global capitalism and the hegemony of classical Western modernity. Instead, balikbayan homes and the indeterminacy imbuing their architecture, and the itinerant practices of the balikbayans inhabiting them, *are* by definition modern.

Precarity is modernity. Anne Allison (2013) defines *precarity* as a particular condition of insecurity produced by late capitalism where both work and life are subject to the indeterminate conditions of constant crisis. This precarity permeates every facet of migrant life and produces a particular sense of itinerancy in how migrants make and experience home. Balikbayans' spaces are distinct from those produced by OFWs, local Filipinos, and even other foreign retirees. Yet all function within the same structure of precarity in the Philippines. Nothing is the same, yet nothing has changed.

To make sense of these complexities, it is important to move away from a view of the home as a literal place where individuals and families reside. It does not simply contain memories and traditions through material practices of consumption and intimacy or its architecture and built environment. To comply with the indeterminate routes of transnational living, a balikbayan home also extends itself beyond its literal walls and encompasses how balikbayans interact with the world outside of the home. And just as the logic of the balikbayan economy operates through patterns of nostalgia and fantasy, the balikbayan home, too, transcends time as much as space. The constitutive imagination of balikbayans' home life upon return occurs again and again, a repeated turning, as Benito Manalo Vergara (2009) argues, through media, social interactions, and stories. Thus, the process of return begins long before balikbayans actually started remaking their homes in the Philippines.

BF Homes and the Story of Migration

Jannero's mumblings were barely intelligible. The taxi driver's words were drowned out by the uproarious grinding noise produced by the road's broken pavement along one of the major roads crisscrossing the BF Homes subdivision in Parañaque City. "Ano po? [What did you say, sir?]" I asked yet again. He sighed. "Ito. Ito ay kung saan nangyari ang Massacre. Ang Visconde Massacre. [Here. Here's where the massacre happened. The Vizconde massacre.]" His finger juts across the passenger side of the car. I immediately recognized the story. Filipinos throughout the diaspora were fixated by the story around the stabbing murders of Estrellita and her two daughters, Carmela and Jennifer. When the wealthy teenager Hubert Webb, the son of a former Philippine senator, was determined to be the primary suspect, public sympathy for the Vizconde family skyrocketed, and even American-born children of Filipino immigrants knew about the tragedy. Three films were even made to capitalize on the public's grim fascination with the event. The most famous of the three was *The Vizconde Massacre Story (God Help Us!)*, starring none other than Kris Aquino, the megafamous talk show host and sister of former president Benigno "Nonoy" Aquino, as Carmela.

The mobility produced by migration begins with stories, widely known tales, and even mumblings like Jannero's. The path of return had been charted long before balikbayans returned to the Philippines. While Filipinos may have been physically away, their presence was continually felt through ongoing conversation (letters and phone calls, and later e-mails and virtual meetings), gifts, and financial support. These connections, given life through Filipino films played in American theaters, *teleserye* on TFC (the Filipino Channel), and *tsismis* (gossip) with friends while shopping in malls, allowed Filipinos to imagine their return in material ways, propelling them to continue sending remittances back to their families and to invest in an indeterminate future. Unlike the haphazard and spontaneous manner in which the departure for and emigration to the United States tends to take place for a host of migrants from different parts of the world, including the Philippines, return is a slow and incremental process. Balikbayans imagine their return through stories and conversations about events in the Philippines and carefully chart each step of their return through patterns of connectivity that are dependent on various modes of technology and social media.

By the time the murders occurred in 1991, the BF Homes had already become a notable geographic marker on Manila's topography. Those Filipinos who had originally emigrated from Luzon, and perhaps even those from elsewhere, had undoubtedly heard of the Homes by the time the massacre occurred. The subdivision is rather large, relative to other subdivisions throughout Metro Manila, its borders cutting across three different cities: Parañaque, Las Piñas, and Muntinlupa. When the subdivision was completely finished in 1970, it was dubbed "the biggest subdivision in Asia." For over two decades, Filipino families, both wealthy and famous, made their homes in the more exclusive barangays within BF Homes's domain. Because of this, it is now what would be considered a typical gated subdivision, enclosed by two gates through which residents can enter and leave. However, the gates and the guards who patrol them are merely aesthetic. Residents and visitors are able to enter and leave the barangay with little to no impediment. Residents pay monthly dues to an association, led by a captain who is responsible for maintaining the condition of the barangay and upholding its bylaws. It is within this subdivision that I situate my study of balikbayans' homes.

Unlike the refracting panorama of Metro Manila, and apart from the newly built Korean-owned businesses sprouting along the barangay's main streets, much of the residential sectors of the BF Homes does not appear to be in a state of constant rebuilding. Outwardly, the changes that are taking place are comparatively subtler, although they are much more visible inwardly. One of the reasons for this is that neighborhood bylaws prohibit houses from exceeding three stories, although a handful of the more prominent neighbors have found ways to build beyond the limit. Many of the homes were built long before this generation of balikbayans began to return in greater number. All the main roads dividing the subdivision into typical suburban grids are relatively well paved, but there are several back roads that are not, even though they are heavily utilized.

Balikbayan homes, like return migrants themselves, vary in design. Depending on their income and familial circumstances, balikbayans may live in their family's home and remain in their home province or choose to relocate closer to an urban center like Manila or Cebu if they decide to establish a new business. While accounts proliferating on the Internet tend to emphasize the lavish new condominiums or expansive lots awaiting the building of a new American-style bungalows, most balikbayans returning to the Philippines to retire prefer to return to homes that have already been built. These homes are not necessarily childhood homes but were purchased much later, when balikbayans first settled in the United States.

Properties like those in the BF Homes subdivision are in many ways ideal for balikbayans. These days, properties in established subdivisions like BF Homes would be unaffordable to most balikbayans. Now, however, many balikbayans can capitalize on decades of supporting their family members, who have resided in these relatively lavish settings, and take over the property once they return. Having invested in their family's estate for several decades prior, they can now utilize their remaining savings to remodel and refurbish older homes. Unlike condominiums in the center of Manila, these multistory homes allow returning Filipinos to live reunited

FIGURE 5.1 Typical balikbayan home in the BF Homes subdivision, 2012. Photo by author.

with family members and also provide ample space for their children and grandchildren to visit.

Inside the home, spaces are formed around the intrinsic value of familial community and the stories, gossip, and jokes that tie families together. The kitchen does not form the center for balikbayan homes. And unlike the traditional communal space of courtyards, where Filipinos came together for conversation and gossip, balikbayan homes replicate their American counterparts. Sociality is centered inside, within the home's domestic space. Unlike the gendered spaces that tend to put Filipino men in the garage and the women around the dinner table, balikbayan homes tend to focus around the living room, where men and women congregate, share stories, and sing karaoke, and where they spill into during large meals.[6] The living room therefore tends to be cluttered with displays, showcasing images from migrants' lives in the United States, their other travels, and their most precious accomplishments—their children. Balikbayan homes remain characteristically Filipino, lively and full of sounds.

Staging Modernity

The additions to Jaime's home had been so recently completed that the brown-tinted beer bottles left by the construction workers still lined one side of his concrete porch. When I entered, the scent of the floor's hardening concrete rushed through the main entrance as I made my way across the threshold. The pile of unopened paint cans that Jaime had attempted to hide away still peeked out from the corner of the living room. Jaime, or "Jhun," is one of many balikbayans who has not officially retired and resettled in the Philippines. Having been forced into early retirement owing to an injury he suffered at work over a decade ago, the former cable technician had been making trips back and forth to Parañaque with his wife, Adele, for the last six years to supervise the remodeling of their second home. Unlike many of the model homes advertised to Filipinos living in the United States on Filipino television and newspapers, and via the Internet, attempting to lure emigrants with promises of "modern living" in their homeland, Jhun's home was surprisingly modest. It wasn't painted in vibrant pastels or outfitted with reflective windows, embellishments that might give a home a sleek, contemporary feel.

The reality of actual return is confounding for developers and architects in the Philippines. The space in Jhun's concrete bungalow was indeed ample. Yet the newly remodeled four-bedroom home lacked almost all of the elements that Filipino developers and advertisers believe balikbayans find appealing. The kitchen included basic counters and room for appliances, but it lacked a colorfully tiled backsplash or even enough space for an American-style stove. The communal spaces lacked any kind of skylight or recess lighting. Instead, both the living and dining rooms were lit by a single lightbulb in each of the metallic white ceiling fans. And while Adele plans on planting a mango tree in the backyard for relatives to harvest each year, they had no plans to install a swimming pool or a water fountain in either yard. Developers, financial institutions, and designers in the Philippines are continually perplexed to realize that balikbayans are actually facsimiles of an American middle-class modernity. They're dumbfounded by the realization that balikbayans are not the wealthy elite for whom they had spent years advertising. Struggling to make a living throughout the continents of North America, western Europe, and Australia, balikbayans often come to the Philippines with far less capital than their reputation lets on.

To be fair, even though Adele and Jhun had been chiseling away at it for some time, the rebuilding project was still unfinished. Yet, each subsequent year, they remain content with their decision to resettle in Parañaque in the future. Not only is the city conveniently located just a short distance away from the Ninoy Aquino International Airport, but it is also their hometown. But because they continue to work on a contractual basis and live in the United States, they have been unable to devote enough time to completing their dream project. Both Adele and Jhun felt that six years was enough, however, to begin showing off much of their hard work to their extended families and friends on this day.

I encountered Adele scurrying around the dining room; sensing that she was in the company of a "Fil-Am," she squealed, "Ma-init naman [It's so hot]."[7] She stretched the upper corners of her mouth to draw out the *i* so that it sounds like a long *e*. Small air conditioners were mounted in only two of the bedrooms of Adele and Jhun's home; the exorbitant cost of installing central air made such a convenience entirely impractical. Therefore, to counter the mid-July heat, which was now beginning to settle in and permeate the home, Jhun requested that his driver purchase four high-powered fans. He hoped that the fans would help to circulate the stagnant air throughout the home's spacious living room and dining space, providing his guests with relief from the oppressive humidity. Of course, his guests, most of whom were relatives who had never left the Philippines and friends from around the neighborhood, were already accustomed to the climate. Balikbayans practice a subtle art of appearing to have accumulated considerable social and economic capital while living abroad, while in fact spending as little as possible.

Balikbayan homes, like Adele and Jhun's, tend to include a separate living space for domestic help, or ya-yas. The presence of domestic servants, in various forms, is perhaps the most pronounced vestige lingering from the previous life of balikbayans. The ya-ya is intrinsic to the familial hierarchy of Filipino families, and even poor families hire poorer Filipinos to care for children and take care of household errands. Before Adele's mother returned to the Philippines to live with the couple, the family's ya-ya, Tessa, had had a room adjacent to the guest restroom on the first floor. Jhun had already made plans to convert a portion of the driveway into an expanded room for Tessa; in the meantime, Tessa was content to sleep in the TV room until her room was built. However, many balikbayans are not moved in the same way. Other ya-yas and domestic helpers resort to sleeping in makeshift spaces like storage closets or share space with the children. While there is less of a demarcation between men and women in the house, ya-yas are confined to particular spaces. If there are multiple bathrooms, they often cannot shower in the same bathroom as the immediate family. Women in the immediate or extended family are not confined to the kitchen because it is usually the ya-ya's space. The domestic help, drivers, and even distant relatives whose main role is to serve the family are almost completely invisible, particularly to guests. *Merienda*, the generous serving of "snacks," appear on the dining table each day, and piles of clean clothing are stacked in each room, but the hands performing the labor are somehow always unseen.

Since many of the residents in BF Homes are upper class and own relatively luxurious homes, the balikbayans who live there can enjoy living in an American-style bungalow without drawing too much attention. Not all balikbayans reside in upper-class barangays. All of them, however, find themselves delicately negotiating the appearance of success through their homes. Undoubtedly, the home remains a physical representation of their accomplishments and class status for them, much as it does for much of the world. Yet balikbayans are also apprehensive about the threat of crime that might come with having a lavishly decorated home. This is a major reason that balikbayan homes tend to resemble those of their neighbors. Unlike their remittance-house counterparts, rebuilt by OFWs and painted in vibrant "Mediterranean" colors, balikbayan homes are indistinct from the homes surrounding them, whether the neighborhood is elite or not. For Joriz Navarro, a balikbayan who had just completed building an entirely new home on the other side of town, security was paramount in his design. Unlike Adele and Jhun, Joriz's entire family, including his three children, moved to the BF Homes after living in the United States for almost two decades. The home's exterior was almost entirely built with new materials, and Joriz was adamant that the surrounding wall would include a traditional sliding iron gate. The gate, the rust painted over several times with a thick white coating, was one of the remaining elements of the family home he had rebuilt. The face of the gate engulfed the front of the home entirely, making it almost impossible to see any portion of the bottom level of the house.

Since balikbayans are already perceived as economically privileged, their performance of class distinctions, paramount to the structure of Philippine society, is much subtler. Rather than relying on their homes to communicate their status outwardly, balikbayans convey their success through throwing large parties, shopping in malls, and treating family members and friends to meals. Just above the gate, the Navarros' family room peered out from the second floor of the house. Nena, Joriz's wife, instructed him to have the room built on the first floor so that the trees surrounding the front yard would block the sunlight from entering and heating the room. Instead, Joriz stubbornly insisted that the view from the room's window allow him to see the street outside, just as their bay windows peered out from their home in South San Francisco. Joriz wanted to gaze at his neighbors as they passed by, attempting to sneak a peek into his window above the gate as his family watched TV or hosted karaoke parties. Perhaps more important, he wanted the neighbors to be able to catch a glimpse of the festivities from outside of the bars and fences around his house.

Distant Kinship

By the afternoon, the sunlight had rushed through the iron bars shielding the window's exterior, warming the room to an uncomfortable temperature. Pointing to the bedroom nearest the home's entrance, Jhun was eager to tell his guests that the room was reserved for his two children as the onlookers inched in, one by one, through the front door. Both boys were still attending college in the United States and would occasionally return with their parents on one of their perennial trips back to the Philippines. Jhun, who had worked for a major cable company in Daly City, California, had been piecing his retirement home together with his wife since 2005. The prospect of return, although accelerated by Adele's mother's declining health, had figured prominently in both Adele and Jhun's minds for a number of years. Eventually, growing anxieties over numerous foreseen expenses and their inability to adequately pay off their home in Daly City and other financial debts finally impelled the couple to begin the search for a property lot in their home province.[8]

In this way, balikbayan homes resemble typical Filipino homes as well as homes throughout Southeast Asia. The home is complete only when it is inhabited by all of the living generations of the family together in one house (see Carsten 1995). The connectivity between families lies at the center of Filipino identity and directly defines their social status in the Philippines (see Miralao 2006, 193; Aguilar 2009, 95). This centrality does not disappear simply because Filipinos have emigrated and lived away from the Philippines for several decades. In fact, sacrifice and duty for family lie at the discursive foundations of how Filipino emigrants and balikbayans rationalize the physical distance between themselves and their family members in the first place (see Asis 1992). Thus, even when family members and especially children are away from the home, balikbayan parents fill each day with errands and routines in preparation for when they will be reunited with their children who are living in the United States and in other places.

Therese Ibarra, who worked as a store manager for a major pharmaceutical franchise in California for several decades, explained, "It's strange. Mark [Therese's husband] and I worked so hard all those years. When we had [the kids], we wanted to give them a good life. The best life possible in the States. So that's why we worked so hard. So now it's weird to be living for ourselves now. Back here in the Philippines. Living for the kids was our life for many years. So now, when Mark asks me what do I want to do today, I immediately think of the kids. What are they doing? What do we need to do for them?" Over the course of several months, while back in Parañaque, Therese and Mark have finished remodeling the living room and guest bathroom. Each weekend, they make the arduous trek through traffic to collect building materials at the Home Depot just north of the BF Homes in Pasay. Therese commented, "The kids will be really happy to see all the changes. They'll be happy that they don't have to share a shower with their mom and dad when they come back to visit. Now they have their own." She smiled while pointing out the new fixtures that were installed in the guest shower.

The traditional household strategy model of migration, the notion that decisions about and movement for migration take place collectively among family members, has long been challenged and complicated by scholarly research in migration studies.[9] Migration patterns among Filipino settlers in the United States are complicated. A married Filipino couple may be fortunate enough to emigrate to the United States together and live with one another initially. However, often one finds stable employment, providing security for themselves and their children for decades, while the other is laid off after several years of working or is simply unable to find work commensurate with their education. In these times of crisis, Filipino families do not always remain physically intact. Yet, because divorce remains deeply taboo within traditional Filipino culture and being legally divorced is sometimes associated with tremendous cultural shame, one spouse may live in the United States, while the other may return to the Philippines. While they are legally married, they live entirely separate lives apart from one another. Family unity may be the ideal, particularly as practiced through heteronormative expressions of kinship, but mobility among Filipinos is complex and is driven by diverse motivations and circumstances.

Other times, however, decisions around migration and return do operate through a household strategy model. Adele and Jhun had always dreamed of returning to the Philippines. They were impelled toward a decision when Adele's mother was forced to return years earlier after being diagnosed with cancer. Without a full-time job and unable to afford health insurance in the United States, Adele and Jhun decided to have Adele's mother return first. In the Philippines, medical care takes place on a pay-as-you-go system. Rather than waiting for a statement from the health insurance provider to arrive in the mail as one would in the United States after undergoing a checkup or procedure, patients in the Philippines must pay before receiving services from a health care provider. Patients will remain in the hospital until their debt is fully settled. While occasional treatments are relatively inexpensive compared with health care services in the United States, there is no system to ensure that patients can reliably receive health care in the Philippines when the expenses mount up. Because of this, many balikbayans choose to keep some form of residence in the United States, through an address with either a child or a sibling. With long-term health insurance, many balikbayans fly back to the United States frequently or live there for part of the year and then return again to the Philippines.

With regard to the decision to have her mother move back to the Philippines, Adele commented, "It's been better that way. Jhun and I can send her money each month to pay for her treatment." Her resignation was clearly communicated by her sullen tone. "Medicine costs a lot in the Philippines but not like it does in the United States, where you don't know how much you're going to spend or what you're even getting." In this way, the balikbayan home does not simply figure as material evidence of one's success. Along with showcasing what Jhun and Adele had achieved over decades of living in the United States, each decision around building the home was primarily motivated by preparation for familial reunification. "[After all], what is success if you cannot take care of your family?" Adele asked.

The ideal of a unified family unit powerfully compels Filipinos to migrate throughout the globe, settle in strange places, and devote tremendous amounts of resources, which are continually remitted back into the Philippine economy. This ideal, which is simply that, also materializes through return migration. Balikbayans design and plan their homes with the ideal of reuniting with their children and, therefore, returning to *the idea* of the life that they had back in the United States.

Itinerant Modernity

One of the most intriguing aspects of remittance landscapes is the accompanying absence that characterizes the space. Once again contrasting these with the traditional "happy atmosphere" of Filipino neighborhoods, Aguilar distinguishes diasporic houses by the "relative absence of children running around the streets" (2009, 89). The ongoing financial necessity propelling a continuous stream of labor sent abroad forces many OFWs to leave their homes unoccupied intermittently throughout the year. Their owners, as Aguilar describes, "have gone off to work" far away in other countries and "will not be returning for a very long time" (89). Balikbayan homes are constituted by a similar affect. Their owners, no longer employed in the United States, are often unprepared to completely relinquish the lifestyle and conveniences associated with living in the United States. Most balikbayans therefore reside in the Philippines for a time before periodically reuniting with family members in the United States. As such, the impact of constantly living, moving, and thinking in between places, even as balikbayans are physically residing in their homes in the Philippines, often leaves balikbayan homes with a similarly residual feeling of absence, itinerancy, and emptiness.

Within the built environment, migrant homes are often characterized by a particular improvisationality. Balikbayan homes are often unfinished; their partly decorated walls and temporary furniture point toward a future permanence but remain incomplete. Front yards and backyards have been taped off and partitioned for future projects.

Absence is another characteristic of balikbayan homes. Absence marks balikbayan homes not so much because the residents are physically absent but because the homes are material vestiges of our contemporary modernity, fixtures of what AbdouMaliq Simone (2004) calls a future "yet to come." As such, in many balikbayan homes, the rooms most inhabited are those lived in by caretakers or distant relatives assigned to manage the home's upkeep, rather than the actual homeowners. Here, long-distance kinship does not simply refer to the distance between balikbayan parents and their children but to the financial circuitry needed to reinforce kinship ties between relatives in order to maintain properties and homes from a distance. Balikbayan homes become a material intervention into dominant conceptions around the life cycle of migration. Because return is often perceived as the final stage of this cycle, the migrant's home, much like their homeland, remains a static fixture, left unchanged by modernity and time's perceived movement forward.

The dominant narrative of globalization tends to emphasize the shrinking nature of the global economy and the increasing interconnectivity of cultural exchange, primarily enabled through innovations in technology and travel. Yet various examples prove that these global connections do not necessarily produce unifying results. They are a reminder, as Anna Lowenhaupt Tsing (2005, 1) suggests, that claims touting the promises of universalism created by globalization "do not actually make everything everywhere same." What Arjun Appadurai (1996) calls the "disjunctive nature of globalization" is not simply that cities and other locales are marginalized or excluded by the rapidly consuming force of globalized economic exchange and its network. It is also that the shape and form of the communication of these global forms of modernity are differentially received by people living throughout the world.

The process of return brings into sharp relief the disjuncture of globalization. For Jhun, this disjuncture was embedded in the homes he attempted to purchase and build:

> At first we wanted to buy a home that was already built. We didn't realize from the [real estate] advertisements how misleading they were until we arrived. Many of the homes were poorly built. I mean, it looks good in the [brochure] pictures. But then you visit the home, and there are no windows in some of the rooms. The walls are done improperly. Sometimes realtors had tenants who were already living there even though the homes were supposedly new ones. Because of all these problems, we decided to purchase a [empty] lot instead and build on it. We knew it would take a lot of time since we don't live here permanently yet.

To add to their headaches, even though Adele had family members who lived nearby and could oversee the contractor and builders working on their home, when they returned each summer Jhun and Adele were disappointed to find that their directives had been ignored or poorly executed.

The exposed plumbing remaining in both of the restrooms attested to each time Jhun had demanded that the contractor have his employees repair their shoddy workmanship. Adele hoped that by offering their home as a place for their relatives to stay, she and Jhun would be assured that construction workers would act responsibly and the work done on the home would be properly supervised. However, Jhun and Adele were constantly let down by their family members:

> What can you do? We live in California, and they live here. It costs a lot of money to call them every day. They don't have a good Internet connection. So they cannot send us pictures of the work that's being done. We don't know what kind of progress is being made. You need to be here every day if you want this to happen properly. You should be here to watch what is happening, but that's impossible. . . . [W]e live in California! Nothing is what you would expect. That's the most difficult thing about moving back here. No matter how many people you talk to, no matter what kind of assurances they give, coming back here is not like coming home. Things are very different. The agents, the ads, everything sounds so good. They say everything to make Filipinos [from the United States] come back home, but once we're here, it's different, we're on our own.

Such snapshots capture glimpses of the larger and more intimate contradictions entangled within the vicissitudes of globalization. As this process continues to intensify and our knowledge of each other in different places *appears* to totalize, the experience of immigrants returning to their homelands attests to the disparate manners in which the cultural manifestations of these forces are projected, commoditized, consumed, and imbibed across the world. These differences, and the ambivalences they produce in turn, are continuously confronting and sometimes even contesting the attempts of global capitalism to unify and commoditize these exchanges. The resulting precarity produced by this disjuncture becomes materialized in the lived experience of balikbayan homes. The balikbayan home conveys not only how globalization has produced transnational connectivities that shape subjects who are physically scattered in between places but also how balikbayans understand and make their present and presence, shaped by an incessant itinerancy and precarity. This is actually what it means to be modern.

6. Domestic Affects » The Philippine Retirement Authority, Retiree Visas, and the National Discourse of Homecoming

Until the mid-2000s, balikbayan tourists and retirees constituted less than 10 percent of visitors to the Philippines. Recently, however, that number has dramatically increased. The cumulative effects of the economic downturn in the U.S. labor and housing markets, the coinciding rise in living and health care costs for a generation of Filipino Americans approaching retirement, and the general perception that the Philippines is becoming "more modern" and therefore "safer" enabled an increase in return migration from the United States. Already by 2009 Filipinos constituted 20 percent of the foreign tourists visiting the Philippines. And of the 3.5 million visitors who arrived to the Philippines in 2010, over 17 percent were Filipino Americans (Melican 2011).

Executives in the Philippine tourism and retirement industries adamantly believe that a marked increase in governmental and corporate investments in the luxury property market will continue to raise the economic profile of the rest of the country. These improvements, according to the Department of Tourism, will alleviate many of the anxieties and insecurities that inhibit Filipinos from visiting or even returning permanently to the Philippines. This optimism helped initiate President Benigno Aquino III's Proclamation 181, which designates 2011–2016 as "the Pinoy

Homecoming Years." The program, the latest configuration of the original Balikbayan Program launched in 1973, renews current visa privileges for balikbayan travelers, but this time the Department of Tourism is focusing its advertising and resources on Filipino American balikbayans.

Perhaps the more significant element distinguishing the homecoming campaign from its predecessor is the structural realignment that will complete the merger of two industries in the Philippines: tourism and retirement. This convergence had already been in progress for over a decade. Now political officials, partnering agencies, and the project's managers believe that this union will become instrumental in drawing balikbayans back to their homeland for retirement, along with attracting non-Filipino foreign retirees to the Philippines. Speaking to the domestic press after Aquino's announcement, tourism secretary Alberto A. Lim further emphasized Proclamation 181's goal of targeting Filipinos living in the United States, explaining that "the Philippine diaspora is one of the largest in the world. Maybe the only one larger is Mexico. Homecoming is natural because there are Filipinos in every country in the world. This applies to all countries, but we want to start in the ones with the biggest number of Filipinos, specifically in North America" (quoted in Melican 2011).

For the Philippine Retirement Authority (PRA), the retirement industry is integral to improving the country's economy by making the Philippines a global retirement haven. Executives and governmental leaders are optimistic that a robust retirement economy will finally reverse labor migrations back to the Philippines and solve the perennial crisis of the brain drain (Marcelo 2006). Therefore, the PRA is positioned to play a crucial role in bringing together the tourism, retirement, and health care industries into a single economic platform. As mentioned in the introduction, Aquino's predecessor, Gloria Macapagal-Arroyo, clearly distinguished this emergent role of the "graying population," asserting that "the PRA should find ways to boost the growth of the booming retirement industry in the Philippines, noting the world's graying population is rapidly increasing. . . . The Philippines is in a very good position to take advantage of this potential because we have the facilities and the manpower. As one of the flagship projects of the Philippine government, I want [the] PRA to boost its efforts to develop and promote the Philippines as a retirement haven and contribute to the increase of foreign investments" (quoted in Pelovello 2008).

Members hope that this reconfiguration will help to ease lingering balikbayan anxieties around returning to and living in the Philippines. "With more aggressive campaigns, we hope an additional 80,000 to 90,000 Filipino-Americans will visit the country this year," Secretary Lim explained. "That will contribute an additional ₱21.8 billion to the economy" (quoted in Melican 2011).

Crucial to the driving force of the imaginative labor inducing Filipinos to send remittances, visit, and return home are the finances and energy invested by governmental institutions to enable Filipinos living and working abroad to see themselves as caretakers of their homeland. In a similar fashion, the retirement industry in the Philippines is reconfigured through a logic that enables balikbayans to see themselves as caretakers who are responsible for the welfare of their homeland. This domesticating logic adheres to the various retirement zones and projects throughout the Philippines, where potential retirees are seen as contributors to the economy and workforce even though they are classed as "retirees."

In an article titled "Philippine Retirement Industry: Who Do We Want to Come?," the head of marketing for Philippine Retirement Incorporated (PRI), Enrique Soriano, reiterated this ideal, claiming, "[Retirees] become productive members of the society. . . . For instance, there are retired professors in other countries that come here, they share their talents" (quoted in Daquiz 2006). Because of their perceived wealth and status accrued overseas, balikbayans are educated through programs hosted by the PRI to see themselves as entrepreneurs who are responsible for continuing to generate revenue for the state. The exceptionalism attributed to balikbayans has come to define not only how balikbayans see themselves within their homeland but how they relate to those who have remained there.

The PRA and the PRI

Situated in the coastal city of Nasugbu, in the province of Batangas, the Village features a number of amenities common to retirement villages, including condominiums, spas and gyms, health clinics, tennis courts, swimming pools, parks, and gardens. "Climate, safety, proximity to medical supplies, highly skilled and caring people, low-cost living, natural attractions, and desirable facilities" represent, according to Edgardo B. Aglipay, the PRA's former chair, fundamental reasons why balikbayans will begin returning to the Philippines for retirement. Aglipay, as controversial as he was prominent, was once the heralded chief of the Philippine National Police and was, in a curious fashion, offered the position to head the PRA by

Macapagal-Arroyo after his retirement in 2005 (see Maragay 2005). As part of his duties as chairperson, Aglipay was responsible for coordinating the government and private sectors to work together to concentrate on the development of retirement villages throughout Baguio, Trinidad, Subic-Clark, Metro Manila (Alabang, Muntinlupa), Laguna, Batangas, Cavite, Cebu, Samal Island, and Cagayan de Oro.

The agency was originally called the Philippine Retirement Park System when it was established by Ferdinand Marcos through Executive Order 1037 in July 1985. In August 2001, pursuing a policy of merging the tourism, retirement, and health industries, Arroyo consolidated the agency under the Board of Investments and officially renamed it the Philippine Leisure and Retirement Authority. Yet it continues to be called the PRA in most discussions and within the media. The PRA exemplifies yet another facet within the Philippine political economy where the distinction between the public and private sectors is unclear, and in many ways absent. As an agency devoted to drawing private investments together with government initiatives, the PRA uneasily straddles the private and state sectors. For instance, while the PRA had officially been transferred out of the Office of the President, it continues to function as a subsection of the state's Department of Trade and Industry, directly under the Board of Investments. While its official primary task is to promote the Philippines as a retirement haven and attract foreign investments from balikbayans and foreign nationals, its actual aims are clearly to accommodate the shared interests of the private and public sectors. The overlap between the two sectors becomes increasingly necessary when the government officially provides only 1 percent of the overall funding for retirement villages. While the Philippine government continues to support the expansion of the retirement industry, the PRA is responsible for providing innovative solutions to finance the building of these multibillion-dollar megaprojects.

The executives of the PRA optimistically believe that the Philippines will be home to almost a million retirees by 2015 (Mollman 2007). Projections also suggest that retirees will contribute US$16.6 billion to the Philippine economy. To achieve this goal, one of the innovative solutions adopted by the PRA was to establish the PRI to help finance the building of retirement villages. While the PRA's primary function is to promote the country as a retirement haven, the PRI regulates the quality of retirement facilities, health care providers, and leisure services to ensure that they meet global standards. "[The] PRI is the private sector. The private sector is addressing all the necessary requirements for us to be able to be globally competitive," explained Mr. Aglipay (quoted in Buco 2006).

The members of the PRI include a plethora of services and retailers registered as "operators of retirement facilities," including leisure and resort destinations, condominium and housing developers, hospitals, health insurance providers, transport and travel services, caregiver training schools, health management organizations, financial institutions, tourism advocates, brokers, builders, health and wellness organizations, and other service providers. According to the PRA, there are 109 accredited merchant facilities and 44 accredited retirement facilities. As collaboration between the PRA and PRI continue to expand, agency officials are able to lobby the state government to lower the price of realty properties, add more incentives for Filipinos abroad to retire in the Philippines, and even make improvements to the general infrastructure of the country.

Speaking at the Philippine Retirement Industry Investment Summit in 2006, the PRI's president, Ernesto M. Ordonez, explained that "this is the first time different market players—hospitals, subdivision developers, golf clubs, etc.—are united, are one" in achieving that shared goal (quoted in Gulane 2006). Ordonez admitted that the ongoing congruency of public and private interests is essential for the Philippines to successfully compete with Malaysia and Thailand, countries that have been receiving almost twenty thousand retirees yearly, and make the Philippines a retirement haven. Among the multinational real estate corporations partnering with the PRA on various initiatives are Ayala Land Inc., Robinsons Land Corporation, Filinvest Land Inc., SM Development Corporation, and Megaworld Corporation, as well as a multitude of insurance firms, transportation companies, and privately subsidized hospitals and clinics.

Depending on the source one consults, there are somewhere between 15,420 to 20,000 registered retirees already in the Philippines. The total investments made by retirees in the country had reached US$107.8 million as of January 2010. With the potential US$4 billion of investments in the retirement industry at stake, the Philippine government has acted quickly and included the development of a number of retirement villages in the government-sponsored Investments Priority Plan of 2006. With the expanding Philippine medical tourism industry and the need to employ the growing surplus of skilled Filipino physicians and nurses, developers are also keen to establish hospitals or clinics within each retirement village. Government agencies hope that through the synchronization of the tourism, retirement, and medical industries balikbayans and other foreign nationals will choose to retire in one of the country's "world-class" retirement villages.

The idea of developing exclusive retirement villages focused on drawing foreign nationals and former Filipino citizens to retire in the Philippines is by no means a recent concept. One of the first retirement projects was established in 1995. Together with the RN Development Corporation, the PRA invested US$65 million in renovating Clark Air Base, allowing former personnel of the base, mainly foreign nationals, to invest their pensions in the development and enjoy the luxuries of living in one of the country's first retirement-focused projects. Inducing foreigners to invest their pensions in foreign economies has since become a priority for state development. According to the rationale of state agents, the low cost of living in developing countries provides an enormous economic incentive for foreigners to spend their pensions in the Philippines rather than in their home countries. Meanwhile, building retirement projects on properties like Clark Air Base, which had been emptied of the majority of its American inhabitants after Mount Pinatubo erupted in 1991, would reinvigorate the local economy and provide Filipinos with much-needed employment.

Once members of the Philippine government understood the immense economic potential posed by linking balikbayans directly to the retirement industry, they immediately began shifting their economic strategies and support toward building retirement villages that would cater not only to foreign nationals but also to balikbayans. Significant to the economic plans of the PRA was the fact that balikbayans are both foreign *and* local. Balikbayans would become a primary target of the retirement industry for three major reasons: (1) Their familiarity with the Philippines meant that their expectations and standards for luxury would remain reasonable within the overall environment of the Philippines. (2) Most Filipinos believe that balikbayans have maintained a significant level of wealth while living and working abroad, and they are seen as possessing serious potential as investors. Aglipay himself had been quoted various times saying that the PRA was focused on Filipino baby boomers born after World War II mainly because they possessed "a great deal of income" (quoted in Apelacio 2007). (3) Finally, balikbayans already desire to return to the Philippines and, according to many developers, only need to be convinced that returning is the right decision. In an interview, Manuel Agripe, an executive with Belle developers, said, "They only really need to be nudged. [What] Filipino would choose to not return if you [gave] them a good reason?"

In December 2003 the Filipino American firm Philippines Real Estate Center (PREC), based in Washington, D.C., was engaged to head the marketing and promotion of the Subic Holiday Villas specifically to Filipinos living in the United States: "'Subic Holiday is targeting retired Fil-Ams as potential clients and we only need 1% of [the] over 2.8 million Fil-Am population for them to be part of this project. It is just our way of saying that Subic Freeport is a good place to welcome balikbayans and continue the quality of life [here that] they are enjoying in the U.S.,' suggested PREC Chairman Michael Gaviola" (*BusinessWorld* 2003b). As at Clark Air Base, government agencies felt that the property around the former military base in Subic Bay was poorly utilized. When the Subic Holiday Villas opened in 2006, retirees were provided with exclusive amenities including schools and recreational opportunities like scuba diving, hiking, and jet skiing through their investments in the Subic Bay Freeport Zone. Residing in the special economic zone also entitled them to utilize the Subic Bay Medical Center, where their health care would be subsidized by a number of prominent American HMOs such as Tricare, Veterans Standards, and Blue Cross Blue Shield.

The primary condition for membership in the Subic Bay Freeport Zone or any other demarcated zone exclusive to retirees is the obtainment of a Special Resident Retiree's Visa (SRRV). The PRA is delegated the responsibility for issuing this special visa, which provides its holders with the privilege of staying in the Philippines permanently and a multiple-entry status. The privileges also include a one-time exemption from customs duties and taxes, as well as exemptions from taxes on pensions and annuities remitted to the Philippines. The SRRV also provides an assortment of tax-free incentives and benefits from a host of partnering establishments such as hotels, resorts, retirement facilities, and restaurants. According to the regulations, foreign nationals between the ages of thirty-five and fifty must deposit a minimum of US$75,000 with one of the PRA-affiliated banks. Those older than fifty are required to deposit a lesser amount, US$50,000. In addition, those who qualify for SRRVs are allowed to bring a spouse and up to two children, provided that they are under the age of twenty-one and single (PRA 2007).

Those who are able to maintain a stable income after retirement through their pensions, however, are required to invest a considerably lower amount. For those fifty years old and above, the deposit amount is then US$10,000, of which $3,000 is kept for funeral expenses, while the rest can be converted into a variety of retirement investments. The minimum pension requirement for a single individual is $800 per month; if one has a spouse, the amount increases to $1,000. According to the PRA, under the "brain gain" program, retired scientists and scholars can have their deposits waived as long as they are willing to teach within their areas of expertise (Daquiz 2006).

More recently, the SRRV was modified specifically to cater to former citizens of the Philippines or balikbayans. According to the stipulations passed in 2003, the Special Investor's Resident Visa allows balikbayans to deposit a minimal amount of just US$1,500. This visa also provides its holders with the privilege of owning up to five thousand square meters of real estate, whether residential, urban, or agricultural property. Along with this modification, the Philippine government encourages balikbayans to act as entrepreneurs through Republic Act No. 9178, or the Act to Promote the Establishment of Barangay Micro-business Enterprise. Balikbayans are also entitled during the duration of their visa to purchase $1,500 worth of goods from any of the government-regulated duty-free shops located around the Philippines.

Asked why the Philippine government instituted a stipulation for balikbayans specifically, J. Antonio Leviste, the PRA's chairperson in 2003, explained, "While working abroad, most of them have remitted money to their relatives at home, thus helping bolster our country's foreign exchange reserves. . . . It's the least we can do for our former compatriots, who are rightly dubbed the modern heroes of our country. . . . Balikbayans are also being enticed back to their country of origin because after earning hard-earned currency abroad, they deserve rest and leisure with some considerations from their countrymen who have benefited from their remittance of foreign currency" (quoted in *BusinessWorld* 2003a). Legislation authorizing the issuing of different visas was essential to facilitating investments by balikbayans in the Philippine economy. However, the duties that balikbayans are obligated to pay do not cease once they return to the Philippines. Instead, many balikbayans are torn about deciding how much they are really willing to invest in the future of their homeland.

"Paying Your Dues": Retirement Associations and Financial Mismanagement

Between 2006 and 2015, PRA and PRI executives had optimistically expected that the cumulative earnings of the 859,250 retirees who were guaranteed to settle in the Philippines alone would amount to US$44 billion (PRA 2007, 9). This was a lofty expectation given that up until 2006, government-sponsored programs maintained by the PRA had been able to entice only about twelve thousand individuals to retire in the Philippines since the agency's establishment in 1985 (Gulane 2006). Yet, since 2006, the number of SRRVs issued to foreign nationals and former Filipino citizens has been steadily increasing. This positive trend has inspired agency executives to continue aggressively targeting retirement communities, particularly those in Asia and Filipinos living in the United States, publishing pamphlets and sending representatives to organize retirement fairs to elicit even more interest. Given the long history of political corruption and graft in the Philippines, concerns have continually arisen regarding the management of retiree investment funds.

For balikbayans, however, the concerns over financial mismanagement are grave, particularly among those who are convinced that corruption is unavoidable in the Philippines.[1] Tensions first came to a head in 1995, when investigative reports discovered that the PRA had lost ₱45.9 million in investment funds. In danger of having his administration mired in controversy so early in his tenure, Fidel Ramos refused to allow the PRA to be dissolved and chose arbitration instead. President Ramos chose Ramon M. Collado as the attorney who would lead the arbitration process and save the PRA from certain demise. Political accountability had long been an issue of concern for people interested in investing in the Philippines.

While I interviewed Gary Lazaro about the PRA, he glibly suggested that he had become an investor in the PRA when most of the SRRV recipients were "European diplomats, Japanese corporate execs, or American retired servicemen," and not balikbayan retirees like him, who have been increasing in number since the mid-2000s. Retiring in the Philippines in 1990, the sixty-nine-year-old golf aficionado had persevered to become a top-level executive at Metlife during the 1970s and 1980s. He decided to leave his plush position at Metlife when a unique opportunity emerged to work alongside his longtime friend Manuel Pangilinan, the chairman of the Philippine Long Distance Telephone Company (PLDT) and once a fellow student at Wharton Business School, which both had graduated from in 1969.

Year	No. of enrollees
2012	2,234
2011	1,615
2010	1,428
2009	2,886
2008	2,396
2007	2,600
2006	1,271
2005	1,259
2004	818
2003	732
2002	593
2001	352
2000	131

Source: Philippine Retirement Authority, *BusinessWorld*.

Gary could easily be spotted perfecting his golf game at the Alabang Country Club, just a few blocks away from his home in the Ayala Alabang Village. Now retired, he frequented the popular club in Muntinlupa four times a week and was happy to respond to any of my questions, provided I was open to spending an evening with him on the golf course. Tapping shreds of grass off the bottom of his shoe against the shiny metallic shaft of his nine iron, "Boboy," as his friends called him, expressed his views on Philippine politics with a healthy mixture of humor and disappointment: "Corruption is in the blood here. It's not like in the United States, where there are checks and balances. Don't get me wrong; there's plenty of [corruption] in the United States. But at least over there, they try to hide it." Through the lit cigarette that he tried to keep from dropping out of his mouth as he talked, Gary murmured:

> You asked me if I would still [have] come here if not for Manuel offering me the job with PLDT. Maybe . . . but I also had a very good life in New York. My wife didn't come to live with me here until years after I first came back. Until 1998. And that was only because of the investment opportunities that came up. Otherwise, I would have just invested my money, you know, bought property in Makati or Palawan like all the other foreigners and returned to the United States after I

stopped working [at PLDT]. I would just manage my properties from the U.S. It's actually much easier to make money in investments in the U.S. [than in the Philippines]. But then we had bigger opportunities to make investments. I decided to retire in Muntinlupa. But I was still very cautious about putting my money with the PRA. You know, they can be very tricky. They tell people that with the visa you can withdraw your deposit at any time. But it wasn't true. You have to know who to talk to. Just like everything here. You always have to know who to talk to. But what if you don't know who to talk to? You're going to lose a lot of money.

Collado's original recommendation to the Philippine government is reflected within Gary's comments. Investors, both foreign and balikbayan, desired more control over their investments. Collado was convinced that the main priority was to garner government support for the creation of an association composed of both foreign and balikbayan retirees that would be responsible for holding the PRA accountable. Through Collado's successful mediation, the Philippine Retirement Authority Members Association Foundation Inc. (henceforth referred to as PRAMA) was established. According to published reports, PRAMA was instituted to

> advocate for the rights of the elderly people in the Philippines. It conducts forum[s], workshop[s], and seminars on Ageing with the collaboration of other non-government organizations and individuals. It aims to develop the Retirement Industry in the country and help consolidate services such as healthcare, geriatric clinics, activity centers, leisure clubs, training center[s] for caregivers and social workers, memorial assistance, and others for the benefit of the elderly people. PRAMA participates in meetings internationally and locally to gather new information on situations and best practices concerning the elderly people. It also occasionally supports activities for the elderly people through grants. (PRA 2009)

In less then ten years, PRAMA enrolled 6,189 foreign retirees, including doctors, engineers, lawyers, management experts, bankers, financial analysts, and businesspeople, among other professions, from fifty-three different countries. Apart from its misleading use of the phrase "elderly people," notably absent from the organization's mission statement is any type of specificity regarding the exact role that PRAMA would eventually play in partnering with state and private entities in developing the retirement industry or the precise manner in which it would "consolidate services." Most important, the statement is silent about its foremost role as a nongovernmental organization responsible for holding the PRA and its partner agencies accountable to retirees for the use of retiree money. The precise motivations that help to explain these strategic absences are illustrative for understanding the apparatuses through which a myriad of governmental and private organizations collude in utilizing tourism as means of economic development and individual profiteering.

Collado also recognized that the PRA continued to lose money because retiree deposits were being dispersed among twenty-three different banks. To gain a more competitive interest rate, the attorney convinced the PRA to concentrate the deposits in only four banks. The value of SRRV deposits immediately increased after the interest rates were modified. After operating losses of ₱45.9 million had been incurred in 1992, the total net income gained by retiree deposits amounted to ₱45.6 million by 1996, owing to Collado's efforts. Previously, retirees had been losing as much as ₱25,000 per day, and about ₱18 million per year, in interest income alone (Cruz 2002). In recognition of PRAMA's successful interventions, the remaining four banks offered PRAMA a 1 percent management fee, which PRAMA decided to share with the PRA.

The PRA and PRAMA officially signed a memorandum of agreement in May 1999, with both parties agreeing to "ensure the effective and efficient promotion and implementation of the Philippine Retirement Program administered by the PRA" (quoted in *BusinessWorld* 1999). The agreement had also set in motion a number of plans to develop business partnerships between investors and local enterprises through small and medium-sized projects backed by the PRA and the Board of Investments. Already early in the establishment of PRAMA, the lines between state, private, and individual investors became muddled, and several of PRAMA's early financial investments had already become convergent with the very entities they were supposed to keep accountable. Such is the history of the Philippine political economy, where, like the development of skyscrapers and condominiums throughout Manila's built landscape, the development of the retirement industry was possible only through the shared interests of political elites and private developers. Again and again, the checks and balances instituted to protect private individuals against government fraud have been all but eliminated.

By 2002 the PRA had accumulated $200 million, of which $60 million had been earned by the association. Yet not all members were satisfied with PRAMA's leadership. It had become the only government-recognized association representing the interests of foreign and former Filipino citizen retirees. In May 2001 a group of retirees, discontented about several leadership issues, split from the association, formed a group called the Concerned Philippine Retirees Group, and formally filed a case against PRAMA. Group members expressed grievances over Collado's apparent authoritarian leadership and his exclusion of a number of association members from voting, which led to his invalid reelection as president. Finally, the most serious of all the grievances was that ₱87 million of the membership funds could not be accounted for by the association's treasury. While the splinter faction could not resolve the financial crisis of the lost investment funds, investors were relieved that membership in PRAMA would no longer be mandatory (General 2002).

While mandatory association memberships are common in the United States, particularly with property ownership, the formation of proprietary associations in the Philippines had its advent with the liberal economic movement that emerged in the country during the 1990s. Given the number of complaints against the association, including this most recent one, several retirees have expressed a clear disinclination to join PRAMA. Gary complained, "I never believed that membership should be mandatory. Especially when you look at both [PRAMA and PRA]. They're the same. You can't tell one from the other." While PRAMA does advocate for various measures, including improvements in health care, for instance, Gary went on to express his annoyance with the association: "Really, their one and only real job is to make sure that the funds that retirees invest into the PRA [aren't] mishandled. They're supposed to make sure that our money isn't stolen. To make sure that when retirees need the money, they can get it. But when you can't even get your money from PRAMA, well, what good are they? What's the difference between them and the government?" When one examines the business dealings of PRAMA one begins to see that there is some truth behind Gary's concerns. The *Manila Standard* reported as far back as 1998 that the PRAMA was using retirement funds to construct retirement villages in Batangas, which executives wanted to call the Golden Village. While retirees were already dissatisfied with their investments, plans were being made to build the retirement village on a 120-hectare property; it would include a number of sports facilities, several medical and dental centers, a market and a shopping arcade, a school, and a church.

The PRAMA and the PRA in particular commonly used the term *world-class* to describe the services and amenities offered within the Golden Village retirement project. According to the organization's representatives, the village would be a "world-class self-contained resort and residential community that offers health services, affordable and convenient housing, active lifestyle amenities such as a marina, a golf course and swimming pools and even a business and commercial center, and investment opportunities to retirees with a monthly pension of $1,200 to $2,000 (in U.S. currency)" (Macabenta 1998). *World-class*, a term constantly repeated throughout retirement brochures and advertisements, denotes the clear attempts that the Philippine retirement industry is making to attract overseas investments and to allay balikbayan paranoia by creating a distinction between retirement villages and the immediate environment surrounding them. There was no difference between the Golden Village and any of the projects planned by the PRA except that PRAMA would call this one its own. Meanwhile, court proceedings continue between PRA and PRAMA; the PRA is accused of preventing PRAMA from withdrawing investment funds and of "elbowing PRAMA out of the interest generated from retirees' funds" at the same time (Locsin 2002).

"There's something to be said for politicians acting like they're good people. Here, politicians act with impunity. How do you trust people like that? How do you do business with someone like that? How can you entrust thousands, hundreds of thousands of dollars of your hard-earned money with people like that?" Barry Fuentes, another balikbayan retiree, asked me in a rhetorical tone. "You know when you meet with your agent at the PRA, they act like it's an honor to have [balikbayans] invest their money with them. But after a while, you understand it's just another way to get more money out of us. You think it's all expenses paid for, like an all-inclusive vacation, like a cruise. That's how they sell it to you at those conventions. But when you're finally here, it's one thing after another. . . . You wonder, where's all this money going?" Regardless of their displeasure with PRAMA and the myriad of problems that persist within the retirement industry, both Barry and Gary enjoy living in Ayala Alabang Village, a quasi–retirement village on the outskirts of Metro Manila in Muntinlupa. In the end, both consider the duties they pay a "necessary evil" for assuring the ease of lifestyle in the Philippines. While one might measure the effects of balikbayan paranoia by observing how its ideology affected the patterning of Metro Manila's dissonant landscape and the fragmented built environment, with its patchwork of developments, the clearest example of the ways in which the Philippine state exploits balikbayan paranoia is in the construction of its retirement landscapes.

Conclusion » Retirement Landscapes
and the Geography of Exception

Recognized by now as a pivotal actor within the country's development
policies, the Department of Tourism has in recent years begun working
closely with land developers and real estate corporations to facilitate and
channel the financial capital of balikbayans back into the Philippines. By
linking the interests of state agencies with those of private investors, the
Philippine government is inventing new ways to persuade balikbayans to
continue being patrons of the state; it seeks to draw overseas Filipinos not
only to visit their homeland but also to invest in property and retire in the
Philippines.

The accumulation of these investments has financed the construction
of retirement villages: massive property developments that are viewed by
many as the future of the Philippines' tourism economy. This chapter discusses the process through which the tourism industry has conjoined itself
with the retirement and health care industries to provide balikbayans with a
solution to their incessant anxiety around returning and settling back home
in the Philippines. Retirement villages therefore represent the contemporary amalgamation of these diverse intersections. Adopting Aihwa Ong's
(2006) concept of "neoliberalism as exception," I describe how these special

economic zones operate outside of the norms of local governance through the legal privileges they are afforded in order to provide their guests with an abundance of unique luxuries.

The structure of retirement landscapes in the Philippines complicates the conceptions of extraterritoriality implicit within zones of exception. Although retirement villages are administrated by the intersecting interests of a number of multinational corporations, with many of them owned by Korean or Japanese investors, the retirement landscape in the Philippines, particularly the retirement villages themselves, continues to be highly regulated by Philippine government policies and the state's own liberal economic objectives. In this way, retirement landscapes represent the manner in which the Philippine government continues to maintain control while catering to flows of competing foreign investments.

Once investors and developers believed they had developed a successful model of retirement villages that would finally convince balikbayans to retire in the Philippines, all that was left was for the Philippine Retirement Authority (PRA) and developers to lobby the Philippine government to institute measures that would further facilitate the settlement of balikbayans in retirement settings. These measures had the effect of granting village owners, operators, and retirees a number of special rights from which local Filipinos were precluded, including those who worked at the retirement facilities. Yet, while the facilities continue to be owned and managed by Japanese or Korean corporations, their services are not limited to a Japanese or Korean clientele. The benefits bestowed on the Philippine government by partly catering to balikbayans keep the government from being inextricably linked with the interests of foreign investors.

Chinese Extraterritoriality

During a lecture for the Free University in Amsterdam, while presenting narratives on China's ever-expanding economic network of overseas labor contracts and use of foreign concessions throughout Southeast Asia and Africa, Lyttleton and Nyíri (2007) noted intriguing observations they recorded while visiting the Golden Boten City, a retirement village adjacent to the border in northern Laos. Opened in early 2008, the Golden Boten City, the "most internationalized modern city in Laos," was financed and developed by the Chinese investment company Fu-Khing; it is situated on four thousand acres of leased land located in one of China's numerous designated Special Economic Zones (SEZs). The retirement village's facilities, which include common retirement amenities such as a shopping district, condominiums, and a golf course, are designed to highlight the hotel-casino complex that lies at the center of the village. More intriguing to Lyttleton and Nyíri, however, was that apart from the sparse number of Thai and Laotian tourists scattered around the village landscape, the vast majority of the complex's staff, from the store merchants to its militarized security, were Chinese contracted labor.

One can imagine the look of surprise on the anthropologists' faces as they were asked to pay with Chinese yuan rather than the inflated Laotian kip. It would seem from Lyttleton and Nyíri's descriptions that even the minutest details of the village bespoke the presence of Chinese governance, including the village's electric sockets, which conducted electricity supplied by Chinese companies. The entire retirement village and the SEZ it is located in have become characteristic features of China's political and economic practice of extraterritoriality.[1] Littleton and Nyiri's experiences in Laos are pertinent to discussing the intermingling of economic interests emerging among economically demarcated regions in Asia clearly. The intertwining of these interests is apparent throughout the production of economic zones in the Philippines' retirement landscapes. Yet, in comparison to Chinese retirement zones such as the Golden Boten City, the particular element distinguishing retirement zones and their outlying communities in the Philippines is the heterogeneity of their residents and the national interests these various communities represent. As migrants who have been specially designated by the Philippine government as privileged citizens, these retirees are afforded a set of rights different from those held by the local Filipino population. Subsequently, the distinct privileges enjoyed by balikbayans and foreign residents have constituted retirement villages and their surroundings into a contested hybrid zone of exceptionalities.

Before I discuss the emergence of retirement landscapes, their designation as SEZs by the Philippine government, and the evidence that these broadening forms of Philippine governmentality point toward a quick policy shift away from U.S.-centric economic dependency, it is worthwhile to juxtapose these contemporary developments with larger discussions around governmentality and economic zones. Much has been written about the contemporary emergence and use of economic zones as zones of political exception and variegated sovereignty throughout regional spaces like East Asia, the Caribbean, and West Africa.[2]

Ong (2006) discusses, for instance, how various Chinese corporations and individuals, within these particular zones of exception, procure a set of exceptional rights owing to their role in producing capital for both the local government and their home government in China. Through complex multilateral agreements among nation-state governments, these individuals and corporations operate with legal immunities owing to their role in aiding capital accumulation for various countries. Ong argues that the lack of accountability that Chinese individuals had within the local legal system, along with their economic privileges such as exemptions from taxes and duties on trade goods, represents a new form of state control practiced by the Chinese government. As Lyttleton and Nyíri's experience in Laos poignantly demonstrates, conversations around these types of extraterritorialized spaces have enormous weight not only for conceptions of citizenship and nation-state sovereignty but also for the creative measures governments take to draw capital into sectors of their economy that would otherwise be unsustainable and to maintain control of the profits accrued by these economic sectors.

Hybrid Zones of Exceptionality in Tagaytay

Relying on Ong's theory of "postdevelopment," Robyn Rodriguez (2010) argues that by contracting Filipinos to work throughout a number of SEZs, particularly through the trading network of the Association of Southeast Asian Nations (ASEAN) states, the Philippine state agrees to relinquish a portion of its sovereignty to corporate entities. At the same time, local elites are allowed to maintain their economic sovereignty owing to their entrenched positions within the long-standing land tenure system and their monopolization of capital holdings. According to Rodriguez, exporting Filipino labor abroad facilitates a number of state interests: "Migration absorbs the excess of laborers that is necessarily produced when the state abandons its sovereignty to multinationals' and multilaterals' demands for export-production; migration is also a 'biopolitical investment' providing employment and income to citizens and thereby preserving the political and economic status of the elite" (16).

In many cases, commitments by Chinese officials and corporate executives to commence building projects in different countries in Africa have entitled the Chinese to all manner of future economic privileges in these countries (Lee 2009). In the case of the Golden Boten City, entrepreneurial partnerships between Laos and China have the effect of strengthening an already sturdy linkage between the two countries. In the Philippines, however, unlike the Golden Boten City, which had become a tourism configuration attracting primarily Laotian, Thai, and mostly Chinese visitors, these retirement zones were produced in such a way that they catered to an array of visitors. The Department of Tourism and the PRA projected that retirees would not only consist of balikbayans or other Americans but also include elderly populations coming from China, Japan, and especially Korea.

Retirement villages rely on the confluence of economic agendas between the tourism, retirement, and medical industries to produce highly competitive touristic environments, which the Philippine government hopes will attract the elderly populations of a number of developed countries and eventually make the Philippines a global retirement haven. As of 2009, of the 207 fully operating SEZs in the Philippines, 11 are specifically demarcated as Tourism Economic Zones (TEZs) or medical tourism centers. While most are concentrated around the periphery of the National Capital Region, retirement landscapes exist in northern Luzon, the Visayas, and Cebu in particular, and in the vacation resorts around the Palawan Islands. Other TEZs are being developed around the provinces of Camarines Sur, and two are being developed in Cavite. Furthermore, plans to continue demarcating SEZs and creating TEZs in places like Davao in Mindanao have become more crucial as means of buttressing economic relations with emerging economies in the Southeast Asian network (Ness 2003, 110–11). The political-economic use of TEZs becomes even more apparent in discussions around developing zones in Mindanao, through which administrators hope to quell terrorist threats (Ness 2005).

At the same time, in order to achieve these goals, the Philippine government is carefully balancing the investments of various foreign groups. While the retirement industry is aggressively targeting former Filipino citizens, especially those in the United States, it is going to similar lengths to cater to foreign investors, particularly those in other Asian countries. For instance, in Tagaytay, Koreans have established several restaurants and an international school designed specifically for English language instruction.[3] Adding to this trend, in February 2001 the Korea-Philippines Friendship Hospital was established just outside of Tagaytay in the major metropolitan city of Cavite. The hospital was largely funded by members of the Korean Investors Association Cavite, a group of Korean businesspeople who have

FIGURE C.1 Filipiniana gated community, a development under construction in Tagaytay, 2009. Photo by author.

benefited from tax incentives created by the CALABARZON (Cavite, Laguna, Batangas, Rizal, and Quezon) economic zone (Kelly 2000).[4]

This growing community of Korean immigrants has largely benefited from special accommodations like the Special Resident Retiree's Visa, study permits, and tax incentives that help to motivate entrepreneurial growth. The rise of Korean investments throughout the region has been received with mixed reviews from local Filipino communities. At the same time, Tagaytay is quickly becoming home to a growing number of balikbayans, who are benefiting from the same incentives and are also building homes or settling in the vibrant retirement communities within Tagaytay. This mixture of local Filipinos, balikbayans, and Koreans is producing an unwieldy geometry of shifting economies. In towns like Tagaytay throughout the Philippines, government initiatives emphasizing foreign investments are creating an environment where the needs of immigrant communities, which include balikbayans, are taking precedence over those of the local Filipino community. A murmur of discontent continues to be expressed among a portion of the local Filipino business owners and workers beneath the surface of the communalism and celebratory overtones expressed by state administrators within the media circuit.

Local Filipinos are resentful toward this incoming group of immigrants in part because of the various exceptions immigrants receive when retiring in the Philippines. One of the privileges included in retirement zones are government incentives that support retirees who do *not* want to retire. Marisol Estrella Calagñan Dalley, a recent "retiree" residing at the Tagaytay Lakeview Estates, adamantly believes that almost all balikbayan retirees are inclined toward not retiring. Marisol explained, her words blurted out in between bouts of laughter:

> At first it seems like a good idea. But if you have spent many years abroad, you'll go crazy if you don't work here. You have to find things that will keep you busy. I thought, well, it would be nice to have a change of pace. I've been working all my life . . . for almost five decades! I came here, and we bought a retirement package here in Tagaytay. I started to get a little crazy, and then I told my husband that I wanted to go back to work. Then he said, "I thought you want[ed] to relax, why did we end up coming back to the Philippines?" I told him, "Well, what do you expect, I've been working all of my life." I'm an independent woman! I can't just sit around the house and make food for my husband.

Marisol was fortunate that her husband had cashed in his investments before the recent stock market crash. Having worked primarily as a caregiver, Marisol had made her way along the outskirts of Rome and London at a young age before finally settling in South San Francisco, where she met her husband, George. Her husband, a native of Utah with roots that go back several decades there, had never set foot outside of the United States until he married Marisol, and only then to visit his in-laws in the Philippines. George never imagined that he would retire in his wife's home country. However, because of Marisol's multinational employment history and inability to find full-time work throughout her years in the United States, her income did not result in enough Social Security to sufficiently supplement George's income. Once Marisol and George were introduced to the idea of retiring in the Philippines, they began carefully planning their future investments in the Tagaytay Lakeview Estates. "Our children were settled, they were married, and even had kids. So they were happy to come and see us once a year. Times are tough [financially], but at least one of our children gets to come during Christmas time," George said while looking compassionately at Marisol. "That's the hardest thing for us, but especially for Mari."

However, the couple refused to stay retired for very long. Benefiting from a lenient bank financing program, the Dalleys used money that George accrued from investments he had acquired through company stock options and opened an Italian restaurant on one of the major boulevards, with a picturesque view of Mount Taal. Decorated with tiny white Christmas lights, the French paneled window looked in on a charming restaurant that seated at most thirty or so customers inside. "It's not practical because when Filipinos come to eat, they bring everyone with them. But it's okay for now because we don't get a lot of customers. Mainly foreigners and [balikbayans]," George said as he prepared a steaming cup of espresso. "That's the only decent cup of espresso that you'll find for miles," he exclaimed while laughing loudly.

Fortunately for Marisol (and George), balikbayans who are looking to invest in a small business are encouraged by recent measures passed in 2002 by the Philippine Congress. According to Republic Act No. 9178, or the Barangay Micro Business Enterprises Act published on the PNB's official website, the Philippine government "promotes the establishment of barangay micro business enterprises (BMBES)" by integrating businesses that typically operated within the informal economy into the mainstream economy. Small businesses like the Dalleys' restaurant are loaned between ₱100,000 to ₱500,000 by designated banks to keep their establishments afloat. While the law is focused on rejuvenating businesses in agriculture and aquaculture, wood and handicrafts, information technology and biotechnology, health care, and education and training sectors, George was careful to mention that the banks had afforded Marisol and him some leeway because they were "retirees." While the assistance provided by the government through the act might appear minor, it made an extraordinary amount of difference to the Dalleys.

It meant that Marisol and George would not have to chance losing a portion of their savings to start the business. Borrowing money from Marisol's impoverished siblings in Cebu was unconceivable. As a balikbayan who was also married to a white American, it would have been a tremendous humiliation for her and loss of face to ask for money from family members in the Philippines when her status as an American citizen meant that she was the one who should act as a patron for her family in the Philippines. Instead, Marisol and George received a loan from a Philippine bank, and Marisol could continue sending money to her relatives even though she and George no longer lived in the United States and as such had no obligation to remit any more money. With less than US$2,000, the minimal amount offered through the microbusiness initiative, one can easily pay a local mall operator and any start-up dues to open a DVD stand or a number of other small operations. That amount of money also far exceeds the annual salary of most Filipinos, including those who operate in small businesses. Yet accommodations like these are more easily accessible to balikbayans and foreign retirees who had officially intended to come to the Philippines to become retirees. Retirement in the Philippine context, however, is a legal status, and not one that precludes individuals from significant employment as it is in the United States.

On a much larger scale, retirement villages are afforded a tremendous amount of leeway by financing institutions and the Philippine government. The SEZs operate in such a way that public entities sometimes operate unofficially as private entities; likewise, private entities often work closely with public ones, making them quasi-private entities. This blurring between sectors lends itself to the tourism and retirement industries, which often depend on the shared interests of both sectors in order to build developments, attract various types of businesses, and function properly. Once the emergent popularity of retirement villages became increasingly recognized by the Philippine government as a means of increasing economic development, Aglipay was quick to lobby the government to include retirement villages within the jurisdiction of the Philippine Economic Zone Authority (PEZA), the government agency responsible for determining and overseeing the incorporation of foreign investments under the Special Economic Zone Act (Ng 2006).[5]

According to its website, PEZA is a government agency that has the responsibility to promote "investments, extend assistance, register, grant incentives to and facilitate the business operations of investors in export-oriented manufacturing and service facilities inside selected areas throughout the country proclaimed by the President of the Philippines as PEZA Special Economic Zones" (Philippine Economic Zone Authority 2010). Projects approved to be exempted from taxation through the SEZ include petrochemical distribution, transport oil depots, health care services, refining of palm oil, information technology facilities, processing of abaca pulp, aircraft maintenance for foreign airlines, and, soon, retirement villages.

Once retirement villages were either included within the provision of economic zones or constituted themselves as a SEZ, they garnered various privileges, including generous tax breaks and the luxury of importing equipment and resources from other countries duty-free. Edgar Habalo, a realtor with Landenmore Properties, a real estate corporation that specializes in selling properties throughout the CALABARZON growth corridor (which includes Tagaytay), explained that these duty-free incentives were critical to the success of retirement villages:

> I'm sure that Fil-Ams enjoy bathing with Neutrogena products and having other specialty items available to them. Right? Well, all of those things aren't available in the Philippines. We have to have them imported, and just having them come through customs is very expensive, let alone just shipping them here. Everything that you enjoy, from the coffees to the detergent. The retirement villas are very aware that foreigners want quality items. And that means items that are from back home in America or Europe. From the United States or from Italy. Not the Philippines. That's the only way that you can entice people to retire here is if they can get all the best things from home here.

Indeed, Edgar's insights were valid on a number of levels. When the PRA attempted to emphasize homestays, a feature of tourism where travelers could stay at the homes of local residents and enjoy eating and interacting with locals rather than being secluded in vacation resorts, the government agency's innovation was short-lived. The PRA quickly realized that the resources and conveniences requested by tourists from their hosts were too costly (*BusinessWorld* 2005). Soon Filipino households were spending two to three times the amount of money they had made in housing a single tourist. Edgar commented, "I know from living in the U.S. for many years that one of the worst things about the Philippines is to need to use the bathroom but there [are] no sanitary napkins. You know, no toilet paper. Am I right? Well, tourist[s] appreciate that in all of our bathrooms we have nice, soft toilet paper. But where do you think we get all of [that] nice fluffy toilet paper? We import it from Hong Kong." As Edgar posed his rhetorical question, he rubbed his thumb against the tips of two fingers as if to say, "Money, it takes lots of money."

It would seem that the entire retirement industry rested uneasily on the truth of Edgar's words. The DOT and PRA have spent a great deal of energy convincing the president, members of Congress, and corporate executives that an extraordinary financial commitment is necessary to entice foreigners, and particularly balikbayans, to retire in the Philippines. The overwhelming confidence and belief exuded by individuals like Aglipay repeatedly appeared in newspapers and speeches. While he, like the rest of his colleagues who cheered on the formation of the retirement industry, continued to convince potential investors that the "good nature of Filipinos" was enough to make foreign nationals and balikbayans feel comfortable retiring in the Philippines, the DOT and PRA continued to fervently push for more investments from the private sector.

By including retirement villages within the list of protected SEZs, the Philippine government is gambling on the enclaves attracting various forms of foreign investment. Once PEZA was established, various touristic enterprises began applying to be categorized as SEZs and included within its umbrella of privileges. The agency's website provides downloadable application forms for various businesses. Business owners need only download an application and fill it out. The deliberation process is long, and inclusion fees are expensive. Yet the apparent accessibility of the agency's website represents the exuberance with which government agencies are receiving the growth of the leisure industry. It also mirrors the overextension of public commitments in Ferdinand Marcos's early tourism projects, which underestimated the daunting costs of building at such an accelerated pace. On the one hand, PRA lobbyists are trying desperately to reduce the cost of initial fees for retiree visas, while, on the other hand, the PRA is trying to reduce the operating costs of retirement villages. Given the history of the Philippine political economy, the final costs will more than likely be placed on the shoulders of the beleaguered Filipino taxpayers.

A recent, yet critical, inclusion into the expanding leisure economy is the emergence of the Philippine Medical Tourism Program and special medical zones. Statistics and research conveying both the enormous expenses incurred for medical care in the United States, and the potential that Americans would be willing to be treated by physicians in the Philippines owing to lower costs, has meant that members of the Philippine government have pushed Congress to open the doors to medical tourism. Eager to offer much-needed quality medical services to foreign and balikbayan retirees, the PRA took this opportunity to merge the Philippine Medical Tourism Program with the retirement village industry. Quoting a study conducted by the Deloitte Center for Health Solutions titled "2008 Survey of Health Care Consumers," agency executives from the Department of Tourism ecstatically presented news that about 750,000 U.S. citizens had traveled abroad to get medical care. Furthermore, the report suggested that this number would increase to six million by 2010 (*BusinessWorld* 2008).

Banking on the report's further conclusion that at least two out of five Americans would be willing to travel abroad for health care, agency executives commenced plans to open state-of-the-art hospitals in retirement villages. Various executives in the PRA lobbied for congressional support by citing evidence that by opening hospitals in the Philippines, the government could finally solve the problem of brain drain in which many skilled Filipinos were forced to work abroad because they could not find work in the Philippines. While discussing the prevalence of Japanese citizens retiring in Southeast Asia, Mika Toyota (2006, 521) explains how as part of the provisions of free trade agreements between Japan and the Philippines in 2006, Japanese sought the services of health care workers and nurses to help provide care to the exponentially growing aging population in Japan. These initiatives had the effect of allowing a limited number of highly qualified Filipinos to enter Japan, beginning with four hundred Filipino nurses and six hundred qualified caregivers starting in 2006.

In 2009, pushed by the crisis of the growing number of elderly people in Japan, Japanese corporations developed plans to open health facilities that would facilitate the movement of the Japanese elderly outside of Japan and to places like the Philippines. For example, the Japanese firm Tokushukai Medical Corporation agreed to invest $100 million in the establishment of a 150-acre health care zone to be placed on reclaimed land. Yet while the hospital is to be named the Benigno Aquino Memorial Hospital, concerns grew when the corporation stipulated that the health care facility would employ only Japanese health care staff and serve a primarily Japanese clientele (Flores 2005).

More than tourists from Japan, visitors from South Korea have in recent years made up the majority of tourism flows to the Philippines, exceeding the number of visitors from the United States, including returning Overseas Filipino Workers. By 2006, over 570,000 South Koreans had visited the

Philippines, and, according to government figures, up to 100,000 South Koreans have settled in the country as permanent residents. Local Filipinos have received this infusion of foreigners with ambivalence. While tourism and immigration by South Koreans, who usually come to the Philippines as part of the increasingly popular English-learning programs, as Christian missionaries, or as aspiring small business owners, are contributing almost half of the financial investments in the Philippine economy (accounting for US$1.2 billion of the $3.5 billion in investment capital that entered the Philippines in 2006), some Filipinos have become unsettled by their growing presence (Damazo 2007). A litany of news reports and editorials have latched onto a range of events, from legal incidents to anecdotal evidence, involving local business owners and residents who are increasingly resentful of South Korean business operators for alleged improper conduct and discrimination toward Filipinos, as well as of tourists who are said to treat local Filipinos badly.[6]

One particularly well-known and reactionary editorialist, Butch del Castillo (2009a, 2009b), wrote a two-part commentary on the "invasion" by tourists and migrants from South Korea. The former president of the widely circulated *Manila Bulletin* suggested that the presence of Koreans is reminiscent of the archipelago's occupation by Japanese soldiers during World War II and that the Koreans are setting up "beachfronts" in the Philippines in order to exploit the country through a number of shady resource extraction projects. Slightly puzzled by the xenophobia ensconced within this analogy, Norman Castro, a Fil-Invest real estate agent, openly welcomed the influx of South Koreans to the Philippines. I first met Norman when he approached me at Shangri-la Plaza, one of the more upscale malls in Mandaluyong and a destination most frequented by foreign tourists, including South Koreans, who opportunistically scour the mall hoping to spot deals on clothes from Hugo Boss or shoes from Salvatore Ferragamo.

Fully aware of the negative sentiment that many Filipinos harbor toward South Koreans, Norman had sympathy for the feelings of his compatriots, but it was clearly measured by a sense of defiant optimism, unlike for del Castillo. Norman commented:

> I think [Filipinos] might be tired of everyone benefiting from our resources. Maybe it's like when a guest overstays their welcome. Then they stay for a few days longer, then the days become months. *Na parang nagiging free loaders na lang sila* [they have become freeloaders

already]. I think some Filipinos think that way. *Iyon siguro ang dahilan kung bakit nagsasawa na sa kanila ang ibang Pino* [Maybe that's why Filipinos have become fed up with them]. *Kasi parang iniisahan tayo ng mga koreano* [because the Koreans are taking advantage of us], so it's like the Filipinos think that they're just ending up getting the short end of the stick, *diba*?

At the same time, Norman appreciated the South Korean clientele, who were more likely than his compatriots to purchase the more lavish units that he and his coworkers offered. His ambivalence represents in many ways the divergent interests of the Philippine state, which is aggressively marketing the Philippines to investors in South Korea, and many among the local population, who find themselves excluded from the benefits of the changes created by these migrations and dismayed to see social inequity in their country remain largely the same.

Changes in demography are especially felt among Filipinos living in smaller provincial towns like Tagaytay. Here the influx of Korean students has opened opportunities for Filipinos to find work tutoring in English or even teaching the language at the Korean-run international school. In Talisay, a tourist area adjacent to Tagaytay City, South Korean–owned Jung Ang Interventure Corporation has made plans for a spa resort around the city's main tourist attraction, the Taal volcano, which has caused controversy among the local communities, who argue that the corporation is violating environmental restrictions.[7] While tensions over the developments by the leisure industry are directly related to ongoing conflicts over land tenure and the sustainability of local livelihoods, they are symptomatic of a much larger history of conflict resulting from foreign occupation. Having already dealt with the centuries-long stratification and oppression unleashed by Spanish and Chinese foreign elites, many Filipinos are wary about the increasing presence and economic interests of Koreans in Tagaytay.

On the other hand, while the purpose of tourism and retirement might be the same among South Koreans and balikbayans, the reception of balikbayans by Filipinos is markedly different. Filipinos often see balikbayans as returning compatriots who have a personal investment in developing the Philippine economy. And their permanent presence in the Philippines functions as evidence of their commitment to improving the country rather than exploiting its resources, in contrast to the Koreans, Japanese, and especially Chinese, who are depicted as taking advantage of Filipinos.[8] The complex and sometimes contradictory political rhetoric constituting balik-bayans as "heroes" has had a similar effect on the ways in which balikbay-ans perceive themselves.

"Why would they resent us? We're Filipino!" Janette Quinoveva, a balik-bayan who had built a vacation home in Tagaytay two years ago, exclaimed. Janette has traveled back and forth to the Philippines each year for the last decade. Like a number of balikbayans, she built a retirement home in Tagaytay, which she uses as a vacation home at least once a year. She told me glibly, "Of course they don't think of us like the Koreans because we're not Korean. Who can blame Filipinos for being angry with Koreans? They come here to the Philippines to learn English and are so, what you say, *kanya-kanya* [stick to themselves].[9] But I am coming home. I didn't grow up [in Tagaytay], but they still know me here."

As I helped Janette lift bag after bag of groceries out of her family's brand-new Toyota SUV and onto the driveway of her expansive property, I could not help but feel the irony of the moment. As she attempted to convince me that the Filipinos around her felt no different about her than they would about any of their other neighbors, simply because they were all born in the Philippines, her lack of awareness kept her from acknowledging the impoverished families whose shanty housing stood directly beside her property. This lack of recognition vividly illustrates the paradox of balik-bayan subjectivity and thus the strength of drawing balikbayans into the country as retirees. The material and financial wealth represented by having an SUV or an estate in Tagaytay alone does not prevent Janette and other balikbayans like her from being able to see themselves as one and the same as Filipinos in the Philippines. But in fact this wealth and the various visa privileges she enjoys together represent her ability to be a transnational subject, a balikbayan who can come back and leave as often she is finan-cially capable of doing so. This ability to return and to exit the Philippines alone produces the exceptional subjectivity that constitutes returning Fili-pinos as balikbayans.

It would appear paradoxical at first that one can be a tourist while simul-taneously being at home, and yet the homogenizing forces epitomized by the discourse around the retirement industry constitute balikbayans into just that. Through a number of measures and privileges, the retirement industry forcefully creates an imaginary, a retirement landscape, where balikbayans can experience a variety of exceptions unlike any of the Fili-pinos living or struggling around them. These discourses are in no way passive, inconspicuous, or hidden but are made blatantly clear as a way of countering the balikbayan paranoia that inhibits Filipinos from wanting to return to the Philippines. Yet it is only in relation to non-Filipinos and other Asians that balikbayans can really effectively become transnational Filipinos returning home.

After decades of fulfilling their duties by faithfully sending home remittances and continuing to invest financially in the Philippines, many balikbayans feel that they are entitled to experience the privileges that come with returning home. However, not every balikbayan can partake in all of the exceptionalities granted through the retirement industry, and the epilogue will describe the various choices balikbayans make principally because many of them cannot afford the costs entailed in being a member of the retirement industry in the Philippines. For most balikbayans, the minimum financial commitment is far more than they could afford, even as Filipinos who had labored in developed countries. The status afforded by adopting a life in a retirement village is only one type of urbanism for balikbayans.

Retirement villages do, however, represent the aggressive manner in which the Philippines continues to regulate migration and utilize tourism (through the retirement industry) as a major tool for economic development. For the Philippine state to successfully achieve this, it depends on the collusion of a number of governmental agencies to create and adopt innovative measures that perpetuate this paradox. As such, the identity of balikbayan can no longer be seen as one primarily accorded to oneself but instead as one that is also construed, codified, and, most important, economically enabled by the Philippine state itself. The retirement landscape has become the hyperrealization of yet another paradoxical unity: the simultaneity of being at once a tourist and a hometown hero.

Epilogue

It is not uncommon to hear Filipinos who have lived in the United States for several decades express an intense sense of ambivalence upon returning to the country where they spent their formative years. When one reads their superficial irritations more closely, one notices that these sentiments are actually interwoven in a complex cloth of emotions. The veil draped over Filipinos in the United States does not disappear when they return to the Philippines.

Deep feelings of regret, embarrassment, and anger tend to be shrouded by seemingly trivial concerns over traffic and dirtiness, clichés of bureaucratic corruption or threats of crime, and, of course, complaints about the oppressive tropical humidity. Never does the difference between the United States and the Philippines become more distinct than when balikbayans return home. Often and inevitably these bitter disappointments and intensely felt anxieties become displaced onto taxi drivers who drive too fast or not fast enough, extended family members who fail to arrive at the airport in a timely fashion, or cashiers and waiters who are too rude or seem eager to exploit balikbayans because of their privileged status. In fact, much of the literature written about Manila, by Filipinos, Filipino Americans, and non-Filipinos alike, is filled with dystopic allusions that heighten these tensions even before most balikbayans reenter their homeland.

For Filipinos who return to Manila, at times the superficial bespeaks the deeper force of a swelling sense of disillusionment. Inside one of the nicer *karinderias* (small restaurants) along Katipunan Avenue, Ezmeralda attempted to explain her first impressions of life back in Manila. A few meters outside the window by our table stood a weathered signboard much like those one would see at an old public high school anywhere in the United States. The letters read "Ateneo de Manila University" in faded blue block letters. Ateneo, as most Filipinos refer to it, has historically been the site where most of Manila's elite students were educated; it was where Ezmeralda had received her degree in business administration with an emphasis in accounting. This degree eventually became her "golden ticket" to the United States. And ever since she arrived in that country thirty-six years ago, she had longed to fulfill her dream of returning to the Philippines and starting a business somewhere in her hometown of Quezon City.

Her manner as proper as her dress, Ezmeralda attempted to hide her dissatisfaction with the environment surrounding us but to little avail. While she spoke, her body moved side to side ever so discreetly in her chair as if to avoid any dirt that might be lurking around the table. Back now for five months, she began speaking to me of her time in the Philippines as she diligently rubbed her metal utensils clean. The sound of disappointment was distinct in her voice. "You think that with all the money we send back to our families and put into this country, that it would be better. I don't know if it will ever get better here. I don't know if I can live here anymore." She had grown unaccustomed to the reality of her old world, and her youthful exuberance had dimmed.

Upon arriving in the Philippines, after picking up one's luggage and exiting Ninoy Aquino International Airport, one is immediately struck by a number of disconcerting images. An army of tour buses and jeepneys speed past, the blaring of their incessant honking breaching the glass of the taxi windows. Everywhere, lines of cars, taxis, buses, and motorcycles form into improvised lanes as they drive, creating driving rules as they go. Then there is the series of dilapidated homes and the shoddy structures of the businesses along the main streets of Parañaque, the town closest to the airport, which appear to be as poorly built as they were decades ago. Finally, there is the uncomfortably familiar encounter with the dirt-covered faces of children meandering in between moving cars, their hands held out for money in exchange for the *sampaguita* (jasmine flower) or chewing gum dangling from their palms. Altogether, these images alone force most balikbayans to sympathize with Ezmeralda's disappointment. Has anything changed in Manila at all? After all, balikbayans have been remitting their money and material goods back to the Philippines for over five decades. Where has all of this money gone?

Ferdinand Marcos had put in place the initial structure for the institutionalization of a balikbayan economy whereby Filipinos living abroad could more easily send money or material goods to the Philippines. Decades later, the rhetoric around balikbayans' obligation to their homeland, endlessly communicated through a throng of Philippine media transmitted through U.S. cable television and newspapers, has not diminished in the least. Now, confronted by these disconcerting images, many Filipinos feel perplexed: haven't their sacrifices changed the country for the better?

Much of the impetus for this project developed from a sliver of conversation between my parents that I happened to witness as an adolescent. The sudden death of my paternal grandfather meant that his family's properties were at risk of being repossessed by the local government since the majority of his children resided in the United States. However, a number of families had been living illegally on my grandfather's properties for several decades. Years later, I would discover that these families had raised their children there, and even some grandchildren were born on this land. It was not simply an issue of reclaiming properties but of further dispossessing the landless poor. Thus, it might be said that the "sacrifices" of balikbayans—material, financial, and emotional remittances that passed between family members and neighbors—were not only failing to make the country better but were, in fact, exacerbating the problems.

· · ·

FORMER PRESIDENT GLORIA MACAPAGAL-ARROYO exudes a deceptive aura of optimism over the future of the Philippines. A barrage of articles on the front pages of Manila's newspapers, along with televised public announcements, express a common rhetoric of economic stability and a confidence that might appear naive during a period of global economic crisis. Government agencies and the media point to various indicators, most notably surges in property and foreign business investments, as a means of sustaining a tone of hopefulness in the face of a growing national debt and global insecurity. This attitude was emblematized by the Millennium Development Goal, in which Macapagal-Arroyo projected that, by 2015, policies instituted by her administration would effectively reduce poverty in the Philippines by half. Of course, one of the central goals of such a tone is to restore and maintain the confidence of the lending institutions that have, over decades, tightened their hold on the political economy in the Philippines, particularly after Marcos's expenditures of state funds. Furthermore, a general improvement in incomes as well as an increase in consumer spending, evidenced by the continual building of mall and condominium enclaves, also helps to bolster the belief that Metro Manila and the Philippines as a whole are benefiting from immense economic growth.

Recent studies, however, convey a contrary and much bleaker economic profile. For instance, Arsenio Balisacan, a professor of economics at the University of the Philippines, claims that the Philippines experienced "modest economic growth in recent years but it did not prevent poverty from rising. Things have really gone worse in the last six to seven years" (quoted in Remo 2009). Balisacan's conclusion reveals another facet of economic globalization and increased market liberalization. Various scholars tend to believe that globalization, rather than producing economic equality, actually widens the distance between social classes. Economic policies focused on reorienting the Philippine economy in a more export-oriented direction have placed downward pressure on wages, continued to devastate the local environment, and further displaced poor communities.

As such, the negative impact of globalization and, subsequently, of the balikbayan economy of return migration it produces is disproportionately felt by the urban poor. The general tone of optimism based on economic indicators of growing incomes and increased spending is deceiving. Regardless how fervently politicians, corporate executives, and economists argue that liberal economic policies have increased the poor's access to consumer goods like electronic equipment or household items like washing machines, the Philippines, where the urban poor are unable to access basic necessities, represents a clear case of how globalization exacerbates inequality (Shatkin 2004).

The urban transformation of Metro Manila and its peripheries has further propelled another problem that primarily affects the urban poor. Recent typhoons have produced catastrophic effects. In 2009 Tropical Storm Ondoy, for example, took a number of communities by surprise and left an enormous number of families homeless, particularly in the cities of Pasig and Marikina. While many communities along coastal regions or adjacent to the two larger rivers around Metro Manila, such as those in Malabon, are accustomed to flooding, communities such as those in the inner regions of Pasig and Marikina were less prepared. Lacking alternative housing, many of these families were forced to reside in temporary housing with extended family members, or, if funds permitted, moved to rented condominiums in other areas around the city, while others had little choice but to stay in the devastated remains of their old homes and neighborhoods.

One of the many factors compounding the ruinous effects of the floods for these families is a concerted effort by corporate developers to keep families from returning to their homes. Exploiting opportunities produced by the evacuation of families from areas throughout Pasig, opportunistic investors have been pressuring the local government to bar families from returning so that the land can be developed for industrial, commercial, and even residential uses. Months after Ondoy, community leaders who once resided along the banks of the Pasig River organized a campaign to resist this eviction process. Central to their argument is that government agencies had continually ignored community members' demands that the government repair dilapidated infrastructure that would have protected them against the effects of heavy precipitation and floods, or that it even provide support to relocate impoverished families to socialized housing closer to their workplaces in the city core. The unforeseen catastrophic effects of the storm, which flooded 80 percent of Metro Manila, created a rather serendipitous opening for developers to seize more property surrounding the city's periphery.

Clearly, community members were aware of the ongoing process of reclaiming land from the urban poor and displacing families further and further away from their livelihoods. As already mentioned, corporations have increasingly been purchasing land in the Bulacan and Rizal provinces to the north and of course the Cavite and Laguna provinces to the south. According to Gavin Shatkin (2008), this process has been perpetuated by (1) a lower minimum wage in the periphery versus in Manila; (2) dropping property prices; (3) government investments in roads, railways, and ports; (4) private investment in provincial development; (5) pro-growth provincial governments; and (6) the movement of educated workers to the periphery.

The intrusion of the balikbayan economy onto land owned or informally inhabited by the urban poor further perpetuates price gouging for property. The commercial and retail developments accompanying the numerous upscale residences being built also enable an increased flexibilization of low-skilled labor. For example, in SM's thirteen thousand stores around the country, 63 percent of its employees are subcontracted, making employees more susceptible to unfair labor practices. Finally, while the business process outsourcing industry continues to increase the wages of educated Filipinos, the vast majority of new property developments are out of the reach of most Filipinos, thereby continuing the affordable housing crisis across the region.

Short of inhabiting Metro Manila and being confronted by its stark imagery face to face, one almost cannot grasp the extent to which social hierarchies and the inequality produced within the city are felt throughout the everyday lives of Filipinos living and working there. While divisions of labor and the attendant reciprocal processes of internal migration and urban flight produced the spatial contours along which the construction of Metro Manila's cities and municipalities was framed, it was centuries of land accumulation and cultural notions based on class division that created the foundation on which a troubling interdependence between the rich and poor continues to propel the society of Manila itself. As such, the physical juxtaposition and lived proximity between the rich and poor in Manila is visible in a way that is unlike in any other city in Southeast Asia (Connell 1999).

A parallel world of informal economies and settlements continues to evolve around Metro Manila, shadowing the flow of massive urbanization throughout the city. Wherever corporate investors and property developers build high-class developments and commercial buildings, an extensive network of highly organized and economically vibrant informal settlements appears. Similar to in most megacities throughout the Global South, the widespread growth of informal settlements was primarily produced by demand for flexible and low-skilled labor created by rapid urban growth, which subsequently led to an exodus of workers from agricultural areas into urban areas. The high cost of land, propelled by the perceived "lack" of housing and increased competition within the urban labor market, further compels rural migrants and the urban poor to settle into informal housing. By 1990 there were more than 650 distinct squatter developments, which housed over 45 percent of Metro Manila's population (Connell 1999).

Policies to develop the Philippine economy through a logic of increased liberalization, particularly by catering to elites and exceptional flows of tourists, visitors, and returnees through the balikbayan economy, maintain the country's position in the global market at the cost of immense social inequality. The balikbayans themselves poignantly convey how the state intentionally produces an ideal and exceptional citizenship, where their duty to the nation becomes intrinsically tied to the welfare of their families who remain in the Philippines. While Vicente L. Rafael (2000) argues that balikbayans, both Overseas Filipino Workers and those who have acquired citizenship and status abroad, express these attachments and loyalties directly through their hometowns and extended families, the Philippine government has cleverly exploited this labor for the purposes of economic development.

Meanwhile, the gulf separating balikbayans and local Filipinos continues to widen with each return. It is undeniable. Just as my mother realized that her return would directly lead to the further displacement of the informal settlers living on the property that our family possessed for generations, the returns of balikbayans are enabling a further deepening of social disparities in the Philippines. Martin Manalansan (2011) argues that the process of return is far from the clear-cut and (ironically) static images prevailing around narratives of migration: "The act of traversing political and geographic borders more often than not conferred cosmopolitan modernity on the returnee. . . . However, these formulations or ideas about diaspora and return were unable to capture the nonlinear and messy itineraries that deviate from the ideal norm" (35). Intending to better the lives of their families, both their immediate family and those back home in the Philippines, balikbayans return to a homeland that is no longer home. Decades of government policies seeking to exploit the returns of balikbayans have transformed their labor into skyscrapers, commercial developments, and entire cities that are, by and large, completely inaccessible to the majority of Filipinos who continue to stay and live in the Philippines.

Yet, by virtue of producing this economy through their material and imaginative laboring, balikbayans' individual contributions and decisions to either remain in the United States or permanently return to the Philippines prove that the processes of globalization are far from predictable or inevitable. Certainly, the coordinates and pathways of these migrations and investments were put in place by historical colonial relationships and contemporary government policies. However, balikbayans, by their own merit, continue to define routes of globalization and pave the way for new migrations, setting the course for a future that is still quite unknown.

Notes

Introduction

1 All amounts are U.S. dollars unless otherwise indicated.

2 Graziano Battistella (2004) explains that the Philippines Overseas Employment Administration maintains records only on *balik-mangagagaw*, or "rehires." These are contracted Filipino laborers who have had their contracts renewed. This creates limitations in calculating a more accurate figure for the actual number of Filipinos who return either temporarily or permanently.

3 For Grewal (2005), space is more of a set of logics than a physical place. This fundamental reconceptualization provides an analytical means to move away from U.S.-centered discourses within cultural and ethnic studies and shift toward the examination of processes of imperialism and governmentality. "America" becomes understood as an *idea* that "produced many kinds of agency and diverse subjects as a discourse of neoliberalism making possible struggles for rights through consumerists' practices and imaginaries that came to be used both inside and outside the territorial boundaries of the United States" (2).

4 Vergara (2009, 14–15) pays particular attention to Tölölyan's quote, "It makes more sense to think of diasporan or diasporic existence as not necessarily involving a physical return but rather a re-turn, a repeated turning to the concept and/or the reality of the homeland and other diasporan kin through memory, written and visual texts, travel, gifts and assistance."

5 Here I am thinking of Lieba Faier's (2013) use of "affective investments" as a conceptual tool for understanding the dialectical process occurring between larger state projects of economic development and the everyday laboring of individual migrants working overseas.

6 The Filipinos were, on the one hand, uniquely skilled and educated so that they were viewed as a desirable pool of migrants who could fill various labor gaps throughout the U.S. economy; on the other hand, many of these migrants were also capable of immigrating to the United States regardless of their lack of skills and education owing to stipulations within the act that allowed family members to be reunited with family who had already settled in various parts of the United

States (Hing 1993; Choy 2003). In fact, the majority of migrants who immigrated to the United States through the Immigration Act of 1965 were permitted to migrate through the family reunification provision. Subsequently, the wave of Filipino immigration after 1965 produced a dual chain of migration to the United States (Liu 1991).

7　This literature will be further elaborated in chapter 6.

8　According to Robert Seguin's (2001) interpretation of this American amalgamation of classlessness, the middle class in America is both an ideology and a performance: "The middle-class, in this way, becomes accessible to a wide range of individuals as long as they possess certain signifiers of cultural capital . . . a social-semantic structure capable of a range of investments, and supporting a range of practices and beliefs" (3–4). See Pido (2012).

9　Gmelch (1980), one of the first scholars to analyze return migration, situates contemporary forms of return migration within patterns of European migration before the turn of the twentieth century. He defined return migration as "the movement of emigrants back to their homelands to resettle" (135). Recently, more scholars, especially in the field of anthropology, have complicated and even contested the characterization of return as a final point within patterns of migration. See, for example, Long and Oxfeld (2004) and Markowitz and Stefansson (2004). Few scholars have explored return migration using an ethnographic approach, but see Smith (2002) and Xiang et al. (2013).

10　Arnisson Andre C. Ortega (2012) examines the case of suburban developments in Canlubang as a means to illustrate occurrences of "actually existing neoliberalism." He is relying on Neil Brenner and Nik Theodore's (2002) particular conceptualization of neoliberal policies and projects, which attempts to explain how the role of city government diminishes and becomes replaced by public-private relations and market-oriented development.

11　For more on these public-private partnerships, see Hackworth (2006) and Ortega (2016) in relation to city planning in the Philippines.

12　The official number is from the U.S. Census, but other reports list up to 4 million. See *Fact Sheet: U.S. Bilateral Relations with the Philippines* (April 28, 2014), U.S. Department of State. These calculations do not include the significant numbers of undocumented Filipinos living in the United States.

13　For a philosophical treatment of the emergence of the idea of the modern and modernity, see Latour (1993).

14　For a discussion on the cultural significance of Manila's highways, see Tadiar (2004). Virilio (2006) uses the metaphor of "vectors" to argue that contemporary technologies have redefined geographic spaces and normal time to the detriment of human rights and well-being.

15　Some Filipinos literally picnic at the mall. In the concrete pavilion adjacent to SM Mall of Asia, one of the largest malls in the country, families often lay picnic blankets on the cement floor and eat together.

Chapter 1: The Balikbayan Economy

1   Some economists have argued that the lack of knowledge of local markets and the cost of obtaining information offsets the benefits of international investing. See, for instance, Eichholtz (1996). The acceleration of information exchange created by the Internet over the last two decades has addressed many of these concerns.

2   According to Thomas Lemke (2002), neoliberalism for Foucault is a rationale of governmentality. It simultaneously totalizes its subjects and individualizes them through ideas like "freedom," "personal responsibility," and "self care." These individual rationalities create a totalizing shift that moves the societal responsibility for conditions such as "illness, unemployment, poverty, and so forth, and for life in society, into the domain for which the individual is responsible and transform[s] it into a problem of 'self care'" (59). See Guevarra (2010) to understand the nursing profession and its migration between the United States and the Philippines through a Foucauldian framework of governmentality and biopolitics.

Chapter 2: The Foreign Local

1   According to Tadiar (2004), the "tawdry dreams" of both Marcos and "ordinary" Filipinos perform a type of imaginative work that produces material effects. The labor of these fantasies effectively sustains the political and economic organization of the Philippine nation-state.

2   A rhetoric of "heroism" and "patriotism," touted in different ways throughout the media and political speeches, particularly in times of domestic crisis, serves to smoothen and propel the continuous flow of Filipinos laboring overseas (see R. Rodriguez 2002).

3   For a detailed discussion of each of these factors, see Tuaño-Amador et al. (2007).

4   See Lee's (2009) discussion of San Gabriel Valley's role as a "global economic outpost."

5   See, for example, Jean Encinas-Franco's "Overseas Filipino Workers (OFWs) as Heroes: Discursive Origins of the 'Bagong Bayani' in the Era of Labor Export" (2015).

6   The case of Flor Contemplacion is one of the paramount examples demonstrating the intense exploitation and vulnerability of OFWs working abroad. In 1995 political outcry was ignited after Contemplacion, a domestic worker in Singapore, was found guilty of murder and executed (see May 1997).

7   Here I am thinking of Ann Laura Stoler's (2002) conceptualization of the colonial gaze of intimacy and domesticity as a national project that governed the behaviors of Dutch men and women during the colonization of Indonesia and Vietnam. This national project of expanding Dutch imperialism through techniques of colonialism "mandated a set of behaviors, a template for living, a

care of the self, an ideal of domesticity" (1). According to Stoler, the pervasive influence of this logic was not relegated to women but, in fact, operated "largely independent of the presence of European women" (1).

Chapter 3: Transnational Real Estate

1   The advertisement is quoted by Tadiar (2004, 43). For an illuminative discussion on the integral role of U.S. print media in supporting pro-expansionist ventures in the Philippines, see Brechin (2006). The *Overland Monthly*, for instance, through a litany of articles, accompanying pictures, and rhetoric of Manifest Destiny, was active in informing the American public of "the Amazing jungles of the Philippines" and their various natural resources waiting to expropriated. In recent decades, English-speaking countries, along with Japan, encouraged by the increased liberalization of trade agreements following the passage of the Foreign Investments Act of 1991 by the Ramos administration (which allowed foreign equity participation of up to 100 percent in a number of unrestricted investment areas) and low setup costs, established numerous corporate offices in Metro Manila (see Cornelio-Pronove and Cheng 1999). While the United States, Japan, and countries in western Europe traditionally accounted for the largest percentage of foreign direct investment until 1997, over the last decade the Philippines has been experiencing a massive surge in foreign investment predominantly from Korea, attracted by investments in English language-learning schools and relatively low-cost properties. In 2003 the Philippine Department of Tourism launched its English as a Second Language Tour Program. The program combines language-learning activities with vacation trips. Although the program caters primarily to East Asian learners in China and Japan, "Koreans make up the bulk of its customers" (Damazo 2007).

2   Perhaps some of the most pervasive practices of speculative capital throughout Southeast Asia and other parts of the Global South are those practiced by the tourism industry. As a means to provide instant foreign investment, ease local unemployment, and regulate the channeling of revenue back to the federal government, one of the first major implementations enforced by Ferdinand Marcos was the creation of the Ministry of Tourism (later renamed the Department of Tourism), the agency Philippine Tourism Authority, and the Philippine Convention Bureau in 1973. Much of political scientist Linda Richter's body of work, in particular, provides an in-depth analysis of how the tourism industry in the Philippines was integral to alleviating international criticism of Marcos's dictatorial regime and his implementation of martial law by presenting the Philippines through a "façade of 'normality'" constructed by the tourism industry. For a thorough discussion on the political use of tourism by the Marcos administration, see Richter (1989).

3   With "presold" or "off-plan" projects, developers often deposit the funds they receive from buyers into an escrow account. Under this arrangement, units are sold at a lower price and with lower monthly payments (compared with com-

pleted projects). Each payment is utilized to pay off the debt incurred by the developer when they purchased the land and also to continue completing the project. As the project moves closer to completion, the prices of the units increase. Both realtors and buyers quickly learn that the sooner they buy the unit, the more value is added to their property, and the original owner can choose to immediately sell the unit or keep it as the value increases. According to Edgar T. Pascual, a Filipino real estate broker and agent operating in the United States, "the guaranteed appreciation is the key that the Filipino Americans are looking for in a pre-sell or off-plan type of realty project. It is not uncommon for one to tender a low 20 percent down payment and to see that amount increase at least twice in a matter of a few months. As sophisticated investors, Filipino Americans know well that their dormant savings do not even earn a decent 4 percent in American banks or in American money market placements" (2003, 40).

4   With a population of 106,000, Daly City had 228 properties in default and 221 in bank ownership or up for auction.

5   Meanwhile, homeowners are able to mitigate the damage to their credit history and partially control their debt. Also, short sales are usually faster and less expensive than foreclosures. They do not extinguish the remaining balance unless the agreement with the lender clearly indicates this on the acceptance of the offer.

6   The significance of having someone to supervise the construction of buildings in the Philippines will be discussed in more detail in the next chapter.

7   Some examples are discussed by María José Álvarez-Rivadulla (2007), Harald Leisch (2002), Rodrigo Salcedo and Alvarao Torres (2004), and Teresa Caldeira (2000).

8   Connell's argument around fortified enclaves in Manila is drawn directly from Caldeira's (2000) *City of Walls*. In her text, Caldeira argues that what makes this period of urbanization significant and unique is that the means through which wealthier Paulistas are self-segregating have become more elaborate and privatized. Amenities like security guards, swimming pools, gyms, and small businesses have created separate worlds both within and apart from the universe of crime and insecurity in São Paulo, similar to a number of enclaves in Metro Manila. Furthermore, Caldeira argues that while these developments and the advertisements selling them are couched in a language of crime, this rhetoric of segregation reveals deeper fears produced by larger political processes of social democratization brought on by globalization and global progressive movements.

9   My conception of the "American dream" within this context includes the aspirations reflected by the increase of single-family detached homes in typically suburban neighborhoods. These aspirations convey the desire for clearly marked lines of social division exhibited within the built environment coupled with liberal notions of property ownership and property rights. Robin M. Leichenko and William D. Solecki (2005) argue that the increasing desire for suburban-style housing parallels a decrease of almost 14 percent in household size in several parts of the developing world between 1970 and 2000. According to these authors, the reasons for this decrease are indicative of patterns of economic glo-

balization, the growing middle class, and an increase in incomes within certain sectors of these societies. With these patterns come a decline in birth rates, the personal choice to live in suburban neighborhoods, and a decline in communal extended-family households.

10 Jane Jacobs's (1996) case study on the placemaking practices of Bengali immigrants in London describes the complex set of practices and subject formation processes that takes place within postcolonial geographies, "a sense of place which is built around vectors of connection and histories of disconnection. . . . [T]he post-colonial geographies have replaced the security of the maps of the past with the uncertainty of touring the unsettled spatialities of power and identity in the present."

Chapter 4: The Balikbayan Hotel

1 See, for instance, V. Smith (1989) and, more recently, discussions on the effects of globalization and militarism on the tourism industry in the Philippines by Gonzalez (2013) and Ness (2005).

2 On ethnic return migrants in Turkey and Spain, see Tsuda (2009).

3 Caldeira's (2000) study on fortified enclaves and the culture of hypersegregation within São Paulo examines how tales of crime and security enable neoliberal governmentality even amid a transformative period of democratization in Brazil.

4 On the ways in which nationalism and racism create "paranoid structures," see Burgin (1996).

5 According to Raymond Williams (1975), a "structure of feelings" is produced as the culmination of various social processes (e.g., culture, politics, historical events, and attitudes) constructing one's social environment at a particular time.

6 Kundiman is a genre of traditional Filipino love songs that was characteristic of Filipino popular music during the 1940s and 1950s before original Philippine music became popular.

7 Filipino street vendors, or naglalakos, commonly carry bañeras, small metal pots used to store food, slung over their shoulders, often balancing the pots on each end of a long wood pole.

8 See Szanton Blanc (1996) for a discussion on the inception of the Balikbayan Program and its political implications for the Marcos administration.

9 See Tadiar (2004) for an in-depth discussion of the significance of the sex industry within the Philippine economy.

10 As a recent example, a *New York Times* article reported on the number of senseless murders committed by perpetrators incensed by their victim's poor karaoke rendition of Frank Sinatra's classic song "My Way" (see Onishi 2010a).

Chapter 5: The Balikbayan House

1   Sarah Lynne Lopez (2015) describes the remittance landscape as spaces where "distinct elements of the built environment [are] altered with migrant dollars" (1).

2   For example, Carol Upadhya (2013) explains that information technology professionals returning to Bangalore are reorganizing the urban infrastructure of Indian cities, for example, widening roads, building overpasses and underpasses, and building new airports, through a logic of "neonationalism." This reenactment of a particular modernity subsequently distinguishes return migrants from their former compatriots in their home country. Sometimes these distinctions are intended, and other times they are unconscious. Lopez (2015, 47) suggests that in building "modern houses, which may have multiple stories, two-car garages, high ceilings, and suburban US floor plans," Mexican transnational migrants inadvertently decide to distinguish themselves from their surroundings in Jalisco.

3   Dierdre McKay (2005), for example, suggests that her OFW interviewees purchase homes and cars, pay for weddings and funerals, and fund tuition for family members in the Philippines in order to "indulge in patterns of local consumption that increase their status" (97).

4   See Silverstein (2004). One might deduce that Bourdieu is reciprocally arguing that, if not for French colonialism, Berber culture would be "rooted."

5   Herzfeld (2016) defines structural nostalgia as a "collective representation of an edenic order—a time before time—in which the balanced perfection of social relations has not yet suffered the decay that affects everything human" (139). Herzfeld's insightful analysis of Bourdieu and other anthropological critiques of the "timeless perfections" of structuralism is that many of these scholars are guilty of inadvertently utilizing the very same logic that they seek to critique. In viewing native cultures as corrupted by capitalism and imperialism, according to Herzfeld, these scholars "overlook the ways in which social actors invent, refashion, and exploit such structures as moral alibis for their contingent actions" (151).

6   This is not to say that balikbayan homes do not exhibit gendered demarcations. Gender tends to be marked around household decisions regarding what the house looks like or how it will be utilized rather than how the spaces are inhabited.

7   "Fil-Am" means Filipino American.

8   In the Tagalog vernacular *province* is a ubiquitous term that simultaneously denotes particular areas such as a home region or town and also offers a counter-distinction to the metropole, namely, Manila.

9   See, for example, Hondagneu-Sotelo's (1994) classical critique of the household strategy model in her discussion of gendered patterns of Mexican migration to the United States.

Chapter 6: Domestic Affects

1   Filomeno V. Aguilar Jr. (2014) notes that the tremendous reluctance and at times blatant apathy that many former Filipino citizens possess toward Philippine politics often derive from the government's history of corruption in electoral politics and financial graft. "By income standards and access to telecommunications technologies, middle class Filipino immigrants in the U.S. are potentially the 'most connected' to the homeland. As it turns out, they are the least likely to get involved in Philippine elections. The disinterest in Philippine politics appears to be the result of a deliberate shunning of the kind of politics that migrants hold in their memory about the homeland, a memory of 'dirty' politics and ineffectual governance—even by emigrants who affirm their Filipino identity, such as the man who never bothered to become a naturalized U.S. citizen yet considered absentee voting as nonsensical (*kahibangan*). The distrust of Philippine political institutions is most palpable" (242).

Conclusion

1   For a concise introduction to contemporary patterns of Chinese extraterritoriality, see Ong (2004). See Scully (1995) for a historical account of extraterritorial practices within the Chinese political economy.

2   Immersed in conversations around Giorgio Agamben's (1998) illuminative concepts of "bare life" and "zones of indistinction," these theorists have begun exploring the relationship between nation-state sovereignty and the variegated rights of the communities inhabiting nation-states. According to Agamben, a zone of indistinction is a territory in which the individuals who reside there possess no claim to the rights of that territory. Because citizenship has the effect of bestowing humanity through the rights it infers, the exclusion of national citizenship for undocumented workers, asylum seekers, and war refugees reduces these to the inhuman condition of bare life. Thus, the sovereign state is, as Aihwa Ong (2006) writes, "the producer both of modern humanity, by giving protection to citizens, and of bare life, by denying it to noncitizens" (22). Unlike Agamben's analysis of particularized zones where individuals were stripped of rights in places where state law had been suspended, a number of scholars, including Ong, were interested in articulating the other side of exception. Ong's recent (2006) work examines how Chinese neoliberal economic policies are producing zones of exception whereby Chinese corporations, investors, and labor migrants utilize sEZs to expand the Chinese economy throughout East and Southeast Asia. For a related discussion on economic zones created by resource extraction in West Africa, see Ferguson (2006) and Watts (2004).

3   It is outside of the scope of this book to discuss the historical waves of Korean immigration into the Philippines, beginning in sparse increments in the eighth century and including the contemporary wave of entrepreneurs and students after the 1980s. According to the Annual Report of Statistics on Immigration

and Emigration Control of the South Korean Ministry of Justice cited in Miralao (2006), from 1985 to 2001 the annual number of registered Koreans immigrating into the Philippines increased by 16 percent (see Miralao 2006).

4 Philip Kelly (2000) might argue that the development led by Korean investors in CALABARZON is emblematic of continual attempts made by key investors and developers to elicit means in order to compete with the National Capital Region as the region's leading economic producer. While commercial and residential projects find it difficult to compete with the market attractiveness of the National Capital Region, the retirement industry is increasingly looking to CALABARZON as a potentially successful alternative.

5 Enacted by the Ramos administration in 1994, Republic Act No. 7916 is an "act providing for the legal framework and mechanisms for the creation, operation, administration, and coordination of special economic zones in the Philippines, creating for this purpose, the Philippine Economic Zone Authority (PEZA), and other purposes" (Philippine Economic Zone Authority 2010).

6 Recently, a spate of articles have appeared in Philippine dailies discussing the "invasion" of South Koreans into the country. See, among others, Damazo (2007), Lopez (2008), *Manila Standard* (2006), and Meinardus (2005).

7 Public demonstrations, led mostly by local residents, fishermen, and farmers who feared that the developments would further deplete Talisay's local economy, were eventually responded to by officials from the Department of Environment and Natural Resources, who initially deemed that Jung Ang's claim to the land was valid. However, after several prominent figures stood up in support of the activists, including Archbishop Ramon Arguellas, the department invalidated Jung Ang's permit to build the resort in Talisay (see Luistro 2007).

8 Various writers in the Philippines have discussed the long-held historical prejudice toward Chinese Filipinos. See, for instance, See (1990).

9 *Kanya-kanya* is a common expression within the Tagalog vernacular that means "unto themselves." Interestingly, while a number of respondents used the expression to discuss the perceived insular settlements of Korean, Japanese, and Chinese immigrants in the Philippines, many of the respondents were just as quick to describe Filipino politics using the same expression. As such, the expression also denotes a disinterest in the larger politics of Philippine society or those whom other interviewees called the *masa*, or masses, of Filipinos.

References

Agamben, Giorgio. 1998. *Homo Sacer: Sovereign Power and Bare Life.* Stanford, CA: Stanford University Press.

Aguilar, Filomeno V. Jr. 1996. "The Dialectics of Transnational Shame and National Identity." *Philippine Sociological Society* 44 (1–4): 101–36.

———. 2009. "Labour Migration and Ties of Relatedness: Diasporic Houses and Investments in Memory in a Rural Philippine Village." *Thesis Eleven* 98 (1): 88–114.

———. 2014. *Migration Revolution: Philippine Nationhood and Class Relations in a Globalized Age.* Singapore: National University of Singapore Press.

Alave, Kristine L. 2007. "Retirement Haven Scheme Hampered by Image Issue." *BusinessWorld*, February 22.

Allison, Anne. 2013. *Precarious Japan.* Durham, NC: Duke University Press.

Álvarez-Rivadulla, María José. 2007. "Golden Ghettos: Gated Communities and Class Residential Segregation in Montevideo, Uruguay." *Environment and Planning A* 39 (1): 47–63.

Anderson, Benedict. 1998. "Cacique Democracy in the Philippines." In *The Spectre of Comparisons: Nationalism, Southeast Asia, and the World.* New York: Verso, 192–226.

Ang, Ien. 1994. "On Not Speaking Chinese: Postmodern Ethnicity and the Politics of Diaspora." *New Formations* 24:1–18.

Apelacio, Cathy. 2007. "RP Best Retirement Haven for Foreign Nationals, Says Gen. Aglipay." *Manila Standard*, March 29.

Appadurai, Arjun. 1996. *Modernity at Large: Cultural Dimensions of Globalization.* Minneapolis: University of Minnesota Press.

Asian Journal. 2009. "Mabuhay Alliance Urges Radical Changes to Prevent Foreclosures and Encourage Filipino American Small Business Development," April 10. http://asianjournalusa.com/mabuhay-alliance-urges-radical-changes-to-prevent-foreclosures-and-encourag-p7002-76.htm.

Asis, Maruja. 1992. "The Overseas Employment Program Policy." In *Philippine Labor Migration: Impact and Policy,* edited by Graziano Battistella and Anthony Paganoni, 68–112. Quezon City, Philippines: Scalabrini Migration Center.

Baguioro, Luz. 2002. "Never Mind the Rising Crime, Let's Go Shopping; Manila Will Pitch Brand-Name Shopping in Makati to Affluent Japanese Women in Its Latest Push for the Tourist Dollar." *Straits Times*, October 25.

Balisacan, Arsenio M., and Hal Hill. 2008. "An Introduction to the Key Issues." In *The Philippine Economy: Development, Policies, and Challenges*, edited by Arsenio M. Balisacan and Hal Hill. Quezon City, Philippines: Ateneo de Manila University Press, 3–44.

Ball, Rochelle. 1997. "The Role of the State in the Globalisation of Labour Markets: The Case of the Philippines." *Environment and Planning A* 29(9): 1603–28.

Battistella, Graziano. 2004. "Return Migration in the Philippines: Issues and Policies." In *International Migration: Prospects in a Global Market*, edited by Douglas S. Massey and J. Edward Taylor, 212–29. New York: Oxford University Press.

Basch, Linda, Nina Glick Schiller, and Christina Szanton Blanc (eds.). 2005. *Nations Unbound: Transnational Projects, Postcolonial Predicaments, and Deterritorialized Nation-States*. New York: Routledge.

Bayani, Sam. 1976. "What's Happening in the Philippines?: Background and Perspectives on the Liberation Struggle." *Far East Reporter*. New York: Maud Russell.

Bello, Walden F. 2005. *The Anti-development State: The Political Economy of Permanent Crisis in the Philippines*. New York: Zed Books.

Bello, Walden F., David Kinley, and Elaine Elinson. 1982. *Development Debacle: The World Bank in the Philippines*. Oakland, CA: Food First Books.

Berman, Marshall. 1988. *All That Is Solid Melts into Air: The Experience of Modernity*. New York: Penguin Books.

Bernal, Buena. 2014. "Balikbayans Comprise 1 of 5 Philippine Tourists." *Rappler*, December 17. http://www.rappler.com/nation/78240-philippine-tourism-balikbayans. Accessed October 1, 2016.

Berry, James, and Stanley McGreal (eds.). 1999. *Cities in the Pacific Rim*. New York: Routledge.

Bonus, Rick. 2000. *Locating Filipino Americans: Ethnicity and the Cultural Politics of Space*. Philadelphia: Temple University Press.

Bourdieu, Pierre. 1970. "The Berber House or the World Reversed." *Social Science Information* 9 (2): 151–70.

———. 1977. *Outline of a Theory of Practice*. Cambridge: Cambridge University Press.

Brechin, Grey. 2006. *Imperial San Francisco: Urban Power, Earthly Ruin*. Berkeley: University of California Press.

Brenner, Neil, and Nik Theodore. 2002. "Cities and the Geographies of 'Actually Existing Neoliberalism.'" *Antipode* 34 (2): 349–79.

Buco, Benjamin V. 2006. "Special Report: Philippine Retirement Industry; PRA and PRI: Hand in Hand in Promoting the Philippines as a Retirement Destination." *Business World*, December 21.

Burgin, Victor. 1996. *In/different Spaces: Place and Memory in Visual Culture*. Berkeley: University of California Press.

Business World. 1999. "MoA Seeks to Develop RP as Ideal Retirement Haven." June 21.

———. 2003a. "Balikbayan Retirees to Get Benefits." May 21.

———. 2003b. "Subic Retirement Village Targets Fil-Am Returnees." October 23.

———. 2005. "Homestay Program." October 11.

———. 2008. "Medical Tourism in the Philippines: An Answer to the Financial Crisis." October 24.

Caldeira, Teresa. 2000. *City of Walls: Crime, Segregation, and Citizenship in São Paulo.* Berkeley: University of California Press.

Caoili, Manuel A. 1999. *The Origins of Metropolitan Manila: A Political and Social Analysis.* Quezon City: University of the Philippines Press.

Capino, Jose B. 2010. *Dream Factories of a Former Colony: American Fantasies, Philippine Cinema.* Minneapolis: University of Minnesota Press.

Carsten, Janet. 1995. "Houses in Langkawi: Stable Structures or Mobile Homes?" in *About the House: Lévi-Strauss and Beyond*, edited by Janet Carsten and Stephen Hugh-Jones. Cambridge: Cambridge University Press

Castells, Manuel. 1996. *The Rise of the Network Society.* Malden, MA: Blackwell.

Choy, Catherine Ceniza. 2003. *Empire of Care: Nursing and Migration in Filipino American History.* Durham, NC: Duke University Press.

———. 2005. "Towards Trans-Pacific Social Justice: Women and Protest in Filipino American History." *Journal of Asian American Studies* 8 (3): 293–307.

Chu, Julie Y. 2010. *Cosmologies of Credit: Transnational Mobility and the Politics of Destination in China.* Durham, NC: Duke University Press.

Cody, Jeffrey W. 2002. *Exporting American Architecture, 1870–2000.* New York: Psychology Press.

Commission on Filipinos Overseas. 2005. *Handbook for Overseas Filipinos.* Seventh edition. Manila, Philippines: CFO.

———. 2013. "Stock Estimate of Overseas Filipinos." http://www.cfo.gov.ph/images /stories/pdf/StockEstimate2013.pdf. Accessed October 5, 2016.

Connell, John. 1999. "Beyond Manila: Walls, Malls, and Private Spaces." *Environment and Planning A* 31 (3): 417–39.

Cornelio-Pronove, Monique, and Chemerie Cheng. 1999. "Metro Manila." In *Cities in the Pacific Rim: Planning Systems and Property Markets*, edited by James Berry and Stanley McGreal, 185–200. New York: Routledge.

Cruz, Neal H. 2002. "Collado Denied Due Process, Human Rights." *Philippine Daily Inquirer*, November 7.

Damazo, Jet. 2007. "Korea Invades the Philippines." *Asia Sentinel*, July 11. http://www .asiasentinel.com/society/korea-invades-the-philippines/.

Daquiz, Ma Suzette R. 2006. "Special Report: Philippine Retirement Industry; Who Do We Want to Come?" *BusinessWorld*, December 21.

Department of Tourism. 2015. *Tourism in the Philippines.* Report. Makati City, Philippines: Department of Tourism.

de Dios, Emmanuel S., and Paul Hutchcroft. 2003. "Political Economy." In *The Philippine Economy: Development, Policies, and Challenges*, edited by Arsenio M. Balisacan and Hal Hill. Quezon City, Philippines: Ateneo de Manila University.

Doeppers, Daniel F. 1984. *Manila, 1900–1941: Social Change in a Late Colonial Metropolis.* Quezon City, Philippines: Ateneo de Manila University Press.

Du Bois, W. E. B. 2008. *The Souls of Black Folk*. Oxford: Oxford University Press

Eckstein, Susan, and Adil Najam (eds.). 2013. *How Immigrants Impact Their Homelands*. Durham, NC: Duke University Press.

Ehrenreich, Ben. 2009. "Foreclosure Fightback." *The Nation*, January 22. http://www.thenation.com/article/foreclosure-fightback#.

Eichholtz, Piet M. A. 1996. "Does International Diversification Work Better for Real Estate Than for Stocks and Bonds?" *Financial Analysts Journal* 52 (1): 56–62.

Encinas-Franco, Jean. 2015. "Overseas Filipino Workers (OFWs) as Heroes: Discursive Origins of the 'Bagong Bayani' in the Era of Labor Export." *Humanities Diliman* 12 (2): 56–78.

Faier, Lieba. 2013. "Affective Investments in the Manila Region: Filipina Migrants in Rural Japan and Transnational Urban Development in the Philippines." *Transactions of the Institute of British Geographers* 38 (3): 376–90.

Ferguson, James. 2006. *Global Shadows: Africa in the Neoliberal World Order*. Durham, NC: Duke University Press.

Flores, Alena Mae S. 2005. "$100m Japanese Medical Facility Rising at Reclaimed Land." *Manila Standard*, February 5.

Francia, Luis. 2001. *The Eye of the Fish: A Personal Archipelago*. Los Angeles: Kaya.

Gagnet, Cathy L. "The World Bank Annual Report 2005." Washington, DC: The World Bank. http://siteresources.worldbank.org/INTANNREP2K5/Resources/51563_English.pdf. Accessed October 1, 2016.

General, Honesto C. 2002. "Trouble in Foreign Retiree's Paradise." *Philippine Daily Inquirer*, June 3.

Gibson, Katherine, and Julie Graham. 1986. "Situating Migrants in Theory: The Case of Filipino Migrant Contract Construction Workers." *Capitalism and Class* 29:130–47.

Gilroy, Paul. 1993. *The Black Atlantic: Modernity and Double Consciousness*. Cambridge, MA: Harvard University Press.

Glick Schiller, Nina, Linda G. Basch, and Christina Szanton Blanc. 1995. "From Immigrant to Transmigrant: Theorizing Transnational Migration." *Anthropological Quarterly* 68 (1): 48–63.

Glionna, John M. 2009. "Philippine Workers Abroad: The Boon Has a Price." *Los Angeles Times*, August 26.

Gmelch, George. 1980. "Return Migration." *Annual Review of Anthropology* 9:135–59.

Gonzalez, Vernadette Vicuna. 2013. *Securing Paradise: Tourism and Militarism in Hawai'i and the Philippines*. Durham, NC: Duke University Press.

Gotham, Kevin Fox. 2009. "Creating Liquidity out of Spatial Fixity: The Secondary Circuit of Capital and the Subprime Mortgage Crisis." *International Journal of Urban and Regional Research* 33 (2): 355–71.

Graham, Stephen, and Simon Marvin. 2001. *Splintering Urbanism: Networked Infrastructures, Technological Mobilities and the Urban Condition*. New York: Routledge.

Grewal, Inderpal. 2005. *Transnational America: Feminisms, Diasporas, Neoliberalisms*. Durham, NC: Duke University Press.

Guevarra, Anna R. 2010. *Marketing Dreams, Manufacturing Heroes: The Transnational Labor Brokering of Filipino Workers.* New Brunswick, NJ: Rutgers University Press.

Gulane, Judy T. 2006. "Plan Positions RP as Retirement Haven." *BusinessWorld*, May.

Hackworth, Jason. 2006. *The Neoliberal City: Governance, Ideology, and Development in American Urbanism.* Ithaca, NY: Cornell University Press.

Haila, Anne. 1997. "The Neglected Builder of Global Cities." In *Cities in Transformation—Transformation in Cities: Social and Symbolic Change of Urban Space,* edited by Ove Källtorp, Ingemar Elander, Ove Ericsson, and Mats Franzén, 51–64. Aldershot, UK: Avebury.

Hawes, Gary. 1987. *The Philippine State and the Marcos Regime: The Politics of Export.* Ithaca, NY: Cornell University Press.

Herzfeld, Michael. 2016. *Cultural Intimacy: Social Poetics and the Real Life of States, Societies, and Institutions.* New York: Routledge.

Hing, Bill Ong. 1993. *Making and Remaking Asian America through Immigration Policy, 1850–1990.* Stanford, CA: Stanford University Press.

Hoang, Kimberly Kay. 2015. *Dealing in Desire: Asian Ascendancy, Western Decline, and the Hidden Currencies of Global Sex Work.* Berkeley: University of California Press.

Holston, James. 1989. *The Modernist City: An Anthropological Critique of Brasilia.* Chicago: University of Chicago Press.

Hondagneu-Sotelo, Pierrette. 1994. *Gendered Transitions: Mexican Experiences of Immigration.* Berkeley: University of California Press.

Jacobs, Jane M. 1996. *Edge of Empire: Postcolonialism and the City.* London: Routledge.

Kelly, Philip. 2000. *Landscapes of Globalization: Human Geographies of Economic Change in the Philippines.* London: Routledge.

Kreifels, Susan. 2009. "Economic Boom Pulls Balikbayans Back Home." *Honolulu Star Bulletin*, October 26.

Krinks, Peter A. 2002. *The Economy of the Philippines: Elites, Inequalities and Economic Restructuring.* New York: Routledge.

Latour, Bruno. 1993. *We Have Never Been Modern.* Cambridge, MA: Harvard University Press.

Lee, Ching Kwan. 2009. "Raw Encounters: Chinese Managers, African Workers and the Politics of Casualization in Africa's Chinese Enclaves." *China Quarterly* 199 (1): 647–66.

Leichenko, Robin M., and William D. Solecki. 2005. "Exporting the American Dream: The Globalization of Suburban Consumption Landscapes." *Regional Studies* 39 (2): 241–53.

Leisch, Harald. 2002. "Gated Communities in Indonesia." *Cities* 19 (5): 341–50.

Lemke, Thomas. 2002. "Foucault, Governmentality, and Critique." *Rethinking Marxism* 14 (3): 49–64.

Lessinger, Johanna. 1995. *From the Ganges to the Hudson: Indian Immigrants in New York City.* Boston: Allyn and Bacon.

Levitt, Peggy. 2001. *The Transnational Villagers*. Berkeley: University of California Press.

Li, Wei. 1998. "Anatomy of a New Ethnic Settlement: The Chinese Ethnoburb in Los Angeles." *Urban Studies* 35 (3): 479–501.

Liu, John M., Paul M. Ong, and Carolyn Rosenstein. 1991. "Dual Chain Migration: Post-1965 Filipino Immigration to the United States." *International Migration Review* 25 (3): 487–513.

Locsin, Joel. 2002. "4 Top Officials Linked to Retirement Fund Scam." *Manila Standard*, October 25.

Long, Lynellyn D., and Ellen Oxfeld (eds.). 2004. *Coming Home?: Refugees, Migrants, and Those Who Stayed Behind*. Philadelphia: University of Pennsylvania Press.

Lopez, Bernardo. 2008. "Upshot: Korean Invasion." *BusinessWorld*, January 17.

Lopez, Sarah Lynn. 2015. *The Remittance Landscape: Spaces of Migration in Rural Mexico and Urban USA*. Chicago: University of Chicago Press.

Luistro, Marlon Alexander. 2007. "Lipa Bishop Wants Total Stop to Taal Spa." *Philippine Daily Inquirer*, June 30.

Lyttleton, Chris, and Pál Nyíri. 2007. "Dams, Casinos and Concessions: Chinese Megaprojects in Laos and Cambodia." In *Engineering Earth: The Impacts of Mega-engineering Projects*, edited by Stanley D. Brunn, 1243–65. New York: Springer.

Maas, Marisha. 2008. "Door-to-Door Cargo Agents: Cultivating and Expanding Filipino Transnational Space." In *Tales of Development: People, Power and Space*, edited by Paulus Gerardus Maria Hebinck, Sef Slootweg, and Lothar Smith, 5–20. Assen, the Netherlands: Van Gorcum.

Macabenta, Greg B. 1998. "Retiring in the Philippines." *BusinessWorld*, September 9.

———. 2008. "Hard Times in America." *BusinessWorld*, June 18.

Magno-Ballesteros, Marife. 2000a. "Land Use Planning in Metro Manila and the Urban Fringe: Implications on the Land and Real Estate Market." Discussion Paper Series No. 2000–20, Philippine Institute for Development Studies, Metro Manila.

———. 2000b. "The Urban Land and Real Estate Market." PhD diss., University of Nijmegen.

Manalansan, Martin. 2003. *Global Divas: Filipino Gay Men in the Diaspora*. Durham, NC: Duke University Press.

———. 2011. "Wayward Erotics: Mediating Queer Diasporic Return." In *Media, Transnationalism, and Asian Erotics*, edited by Purnima Mankekar and Louisa Schein, 33–52. Durham, NC: Duke University Press.

Manapat, Ricardo. 1991. *Some Are Smarter Than Others: The History of Marcos' Crony Capitalism*. Putnam Valley, NY: Aletheia.

Manila Standard. 2006. "Korea Invasion." March 4.

Maragay, Fel V. 2005. "GMA Won't Extend Aglipay's Term." *Manila Standard*, January 21.

Marcelo, Samantha Leslie L. 2006. "Special Feature: Old Is In (Could RP Be the Next Retirement Haven?)." *BusinessWorld*, June 9.

Marcos, Imelda. 1985. *Metropolitan Manila: Towards a City of Man, Total Human*

Resource Development. Quezon City, Philippines: National Media Production Center.

Markowitz, Fran, and Anders H. Stefansson (eds.). 2004. *Homecomings: Unsettling Paths of Return.* Lanham, MD: Rowman & Littlefield.

Marx, Karl. 1978. "Communist Manifesto." In *The Marx-Engels Reader,* edited by Robert C. Tucker, 476. New York: Norton.

Matejowsky, Ty. 2012. "Labor Migration, Overseas Remittances, and Local Outcomes in the Contemporary Philippines." In *Migration and Remittances during the Global Financial Crisis and Beyond,* edited by Ibrahim Sirkeci, Jeffrey H. Cohoen, and Dilip Ratha, 315–18. Washington, DC: World Bank.

May, Ronald James. 1997. "The Domestic in Foreign Policy: The Flor Contemplacion Case and Philippine-Singapore Relations." *Pilipinas* 29:63–76.

McCoy, Alfred W. 2009. *An Anarchy of Families: State and Family in the Philippines.* Madison: University of Wisconsin Press.

McKay, Deirdre. 2005. "Reading Remittance Landscapes: Female Migration and Agricultural Transition in the Philippines." *Geografisk Tidsskrift-Danish Journal of Geography* 105 (1): 89–99.

———. 2006. "Translocal Circulation: Place and Subjectivity in an Extended Filipino Community." *Asia Pacific Journal of Anthropology* 7 (3): 265–78.

McMichael, Philip. 2012. *Development and Social Change: A Global Perspective.* Los Angeles: Sage.

Meinardus, Ronald. 2005. "'Korean Wave' Sweeps the Philippines." *Japan Times,* December 19.

Melican, Nathaniel R. 2011. "Tourism Dep't Wants More Balikbayans." *Business-World,* June 10.

Menjivar, Cecilia, Julie DaVanzo, Lisa Greenwell, and R. Burciaga Valdez. 1998. "Remittance Behavior among Salvadoran and Filipino Immigrants in Los Angeles." *International Migration Review* 32 (1): 97–126.

Miralao, Virginia A. 2006. "Understanding the Korean Diaspora in the Philippines." In *Exploring Transnational Communities in the Philippines,* edited by Virginia A. Miralao and Lorna P. Makil. Quezon City, Philippines: Philippine Migration Research Network and Philippine Social Science Council.

Mitchell, Timothy. 2000. "The Stage of Modernity." In *Questions of Modernity,* edited by Timothy Mitchell, 1–34. Minneapolis: University of Minnesota.

Mollman, Steve. 2007. "The Perfect Place." *Wall Street Journal,* April 6.

National Statistical Coordination Board (NSCB). 2003. *Philippine Statistical Yearbook.* Makati City, Philippines: NSCB.

National Statistics Office. 2004. "2003 Gross Regional Domestic Product (GRDP) Estimates Based on the New Regional Configuration." *Philippine Statistics Authority,* July 12. http://nap.psa.gov.ph/grdp/2003/default.asp.

———. 2007. "2007 Census of Population Reports." *Philippine Statistics Authority.* https://psa.gov.ph/statistics/census/population-and-housing/2007-PopCen. Accessed October 1, 2016.

Ness, Sally Ann. 2003. *Where Asia Smiles: An Ethnography of Philippine Tourism.* Philadelphia: University of Pennsylvania Press.

———. 2005. "Tourism–Terrorism: The Landscaping of Consumption and the Darker Side of Place." *American Ethnologist* 32 (1): 118–40.

Ng, Jennifer A. 2006. "Retirement Body Turns to Real Estate Developers." *BusinessWorld*, May 25.

Nierras, Jaime, Lilia Cassanova, and Linda Hornilla. 1992. "Improving the Urban Planning and Management Process and Performance: Metro Manila." *Regional Development Dialogue* 13 (1): 122–48

Nikolits, Daniel. 2015. "The World Bank Annual Report 2015." Washington, DC: The World Bank. https://openknowledge.worldbank.org/handle/10986/22550. Accessed October 1, 2016.

Ocampo, Romeo B. 1995. "The Metro Manila Mega-region." In *The Mega-urban Regions of Southeast Asia*, edited by Terence McGee and Ira Robinson, 282–95. Vancouver: University of British Columbia.

Office of the Press Secretary. 2014. "Fact Sheet: United States-Philippines Bilateral Relation." April 28. Washington, DC: White House.

Olds, Kris. 2001. *Globalization and Urban Change: Capital, Culture, and Pacific Rim Mega-projects.* Oxford: Oxford University Press.

Ong, Aihwa. 2004. "The Chinese Axis: Zoning Technologies and Variegated Sovereignty." *Journal of East Asian Studies* 17 (4): 69–96.

———. 2006. *Neoliberalism as Exception: Mutations in Citizenship and Sovereignty.* Durham, NC: Duke University Press.

Onishi, Norimitsu. 2010a. "Sinatra Song Often Strikes Deadly Chord." *New York Times*, February 6.

———. 2010b. "Toiling Far from Home for Philippine Dreams." *New York Times*, September 18.

Ortega, Arnisson Andre C. 2012. "Desakota and Beyond: Neoliberal Production of Suburban Space in Manila's Fringe." *Urban Geography* 33 (8): 1118–43.

———. 2016. *Neoliberalizing Spaces in the Philippines: Suburbanization, Transnational Migration, and Dispossession.* Lanham, MD: Rowman & Littlefield

Parreñas, Rhacel Salazar. 2001a. *Servants of Globalization: Women, Migration, and Domestic Work.* Palo Alto, CA: Stanford University Press.

———. 2001b. "Transgressing the Nation-State: The Partial Citizenship and 'Imagined (Global) Community' of Migrant Filipina Domestic Workers." *Signs: Journal of Women in Culture and Society* 26 (4): 129–54.

———. 2008. *The Force of Domesticity: Filipina Migrants and Globalization.* New York: New York University Press.

———. 2012. "The Reproductive Labour of Migrant Workers." *Global Networks* 12 (2): 269–75.

Pascual, Edgar T. 2003. *How to Profit from the $27 Billion Filipino American Market.* Quezon City, Philippines: Giraffe Books.

Pelovello, Roy. 2008. "Retirement Agency Gets Extra Function." *Manila Standard.*

Philippine Economic Zone Authority. 2010. Special Economic Zone Act. http://www
.peza.gov.ph/index.php?option=com_content&view=article&id=97&Itemid=55.

Philippine News. 1989. "Safe Guidelines for the Bartkbayan." May 31–June 6, p. 12.

Pido, Eric J. 2012. "The Performance of Property: Suburban Homeownership as a
Claim to Citizenship for Filipinos in Daly City." *Journal of Asian American Studies*
15 (1): 69–104.

PRA (Philippine Retirement Authority). 2007. "Aglipay's Twin Strategy to Achieve
Retirement Goals." *Philippine Retirement News*, June, 1.

Rabinow, Paul. 1989. *French Modern: Norms and Forms of the Social Environment.*
Cambridge, MA: MIT Press.

Rafael, Vicente L. 2000. *White Love and Other Events in Filipino History.* Durham,
NC: Duke University Press.

Reed, Robert. 1993. "From Suprabarangay to Colonial Capital: Reflections on the
Hispanic Foundation of Manila." In *Forms of Dominance: On the Architecture and
Urbanism of the Colonial Experience*, edited by Nezar AlSayyad, 45–81. London:
Avebury.

Remo, Michelle. 2009. "RP Gains Said to Translate to Rise in Number of Poor
People." *Philippine Daily Inquirer*, November 15.

Republic of the Philippines Bureau of Immigration. 2016. "Balikbayan Privilege." *The
Official Gazette: The Official Journal of the Republic of the Philippines.* http://www
.immigration.gov.ph/faqs/visa-inquiry/balikbayan-previlege. Accessed October 1,
2016.

Richter, Linda K. 1982. *Land Reform and Tourism Development: Policy-Making in the
Philippines.* Cambridge, MA: Schenkman.

———. 1989. *The Politics of Tourism in Asia.* Honolulu: University of Hawai'i Press.

Rimmer, Peter, and Howard Dick. 2009. *The City in Southeast Asia: Patterns, Processes and Policy.* Honolulu: University of Hawai'i Press.

Rodis, Rodel. 2008. "The 'F' Word." *AsianWeek*, November 15. http://www.asianweek
.com/2008/11/18/the-f-word/.

Rodriguez, Edgard R. 1998. "International Migration and Income Distribution in the
Philippines." *Economic Development and Cultural Change* 46:329–51.

Rodriguez, Robyn. 2002. "Migrant Heroes: Nationalism, Citizenship and the Politics
of Filipino Migrant Labor." *Citizenship Studies* 6 (3): 341–56.

———. 2010. *Migrants for Export: How the Philippine State Brokers Labor to the
World.* Minneapolis: University of Minnesota Press.

Rofel, Lisa. 1999. *Other Modernities: Gendered Yearnings in China after Socialism.*
Berkeley: University of California Press.

Sajor, Edward. 2003. "Globalization and the Urban Property Boom in Metro Cebu,
Philippines." *Development and Change* 34 (4): 713–41.

Salazar, Tessa. 2008. "40% of Filinvest's Mountain Suburb Buyers from Overseas."
Philippine Daily Inquirer, September 6. http://www.inquirer.net/specialreports
/propertyguide/aroundtown/view.php?db=1&article=20080906-158970&pageID
=2. Accessed October 6, 2010.

Salcedo, Rodrigo, and Alvaro Torres. 2004. "Gated Communities in Santiago: Wall or Frontier?" *International Journal of Urban and Regional Research* 28 (1): 27–44.

San Francisco Examiner. 2009. "Daly City Foreclosure Rate Highest in County." March 31.

San Juan, Epifanio Jr.. 1998. *From Exile to Diaspora: Versions of the Filipino Experience in the United States.* Boulder, CO: Westview Press.

Sassen, Saskia. 2001. *The Global City: New York, London, Tokyo.* Princeton, NJ: Princeton University Press.

Schein, Louisa. 1999. "Diaspora Politics, Homeland Erotics, and the Materializing of Memory." *positions* 7 (3): 697–731.

Schmitt, Richard. 1987. *Introduction to Marx and Engels and a Critical Reconstruction.* Boulder, CO: Westview.

Scully, Eileen P. 1995. "Taking the Low Road to Sino-American Relations: 'Open Door' Expansionists and the Two China Markets." *Journal of American History* 82 (1): 62–83.

See, Teresita Ang. 1990. *The Chinese in the Philippines: Problems and Perspectives.* Manila, Philippines: Kaisa Para Sa Kaunlaran.

Seguin, Robert. 2001. *Around Quitting Time: Work and Middle-Class Fantasy in American Fiction.* Durham, NC: Duke University Press.

Shatkin, Gavin. 2004. "Planning to Forget: Informal Settlements as 'Forgotten Places' in Globalising Metro Manila." *Urban Studies* 41 (12): 2469–84.

———. 2008. "The City and the Bottom Line: Urban Megaprojects and the Privatization of Planning in Southeast Asia." *Environment and Planning A* 40 (2): 383–401.

Silverstein, Paul A. 2004. "Of Rooting and Uprooting: Kabyle Habitus, Domesticity, and Structural Nostalgia." *Ethnography* 5 (4): 553–78.

Simone, AbdouMaliq. 2004. *For the City Yet to Come: Changing African Life in Four Cities.* Durham, NC: Duke University Press.

Smith, Andrea. 2002. *Europe's Invisible Migrants: Consequences of the Colonists' Return.* Amsterdam: Amsterdam University Press.

Smith, Michael P. 2001. *Transnational Urbanism: Locating Globalization.* Malden, MA: Blackwell.

Smith, Valene L. (ed.). 1989. *Hosts and Guests: The Anthropology of Tourism.* Philadelphia: University of Pennsylvania Press.

Stoler, Ann Laura. 2002. *Carnal Knowledge and Imperial Power: Race and the Intimate in Colonial Rule.* Berkeley: University of California Press.

Szanton Blanc, Cristina. 1996. "*Balikbayan*: A Filipino Extension of the National Imaginary and of State Boundaries." *Philippine Sociological Review* 44 (1–4): 178–93.

Tadiar, Neferti X. M. 2004. *Fantasy Production: Sexual Economies and Other Philippine Consequences for the New World Order.* Hong Kong: Hong Kong University Press.

Tan, Edward L. 2005. *Real Estate Buyer Profile and Behavior: Helps You Understand the Overseas Filipino Workers' Buyer Behavior.* Mandaluyong City, Philippines: Miracle.

Tenorio, Bum D. Jr., Dulce Arguelles, and Florencio P. Narito. 1998. "30,000 Balik-bayans Stay Away." *Manila Standard*, September 24.

Tölölyan, Khachig. 1996. "Rethinking Diaspora(s): Stateless Power in the Trans-national Moment." *Diaspora* 5 (1): 3–36.

Toyota, Mika. 2006. "Ageing and Transnational Householding: Japanese Retirees in Southeast Asia." *International Development Planning Review* 28 (4): 515–31.

Toyota, Mika, and Biao Xiang. 2012. "The Emerging Transnational 'Retirement Industry' in Southeast Asia." *International Journal of Sociology and Social Policy* 32 (11/12): 708–19.

Tsing, Anna Lowenhaupt. 2005. *Friction: An Ethnography of Global Connection.* Durham, NC: Duke University Press.

Tsuda, Takeyuki (ed.). 2009. *Diasporic Homecomings: Ethnic Return Migration in Comparative Perspective.* Palo Alto, CA: Stanford University Press.

Tuaño-Amador, Maria Cyd N., Racquel A. Claveria, Vic K. Delloro, and Ferdinand S. Co. 2007. "Philippine Overseas Workers and Migrants' Remittances: The Dutch Disease Phenomenon and the Cyclicality Issue." *Bangko Sentral Review* (January): 1–23.

Upadhya, Carol. 2013. "Return of the Global Indian: Software Professionals and the Worlding of Bangalore." In *Return: Nationalizing Transnational Mobility in Asia*, edited by Biao Xiang, Brenda Yeoh, and Mika Toyota, 141–61. Durham, NC: Duke University Press.

Van Naerssen, Ton, Michel Ligthart, and Flotilda N. Zapanta. 1996. "Managing Metropolitan Manila." In *The Dynamics of Metropolitan Management in Southeast Asia*, edited by Jürgen Rüland, 168–206. Singapore: Institute of Southeast Asian Studies.

Vergara, Benito Manalo. 2009. *Pinoy Capital: The Filipino Nation in Daly City.* Phila-delphia: Temple University Press.

Virilio, Paul. 2006. *Speed and Politics.* Los Angeles: Semiotext(e).

Watts, Michael. 2004. "Resource Curse? Governmentality, Oil and Power in the Niger Delta, Niger." *Geopolitics* 9 (1): 50–80.

Weekley, Kathleen. 2004. "Saving Pennies for the State: A New Role for Filipino Migrant Workers?" *Journal of Contemporary Asia* 34 (3): 349–63.

Williams, Raymond. 1975. *The Country and the City.* Oxford: Oxford University Press.

Xiang, Biao, Brenda Yeoh, and Mika Toyota (eds.). 2013. *Return: Nationalizing Transnational Mobility in Asia.* Durham, NC: Duke University Press.

Index

Aglipay, Edgar, 18, 161, 195, 197
American Dream, 133–34
Appadurai, Arjun, 7, 13, 188–89
Aquino, Benigno "Ninoy," 192
Aquino, Corazon, 23, 160, 196; liberalizing policies, 60. *See also* neoliberalism
Asian Development Bank, 47
Asian Financial Crisis, 1997, 96–98
Ayala Land Inc., 46, 63, 106, 108, 111, 198, 210

balikbayan economy, 15, 17, 28, 39, 99, 236
balikbayan landscape, definition, 25, 40–41; architecture, 187–90
balikbayan paranoia, 153–54, 163; gender, 163–64
Balikbayan policy, 67, 69–70, 158–59
balikbayans, xi; balikbayan boxes, 73, 82; Balikbayan Law, 72; definition, 4, 60, 69–72; differentiation from overseas Filipino workers (OFW), 4, 91; program, 74; "ugly," 90, 150. *See also* overseas Filipino workers
Bangko Sentral ng Pilipinas (BSP), 66, 73, 79, 84
Bello, Walden, 50
BF Homes, 174–78
bird dogs, 96, 125–27
Bonus, Rick, x, 89

Bourdieu, Pierre: Berber House, 172–73; home, 169
Burgin, Victor, 153
business process outsourcing (BPO), 63
bypass-implant urbanism, 26

CALABARZON region, 23, 42
Caldeira, Teresa, 1, 152–53
central business district (CBD), 63, 96, 106, 127–28
Chamber of Real Estate and Builders Association (CRBA), 57
Chinese extraterritoriality, 213–14. *See also* Ong, Aihwa
class: American middle class, 12; property buyers in the Philippines; 109
crime, 152–53, 163, 165
Commission of Filipinos overseas, 17, 74

Daly City, 30, 73, 83, 95–96, 124
debt financing, 16–7, 23
Department of Tourism, 4, 69, 167, 192, 211, 216
Du Bois, W. E. B, x–xi

economy of appearances, 101–3, 110, 159–60. *See also* Tsing, Anna Lowenhaupt
elite rulers, 44

Faier, Lieba, 171
family: home design, 183–86; kinship, 88–89; migration strategy, 184
The Filipino Channel (TFC), 29, 116, 148, 162
foreign investment, 40–41, 54, 105–6; Asian, 212; Foreign Investments Act of 1991, 74
Fort Bonifacio Global City, 40, 169

global cities, 56
globalization, 14–15, 55, 188, 190
Global South, 1, 28, 241
Golden Boten City, 214–16
Great Recession and Subprime Mortgage Crisis, 2007, 30–31, 98, 113

home, 9, 13
Housing and Land Use Regulatory Board, 21

IloIlo City, 64–65
imagination, 7; imaginative laboring, 8, 14, 17, 33, 65, 75
Immigration Act, 1965, viii, 12, 18, 97, 105; dual chain migration; ix
International Monetary Fund, 20, 48–51
invisibility, x

Laos, 213–14
Local Autonomy Act of 1959, 46
Lucio Tan Group, 120, Eton, 108

mabuhay, 156–57
Mabuhay Manor, 146–48, 150–55
Macapagal-Arroyo, Gloria, 1–2, 15–16, 195, 237
Makati, 46–47, 63
malls, 26, 103, 127
Manila, 41, 45–46; American colonial rule, 42, 45; Spanish colonial rule, 43–44; World War II, 45
Manila Metro Rapid Transit System (MRT), 26
Marcos, Ferdinand, 41, 47, 53, 59, 196, 236; land reform, 22–23; martial law, 50; "New Society," 53
Marcos, Imelda, 20–21
Marx, Karl, 6
microbusiness, 221
Mitchell, Timothy, 8–9, 19–20
modernity, 8–9, 19, 27–28, 63–64; design, 171, 179–82

National Capital Region (NCR), 38, 41, 53, 160
neoliberalism: actually existing neoliberalism, 16; as discourse, xi; early liberal policies, 24; Foucault, 61; neoliberal urban governance, 21
Ninoy Aquino International Airport (NAIA), 62, 93, 162, 235
North American Free Trade Agreement (NAFTA), 44
nostalgia, 13

Ong, Aihwa: neoliberalism as exception, 211–12; zones of exception, 214–15
overseas Filipino workers, 61, 101, 165, 169, 226; labor export policy, 59–60; Migrant Workers and Overseas Filipinos Act, 1995, 91; "new heroes," 91

Payne-Aldrich Act, 1909, 44
Philippine Overseas Employment Administration (POEA), 92
Philippine Retirement Authority (PRA), 3–4, 18, 161, 193–99
Philippine Retirement Authority Members Association Foundation Inc. (PRAMA), 205–11

Philippine Retirement Inc. (PRI), 161, 194–99
precarity, 28, 171, 173
property development, 46; Condominium Act, 1996, 56; The Investors Lease Act, 1993, 55; property markets, 56–58, 105–6

Quezon City, 45–46

Rafael, Vicente L., 65, 150, 167, 241–42
real estate, study of, 57
real estate advertisements, 127–35
realtors, 31, 111–16; Philippines Real Estate Center (PREC), 200; transnational realtors, 106–7, 118–21, 125–7. See also bird dogs
remittances, 40, 66–68, 75–97; obligation to send, 62, 75; relief provided by, 64–65, 68, 239; remittance landscape, 77, 170; remittance-sending companies, 73, 79–80
repeated turning, 8, 10–11, 67
retirement haven, 193
retirement villages, 3, 211, 224, 231
return migration: theories of, 165

sex industry, 160
Special Economic Zones (SEZS), 221; Philippine Economic Zone Authority, 222, 224; Tourism Economic Zones (TEZS), 216
Special Resident Retirement Visa (SRRV), 72, 199–206

speculative capital, 101–3
structural adjustment, 51–52
structures of feeling, 12, 81
Subic Bay, 200
suburbanization: 105. See also Local Autonomy Act of 1959

Tadiar, Neferti X., 75, 109
Tagaytay, 136, 215–20; Koreans in, 217, 227–29
tourism; performance of 156–57; programs, 159; medical, 216, 224–7. See also economy of appearances
transnational connectivity, 9, 14, 82
transnationalism, 66
transnational urbanism, 38, 58
Tsing, Anna Lowenhaupt, 8, 99, 101, 107
Typhoon Fengshen, 64–65
Typhoon Ondoy, 238–39

urbanization in Southeast Asia, 54–56
Urban Land Reform Programme, 1979, 21
urban poor, 165, 238
U.S. neocolonialism, 81–82

Vergara, Benito M., x, 10, 174
Vizconde Massacre, 174–75

word-play, 162
World Bank, 20, 48–51